ACE RACE ™

VOLUME 1

PALE BLUE DOT

PETER CALLOWAY co-creator & writer

ALEX SHIBAO co-creator & artist

NATÁLIA MARQUES colorist

MARSHALL DILLON letterer

ALEX SHIBAO front & original covers

JUAN DOE & DECLAN SHALVEY variant covers

DYLAN TODD logo designer

COREY BREEN book designer

MIKE MARTS editor

AFTERSHOCK ™

MIKE MARTS - Editor-in-Chief • JOE PRUETT - Publisher/CCO • LEE KRAMER - President • JON KRAMER - Chief Executive Officer
STEVE ROTTERDAM - SVP, Sales & Marketing • DAN SHIRES - VP, Film & Television UK • CHRISTINA HARRINGTON - Managing Editor
MARC HAMMOND - Sr. Retail Sales Development Manager • RUTHANN THOMPSON - Sr. Retailer Relations Manager • BLAKE STOCKER - Chief Financial Officer
AARON MARION - Publicist • LISA MOODY - Finance • RYAN CARROLL - Development Coordinator • STEPHAN NILSON - Publishing Operations
CHARLES PRITCHETT - Comics Production • COREY BREEN - Collections Production • TEDDY LEO - Editorial Assistant
STEPHANIE CASEBIER & SARAH PRUETT - Publishing Assistants

AfterShock Logo Design by COMICRAFT

Publicity: contact AARON MARION (aaron@publichausagency.com) & RYAN CROY (ryan@publichausagency.com) at PUBLICHAUS
Special thanks to: IRA KURGAN, MARINE KSADZHIKYAN, ANTONIA LIANOS & JULIE PIFHER

Follow us on social media 🐦 📷 f

I N T R O D U C T I O N

So, hi.

You're reading this! I can't tell you how exciting that is for me. I've been a writer for a while, lucky enough to make a living at it. But I've never lost the joy that comes with getting to share a story with the world.

And this is a story about our world. Or, more specifically, the race to get *off* it. This particular story started as a worry: that humanity, on a global, societal level, had lost its capacity for exploration. I don't just mean in space, either. In the sciences, the arts, the histories.

Then I realized, no, that's not true. It's just not *governments* doing it anymore. It's now the purview of private citizens, driven by curiosity, driven by exhilaration, driven by the desire to *go out and do something.* That realization came with hope. And hope is where I want to spend my time.

That's a fairly long way of saying: this is a story about exploration. But it's also about hope. And the human capacity for risk in order to do both.

So from my keyboard to Alex's pencil (and inks!) to your hands, I want to say thank you for exploring the book. I hope you enjoy it.

PETER CALLOWAY
June, 2019

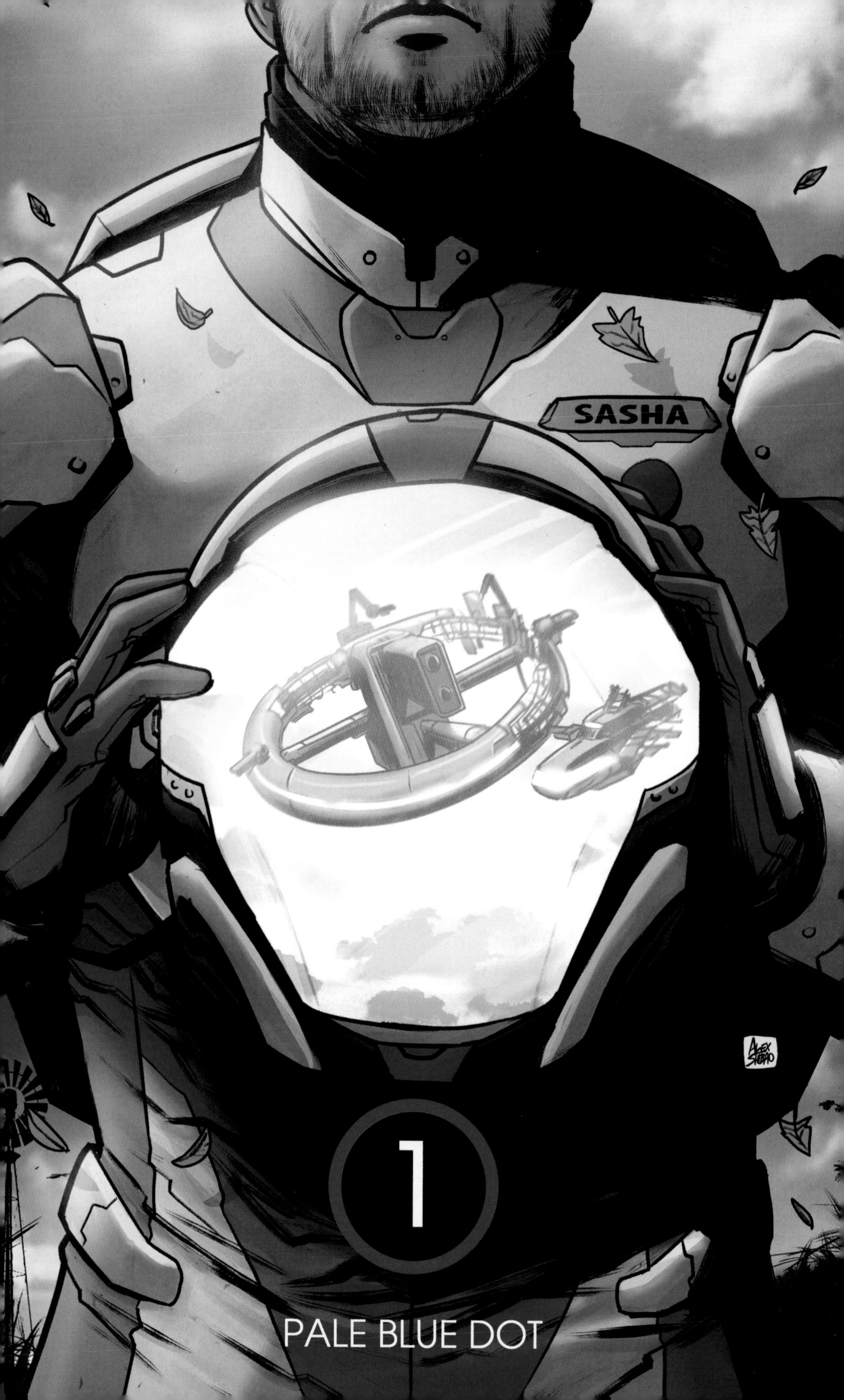
SASHA

1

PALE BLUE DOT

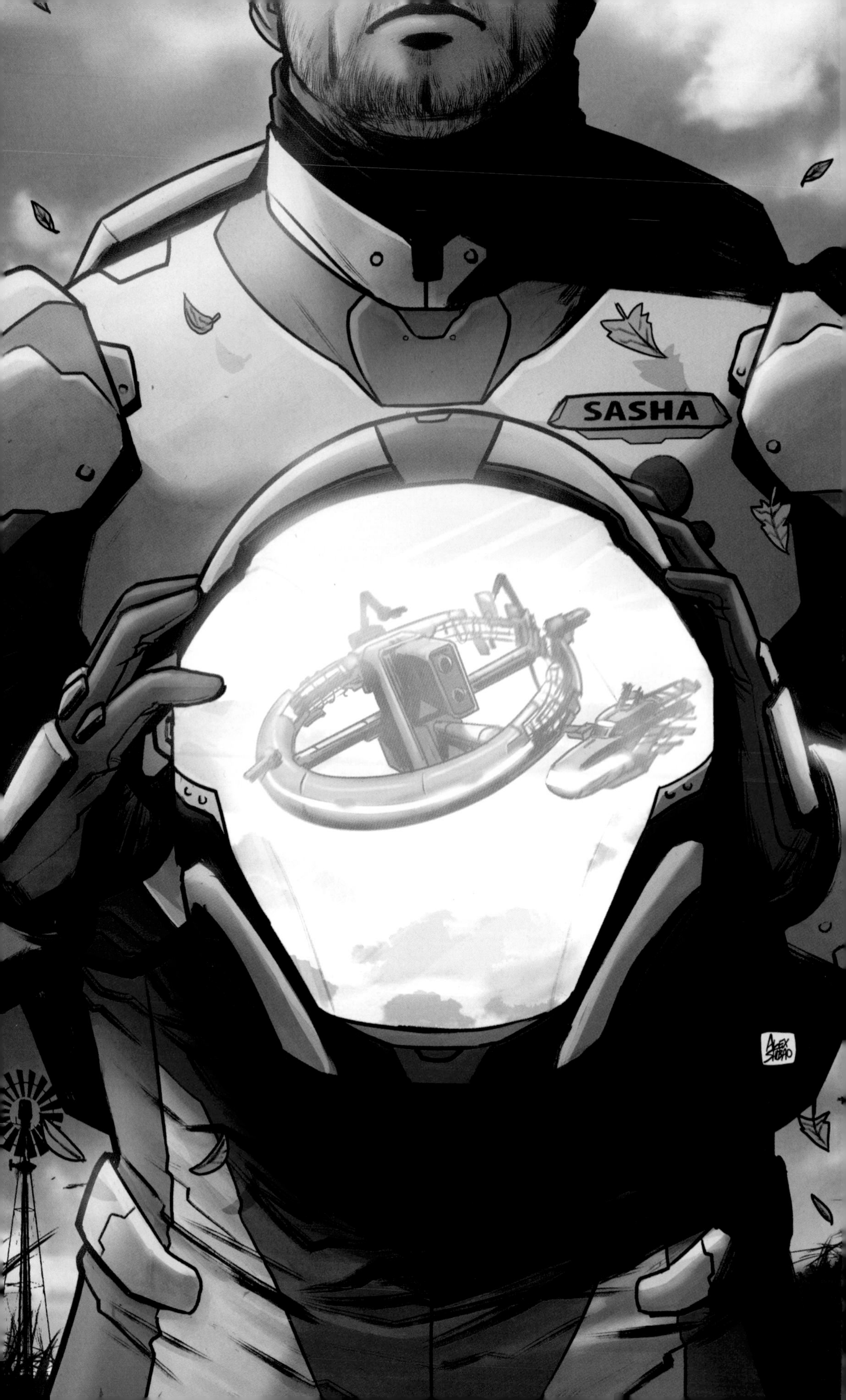
SASHA
ALEX SHIBAO

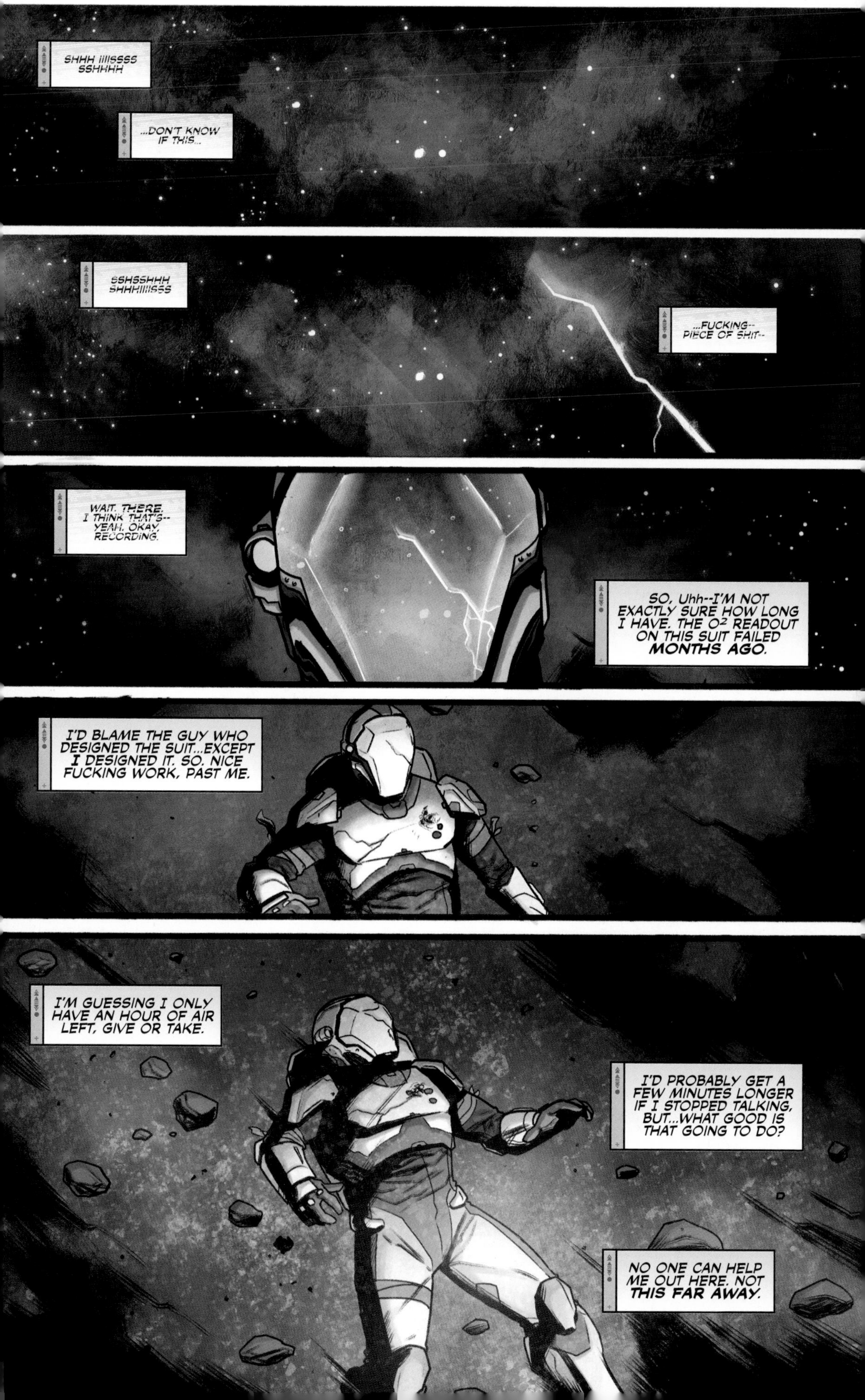
SHHH iiiiSSSS SSHHHH
...DON'T KNOW IF THIS...
SSHSSHHH SHHHIIIISSS
...FUCKING-- PIECE OF SHIT--
WAIT. THERE. I THINK THAT'S-- YEAH. OKAY, RECORDING.
SO, Uhh--I'M NOT EXACTLY SURE HOW LONG I HAVE. THE O² READOUT ON THIS SUIT FAILED MONTHS AGO.
I'D BLAME THE GUY WHO DESIGNED THE SUIT...EXCEPT I DESIGNED IT. SO. NICE FUCKING WORK, PAST ME.
I'M GUESSING I ONLY HAVE AN HOUR OF AIR LEFT, GIVE OR TAKE.
I'D PROBABLY GET A FEW MINUTES LONGER IF I STOPPED TALKING, BUT...WHAT GOOD IS THAT GOING TO DO?
NO ONE CAN HELP ME OUT HERE. NOT THIS FAR AWAY.

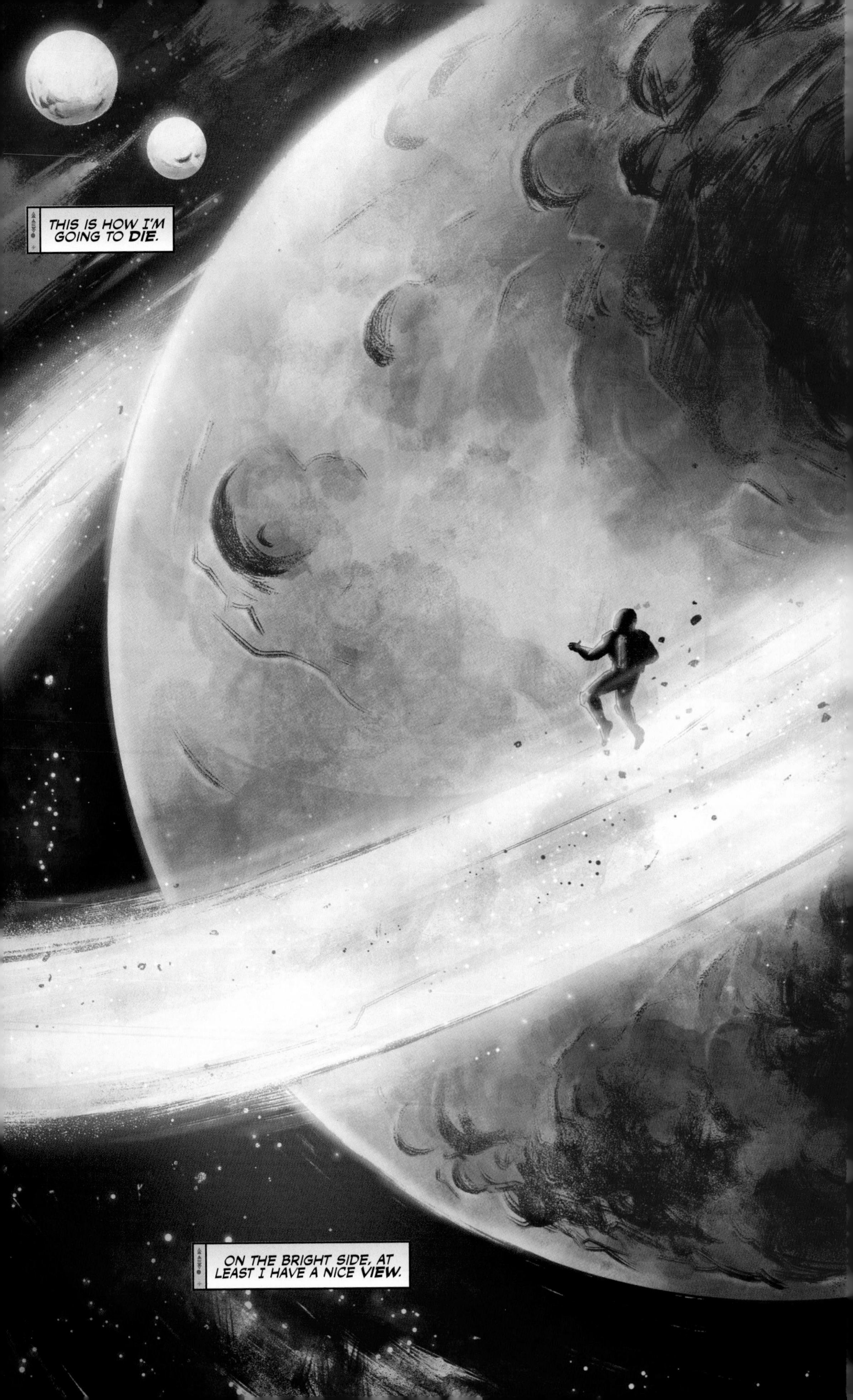
THIS IS HOW I'M GOING TO DIE.
ON THE BRIGHT SIDE, AT LEAST I HAVE A NICE VIEW.

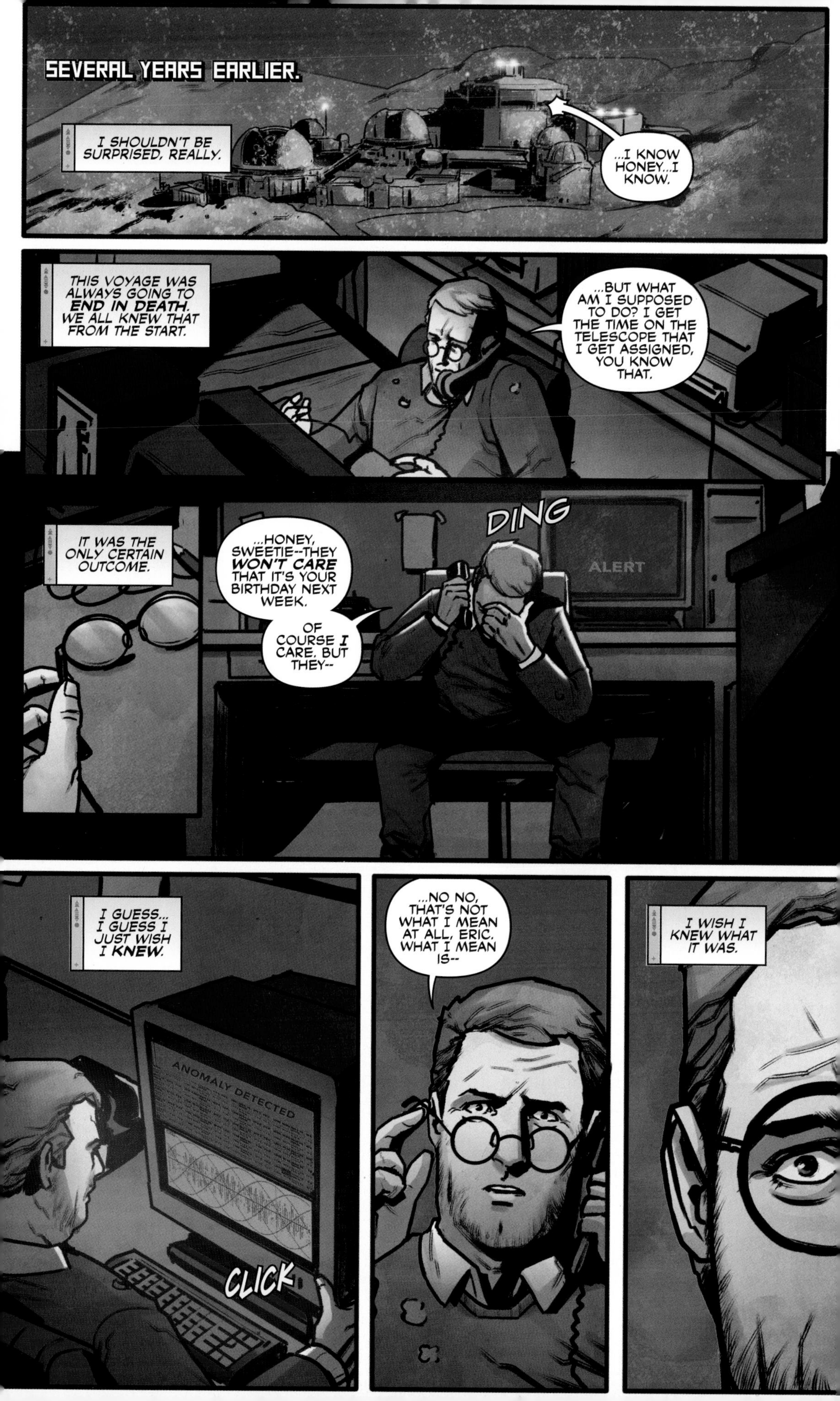
SEVERAL YEARS EARLIER.
I SHOULDN'T BE SURPRISED, REALLY.
...I KNOW HONEY...I KNOW.
THIS VOYAGE WAS ALWAYS GOING TO END IN DEATH. WE ALL KNEW THAT FROM THE START.
...BUT WHAT AM I SUPPOSED TO DO? I GET THE TIME ON THE TELESCOPE THAT I GET ASSIGNED, YOU KNOW THAT.
IT WAS THE ONLY CERTAIN OUTCOME.
...HONEY, SWEETIE--THEY WON'T CARE THAT IT'S YOUR BIRTHDAY NEXT WEEK.
OF COURSE I CARE. BUT THEY--
DING
ALERT
I GUESS... I GUESS I JUST WISH I KNEW.
ANOMALY DETECTED
CLICK
...NO NO, THAT'S NOT WHAT I MEAN AT ALL, ERIC. WHAT I MEAN IS--
I WISH I KNEW WHAT IT WAS.

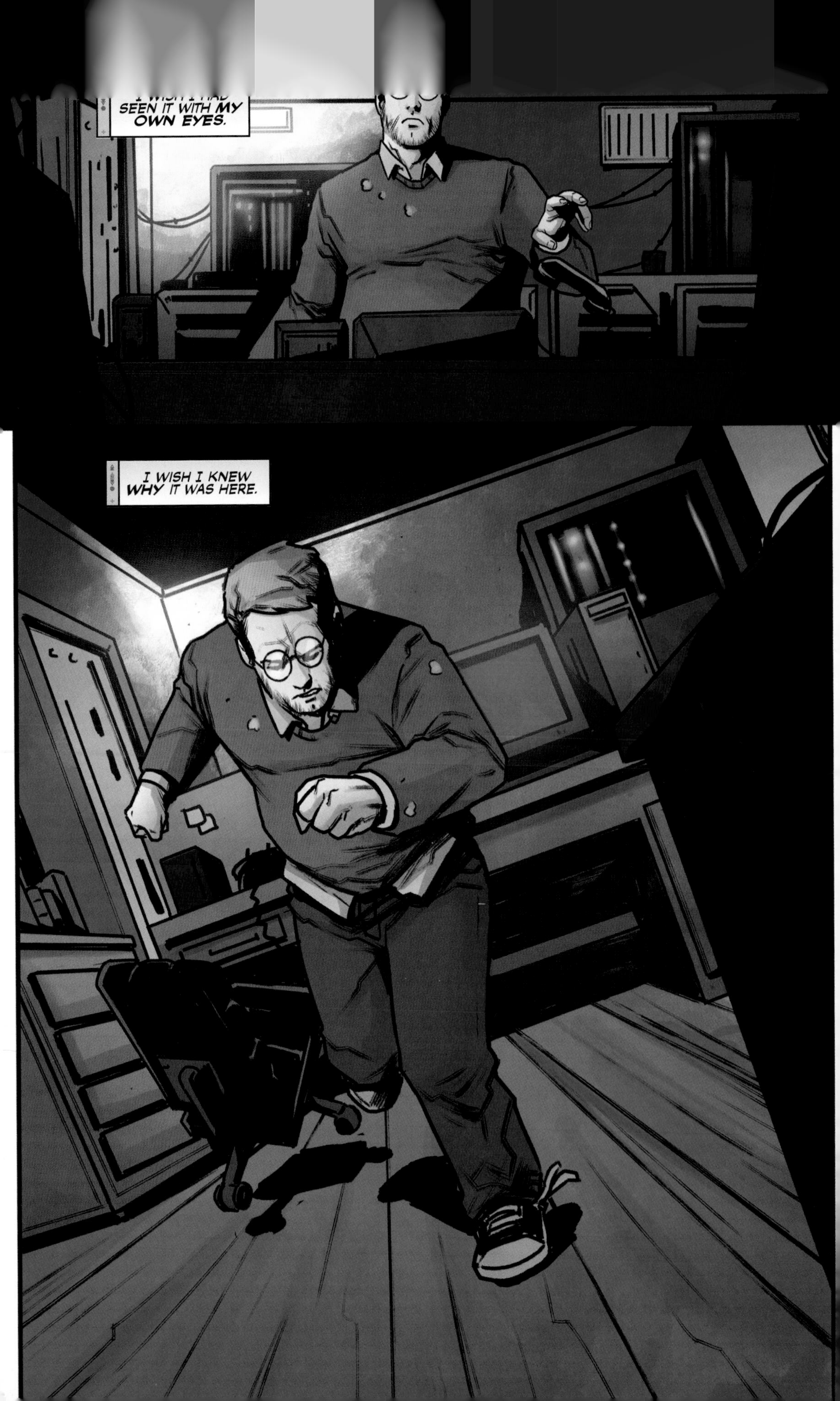
SEEN IT WITH MY OWN EYES.
I WISH I KNEW WHY IT WAS HERE.

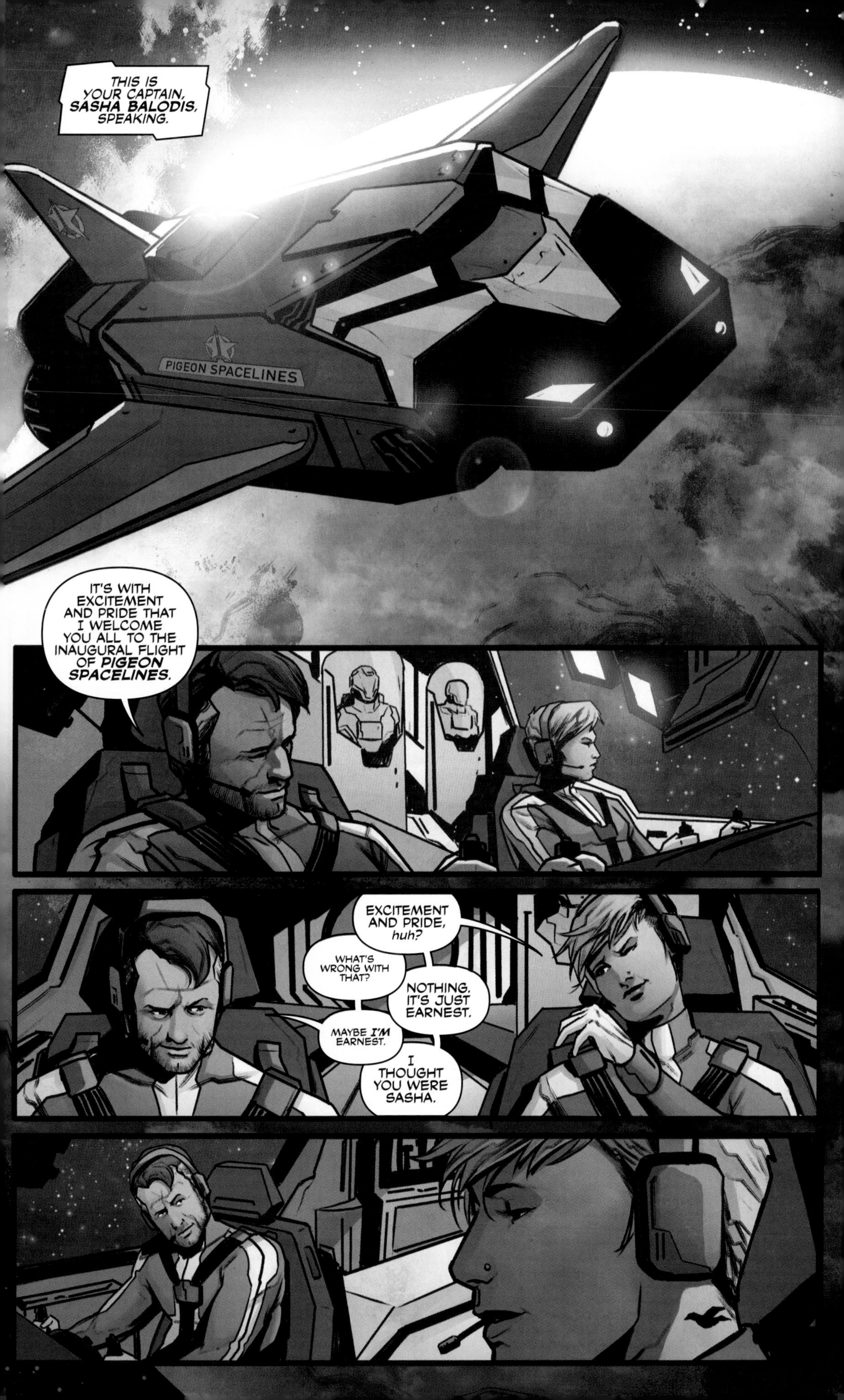
THIS IS YOUR CAPTAIN, SASHA BALODIS, SPEAKING.
PIGEON SPACELINES
IT'S WITH EXCITEMENT AND PRIDE THAT I WELCOME YOU ALL TO THE INAUGURAL FLIGHT OF PIGEON SPACELINES.
EXCITEMENT AND PRIDE, huh?
WHAT'S WRONG WITH THAT?
NOTHING. IT'S JUST EARNEST.
MAYBE I'M EARNEST.
I THOUGHT YOU WERE SASHA.

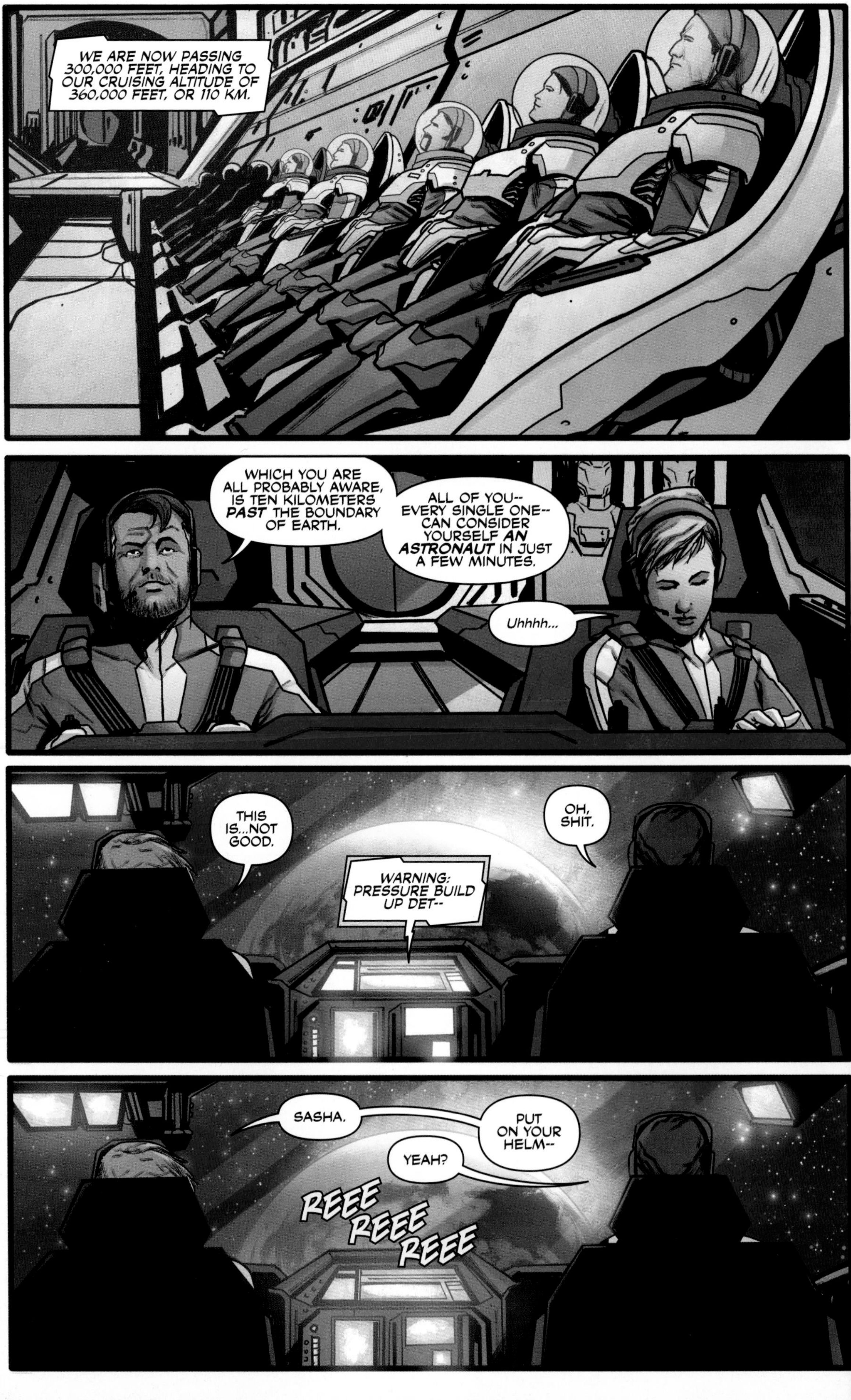
WE ARE NOW PASSING 300,000 FEET, HEADING TO OUR CRUISING ALTITUDE OF 360,000 FEET, OR 110 KM.
WHICH YOU ARE ALL PROBABLY AWARE, IS TEN KILOMETERS PAST THE BOUNDARY OF EARTH.
ALL OF YOU-- EVERY SINGLE ONE-- CAN CONSIDER YOURSELF AN ASTRONAUT IN JUST A FEW MINUTES.
Uhhhh...
THIS IS...NOT GOOD.
OH, SHIT.
WARNING: PRESSURE BUILD UP DET--
SASHA.
YEAH?
PUT ON YOUR HELM--
REEE REEE REEE

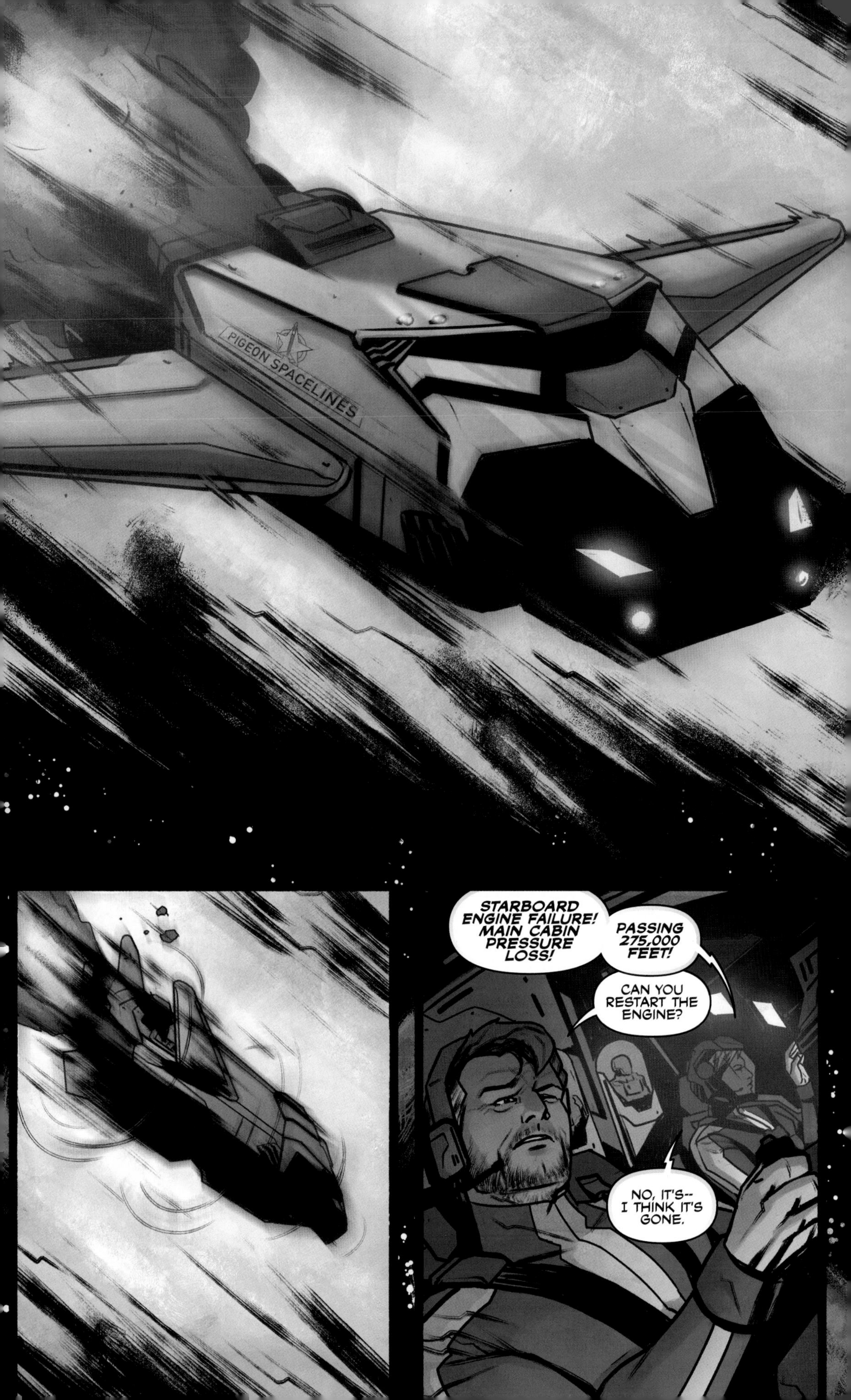
PIGEON SPACELINES
STARBOARD ENGINE FAILURE! MAIN CABIN PRESSURE LOSS!
PASSING 275,000 FEET!
CAN YOU RESTART THE ENGINE?
NO, IT'S-- I THINK IT'S GONE.

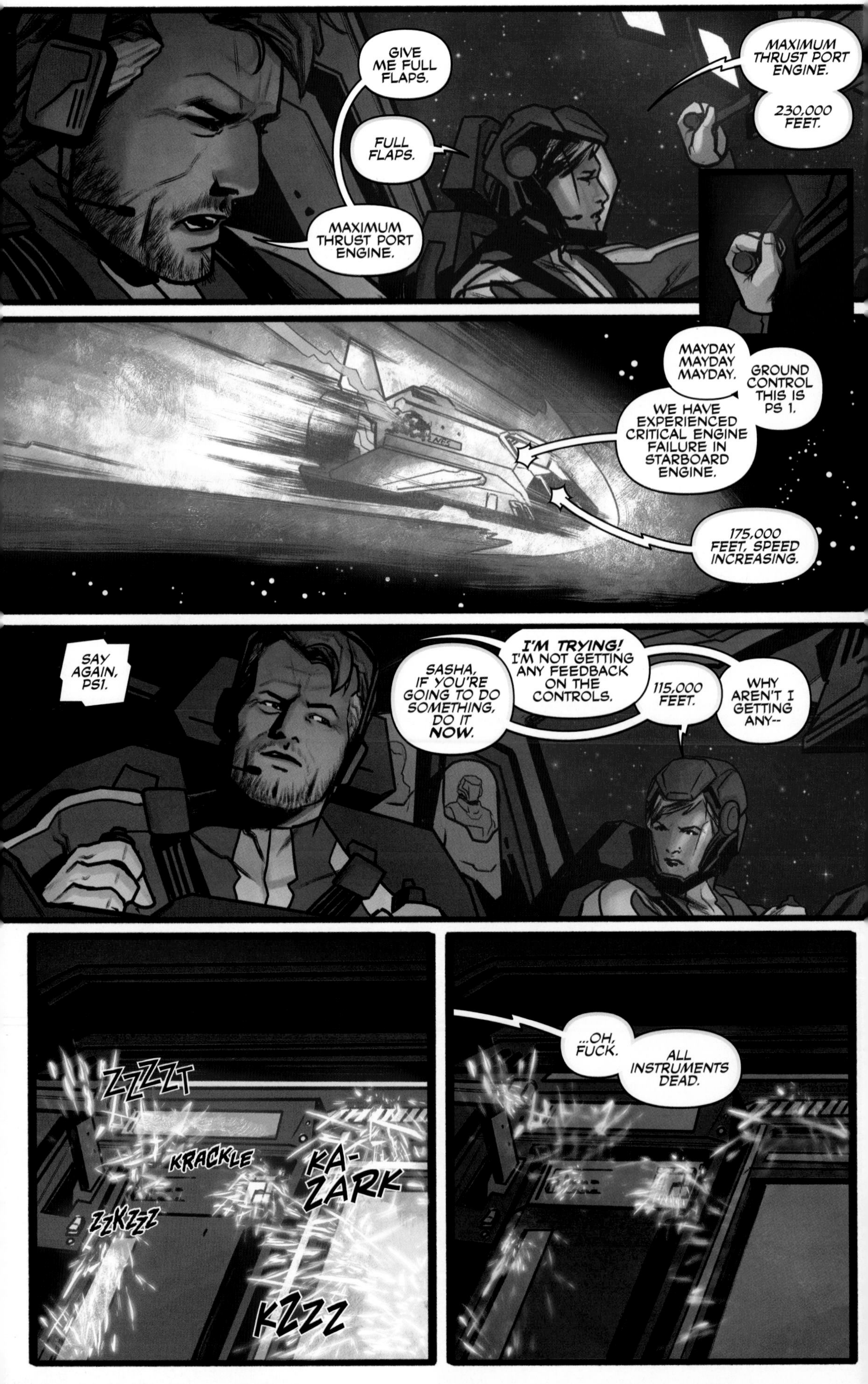

GIVE ME FULL FLAPS.
FULL FLAPS.
MAXIMUM THRUST PORT ENGINE.
MAXIMUM THRUST PORT ENGINE.
230,000 FEET.
MAYDAY MAYDAY MAYDAY.
GROUND CONTROL THIS IS PS 1.
WE HAVE EXPERIENCED CRITICAL ENGINE FAILURE IN STARBOARD ENGINE.
175,000 FEET, SPEED INCREASING.
SAY AGAIN, PS1.
SASHA, IF YOU'RE GOING TO DO SOMETHING, DO IT NOW.
I'M TRYING! I'M NOT GETTING ANY FEEDBACK ON THE CONTROLS.
115,000 FEET.
WHY AREN'T I GETTING ANY--
ZZZZT
KRACKLE
KA-ZARK
ZZKZZZ
KZZZ
...OH, FUCK.
ALL INSTRUMENTS DEAD.

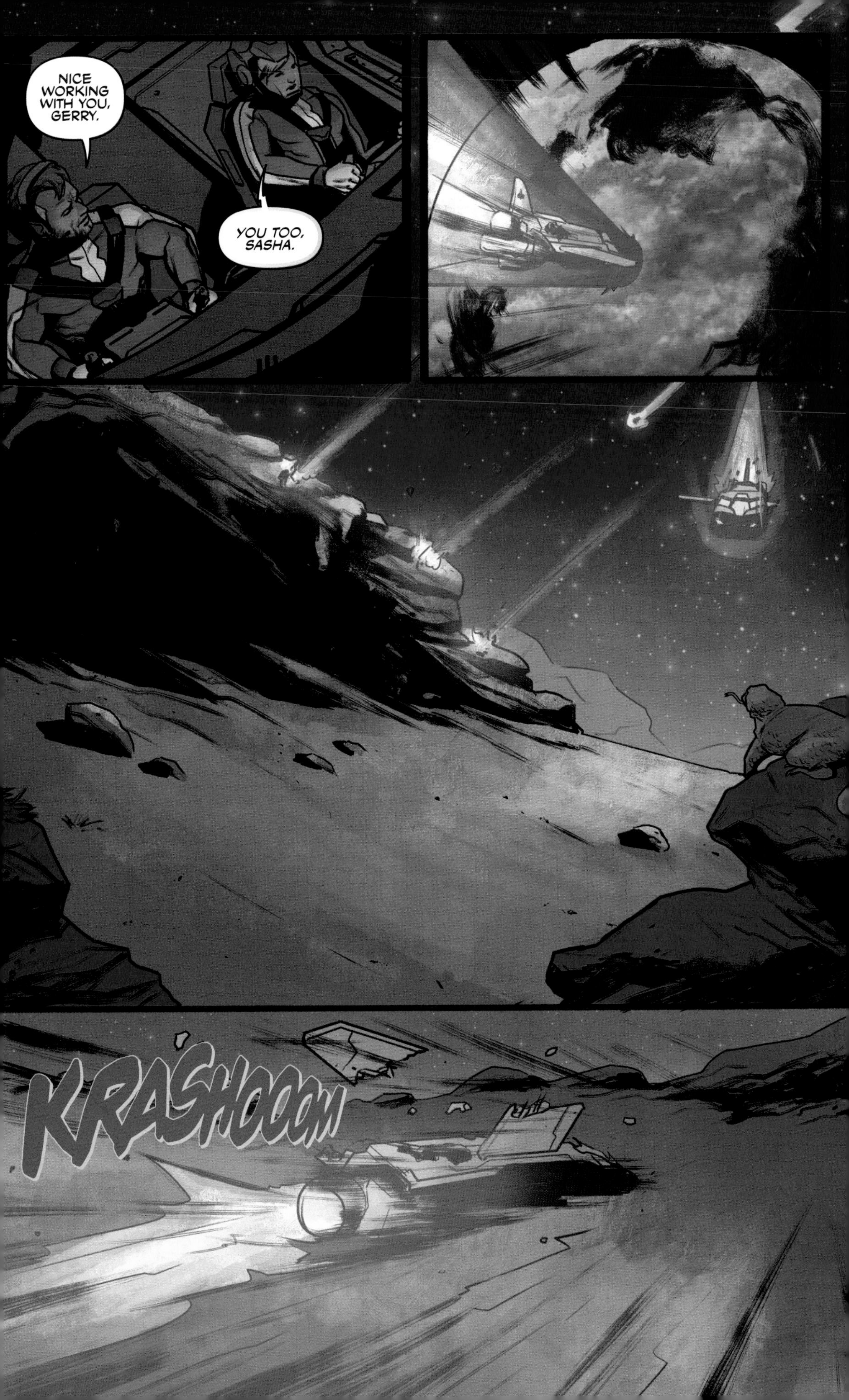
NICE WORKING WITH YOU, GERRY.
YOU TOO, SASHA.
KRASHOOOM

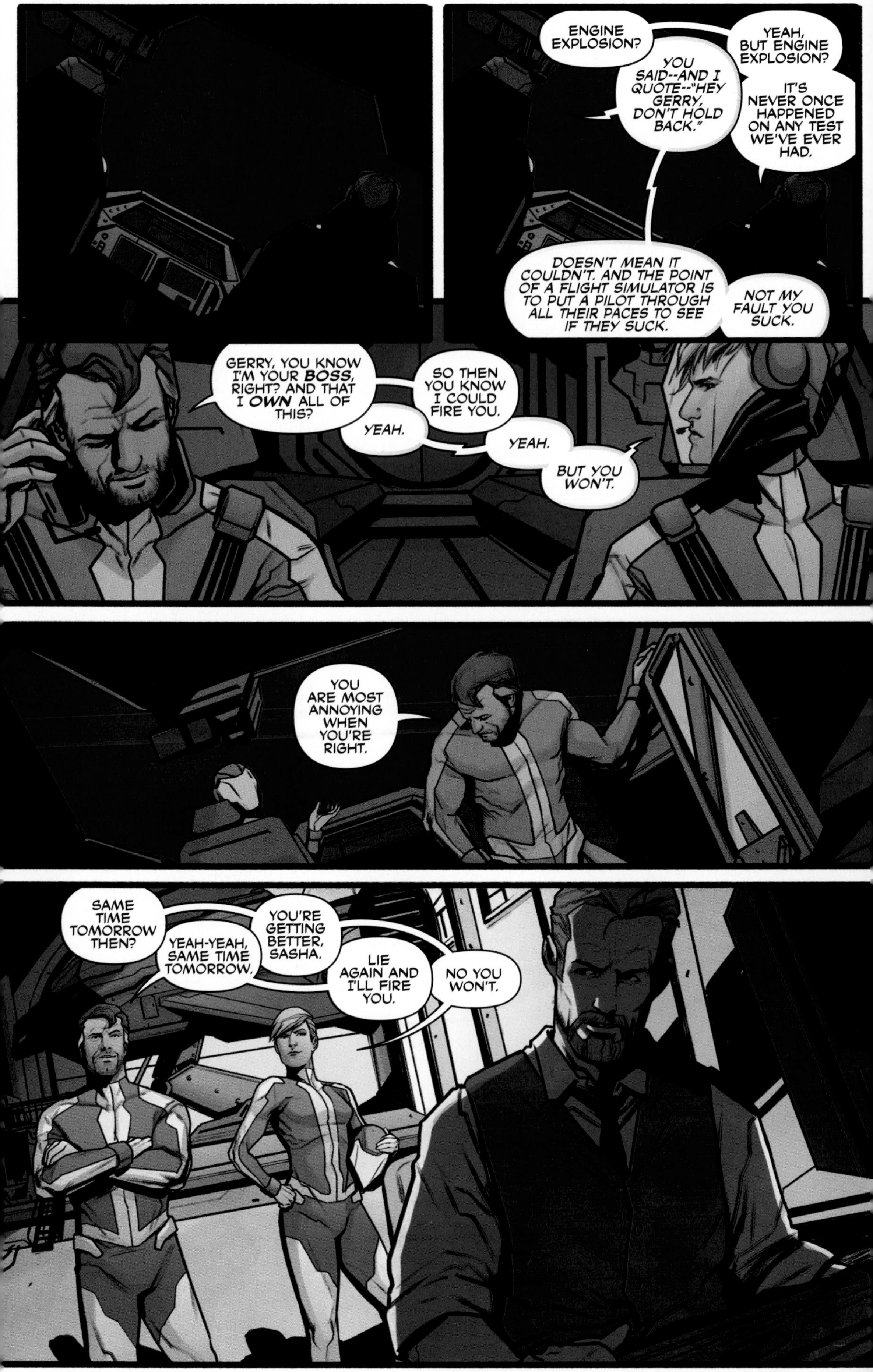
ENGINE EXPLOSION?
YOU SAID--AND I QUOTE--"HEY GERRY, DON'T HOLD BACK."
YEAH, BUT ENGINE EXPLOSION?
IT'S NEVER ONCE HAPPENED ON ANY TEST WE'VE EVER HAD.
DOESN'T MEAN IT COULDN'T. AND THE POINT OF A FLIGHT SIMULATOR IS TO PUT A PILOT THROUGH ALL THEIR PACES TO SEE IF THEY SUCK.
NOT MY FAULT YOU SUCK.
GERRY, YOU KNOW I'M YOUR BOSS, RIGHT? AND THAT I OWN ALL OF THIS?
YEAH.
SO THEN YOU KNOW I COULD FIRE YOU.
YEAH.
BUT YOU WON'T.
YOU ARE MOST ANNOYING WHEN YOU'RE RIGHT.
SAME TIME TOMORROW THEN?
YEAH-YEAH, SAME TIME TOMORROW.
YOU'RE GETTING BETTER, SASHA.
LIE AGAIN AND I'LL FIRE YOU.
NO YOU WON'T.

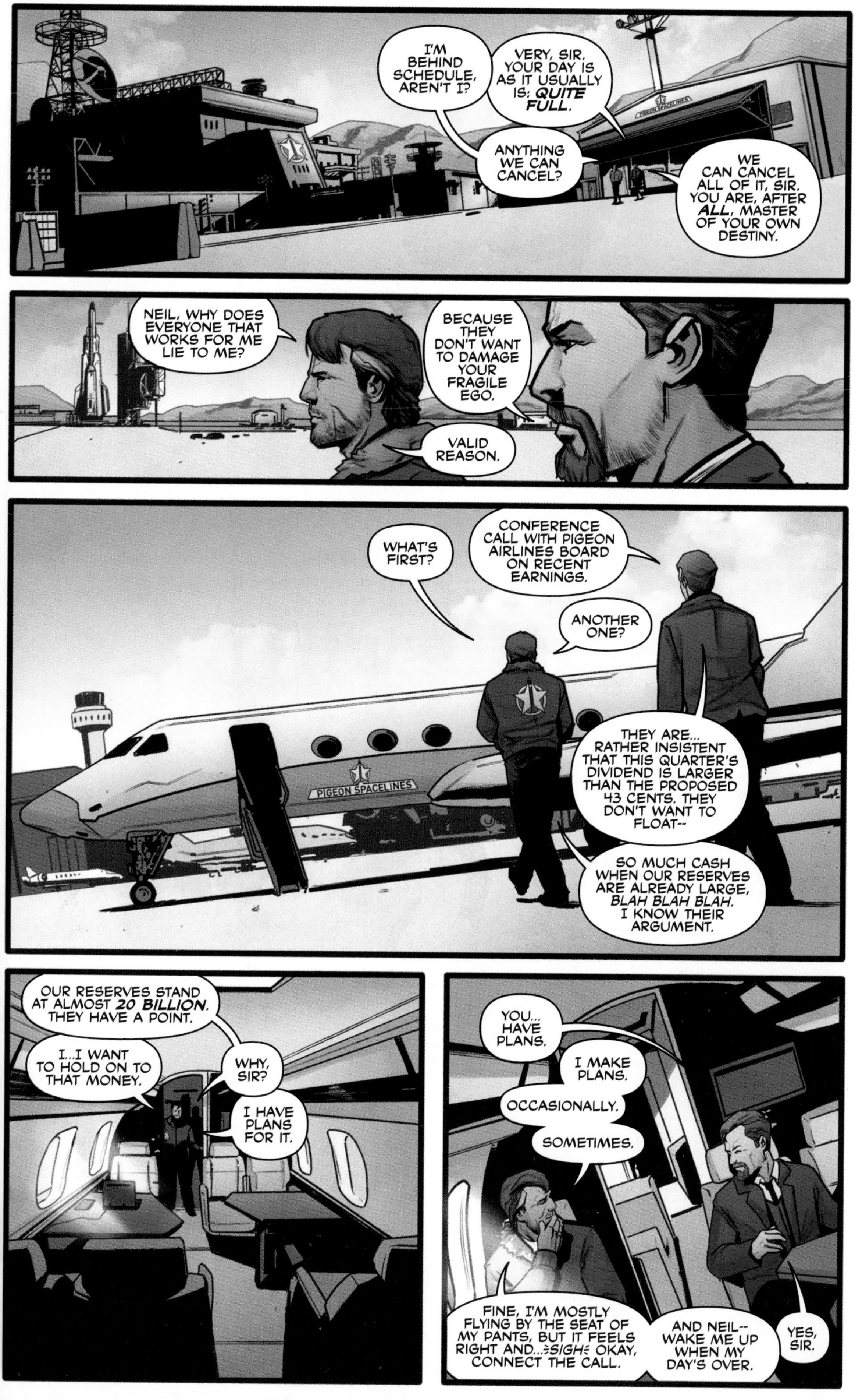

I'M BEHIND SCHEDULE, AREN'T I?
VERY, SIR. YOUR DAY IS AS IT USUALLY IS: **QUITE FULL**.
ANYTHING WE CAN CANCEL?
WE CAN CANCEL ALL OF IT, SIR. YOU ARE, AFTER **ALL**, MASTER OF YOUR OWN DESTINY.
PIGEON SPACELINES
NEIL, WHY DOES EVERYONE THAT WORKS FOR ME LIE TO ME?
BECAUSE THEY DON'T WANT TO DAMAGE YOUR FRAGILE EGO.
VALID REASON.
WHAT'S FIRST?
CONFERENCE CALL WITH PIGEON AIRLINES BOARD ON RECENT EARNINGS.
ANOTHER ONE?
THEY ARE... RATHER INSISTENT THAT THIS QUARTER'S DIVIDEND IS LARGER THAN THE PROPOSED 43 CENTS. THEY DON'T WANT TO FLOAT--
SO MUCH CASH WHEN OUR RESERVES ARE ALREADY LARGE, *BLAH BLAH BLAH*. I KNOW THEIR ARGUMENT.
PIGEON SPACELINES
OUR RESERVES STAND AT ALMOST ***20 BILLION***. THEY HAVE A POINT.
I...I WANT TO HOLD ON TO THAT MONEY.
WHY, SIR?
I HAVE PLANS FOR IT.
YOU... HAVE PLANS.
I MAKE PLANS.
OCCASIONALLY.
SOMETIMES.
FINE, I'M MOSTLY FLYING BY THE SEAT OF MY PANTS, BUT IT FEELS RIGHT AND... *SIGH* OKAY, CONNECT THE CALL.
AND NEIL-- WAKE ME UP WHEN MY DAY'S OVER.
YES, SIR.

8:17 AM

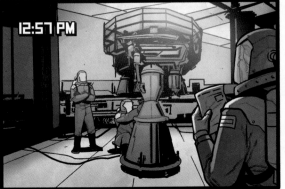

12:57 PM

4:48 PM

9:35 PM

United Nations Arts
and
Science Advisory Council Gala

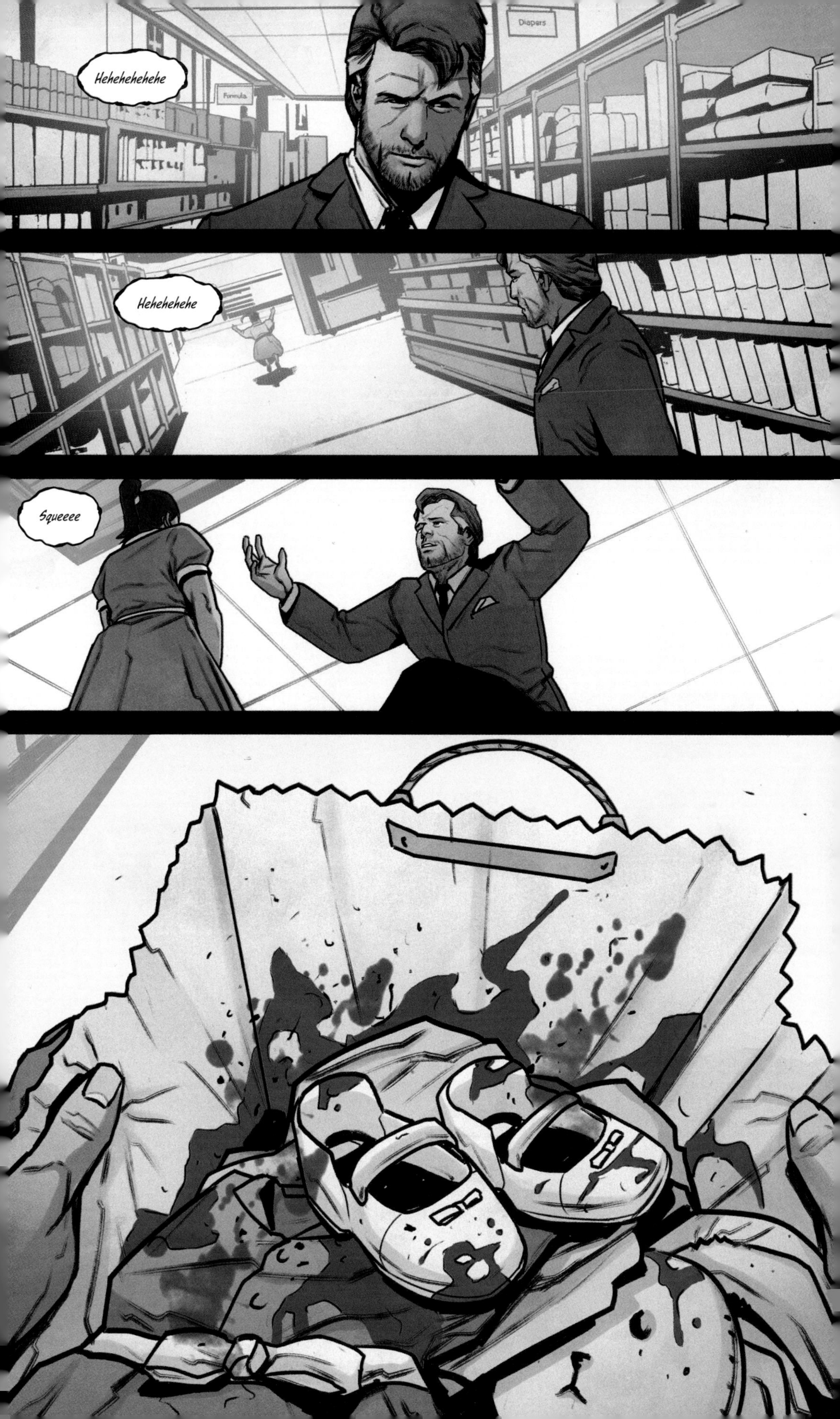
Hehehehehehe
Formula
Diapers
Hehehehehe
Squeeee

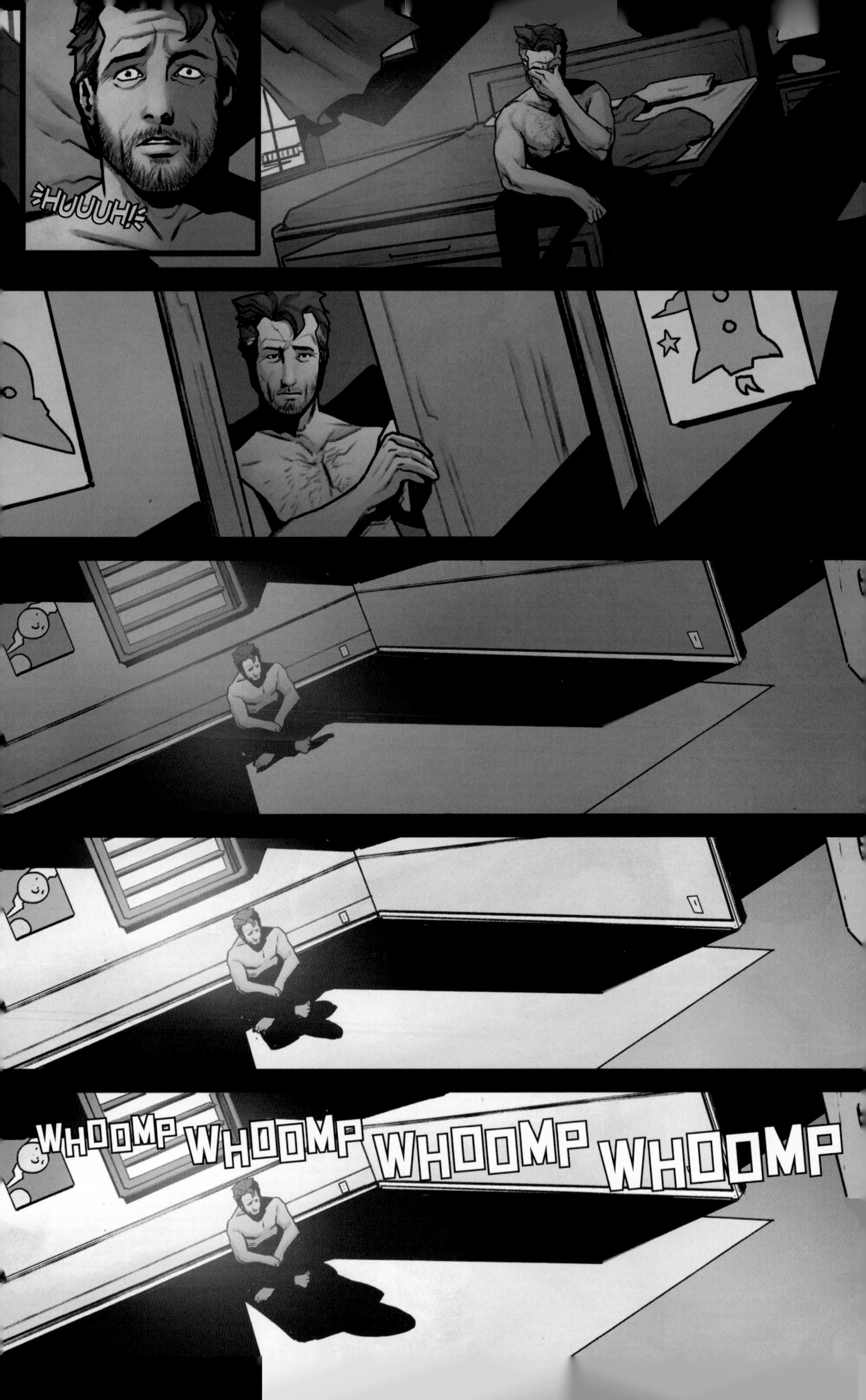
HUUUH!
WHOOMP WHOOMP WHOOMP WHOOMP

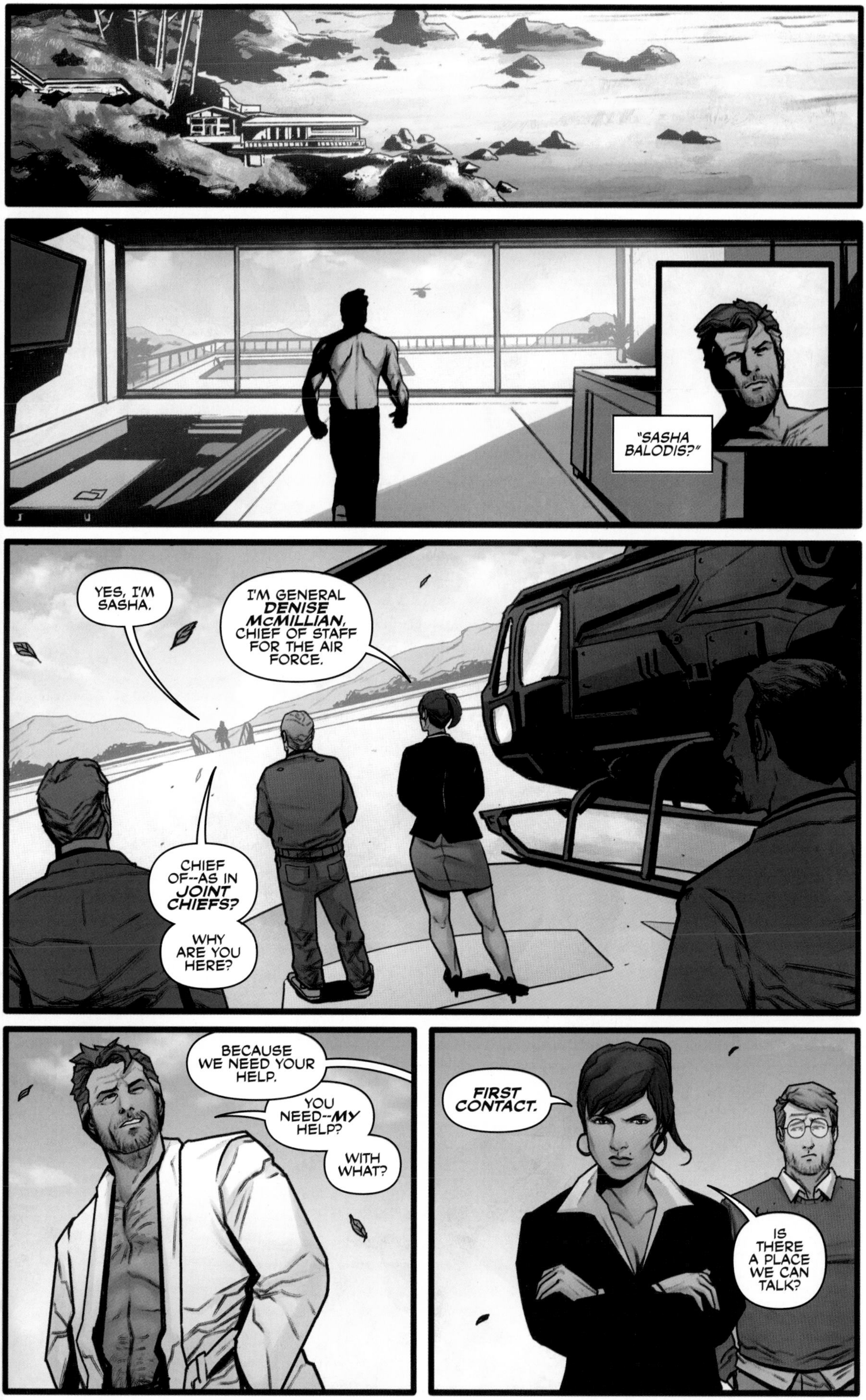
"SASHA BALODIS?"
YES, I'M SASHA.
I'M GENERAL DENISE McMILLIAN, CHIEF OF STAFF FOR THE AIR FORCE.
CHIEF OF--AS IN JOINT CHIEFS?
WHY ARE YOU HERE?
BECAUSE WE NEED YOUR HELP.
YOU NEED--MY HELP?
WITH WHAT?
FIRST CONTACT.
IS THERE A PLACE WE CAN TALK?

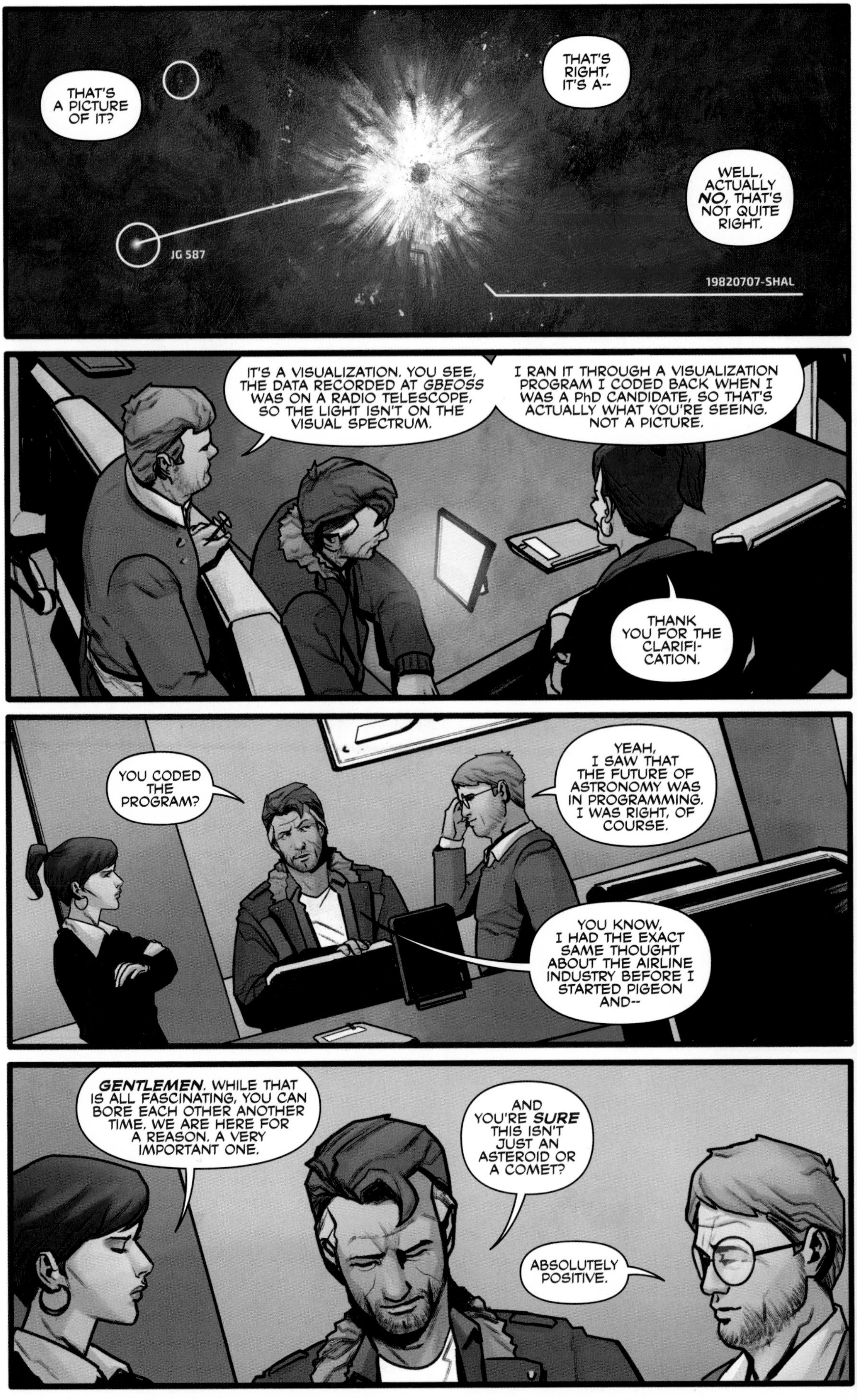
THAT'S A PICTURE OF IT?
THAT'S RIGHT, IT'S A--
WELL, ACTUALLY NO, THAT'S NOT QUITE RIGHT.
JG 587
19820707-SHAL
IT'S A VISUALIZATION. YOU SEE, THE DATA RECORDED AT GBEOSS WAS ON A RADIO TELESCOPE, SO THE LIGHT ISN'T ON THE VISUAL SPECTRUM.
I RAN IT THROUGH A VISUALIZATION PROGRAM I CODED BACK WHEN I WAS A PhD CANDIDATE, SO THAT'S ACTUALLY WHAT YOU'RE SEEING. NOT A PICTURE.
THANK YOU FOR THE CLARIFI-CATION.
YOU CODED THE PROGRAM?
YEAH, I SAW THAT THE FUTURE OF ASTRONOMY WAS IN PROGRAMMING. I WAS RIGHT, OF COURSE.
YOU KNOW, I HAD THE EXACT SAME THOUGHT ABOUT THE AIRLINE INDUSTRY BEFORE I STARTED PIGEON AND--
GENTLEMEN. WHILE THAT IS ALL FASCINATING, YOU CAN BORE EACH OTHER ANOTHER TIME. WE ARE HERE FOR A REASON. A VERY IMPORTANT ONE.
AND YOU'RE SURE THIS ISN'T JUST AN ASTEROID OR A COMET?
ABSOLUTELY POSITIVE.

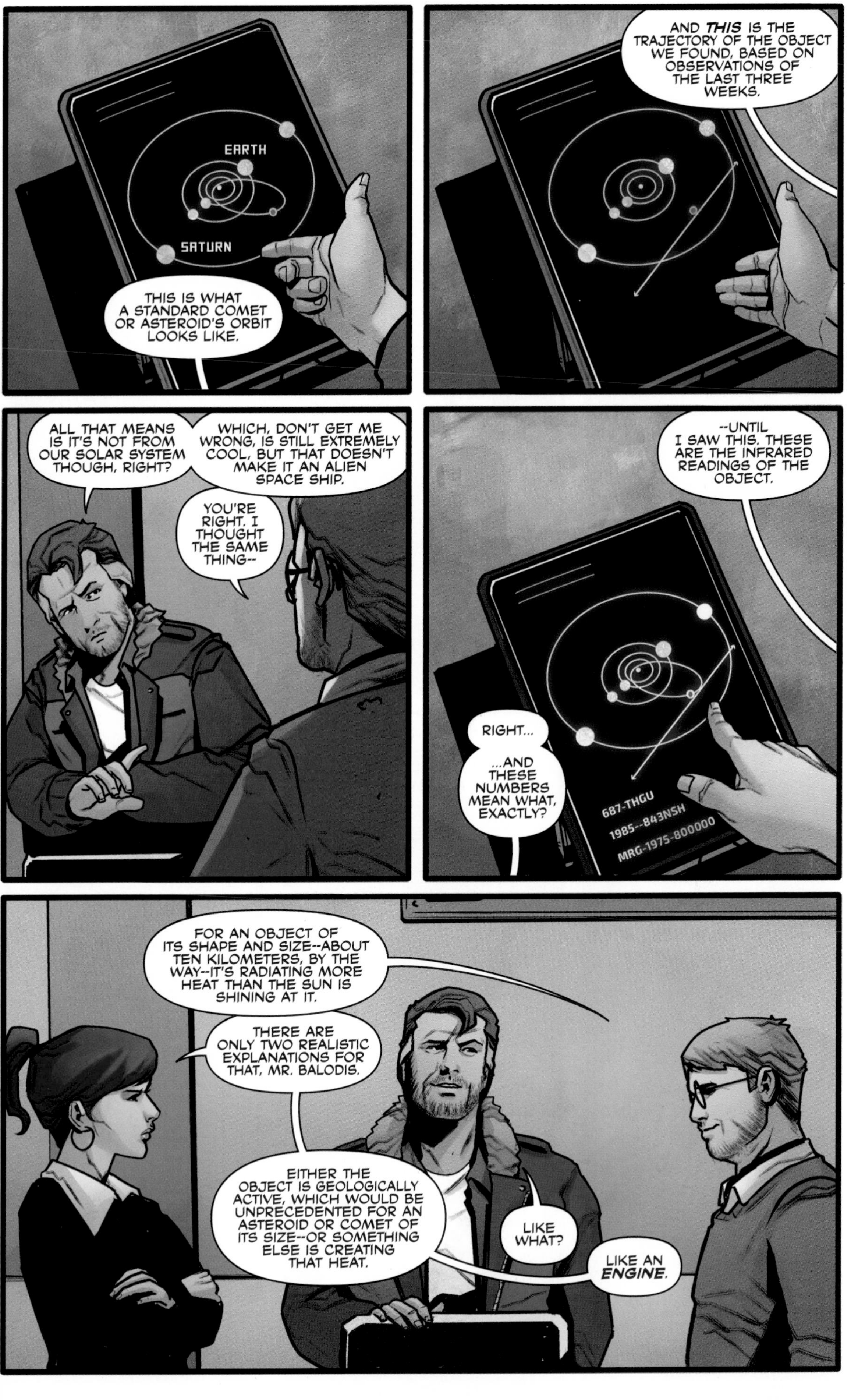
EARTH
SATURN
THIS IS WHAT A STANDARD COMET OR ASTEROID'S ORBIT LOOKS LIKE.
AND THIS IS THE TRAJECTORY OF THE OBJECT WE FOUND, BASED ON OBSERVATIONS OF THE LAST THREE WEEKS.
ALL THAT MEANS IS IT'S NOT FROM OUR SOLAR SYSTEM THOUGH, RIGHT?
WHICH, DON'T GET ME WRONG, IS STILL EXTREMELY COOL, BUT THAT DOESN'T MAKE IT AN ALIEN SPACE SHIP.
YOU'RE RIGHT. I THOUGHT THE SAME THING--
--UNTIL I SAW THIS. THESE ARE THE INFRARED READINGS OF THE OBJECT.
RIGHT...
...AND THESE NUMBERS MEAN WHAT, EXACTLY?
687-THGU
1985--843NSH
MRG-1975-800000
FOR AN OBJECT OF ITS SHAPE AND SIZE--ABOUT TEN KILOMETERS, BY THE WAY--IT'S RADIATING MORE HEAT THAN THE SUN IS SHINING AT IT.
THERE ARE ONLY TWO REALISTIC EXPLANATIONS FOR THAT, MR. BALODIS.
EITHER THE OBJECT IS GEOLOGICALLY ACTIVE, WHICH WOULD BE UNPRECEDENTED FOR AN ASTEROID OR COMET OF ITS SIZE--OR SOMETHING ELSE IS CREATING THAT HEAT.
LIKE WHAT?
LIKE AN ENGINE.

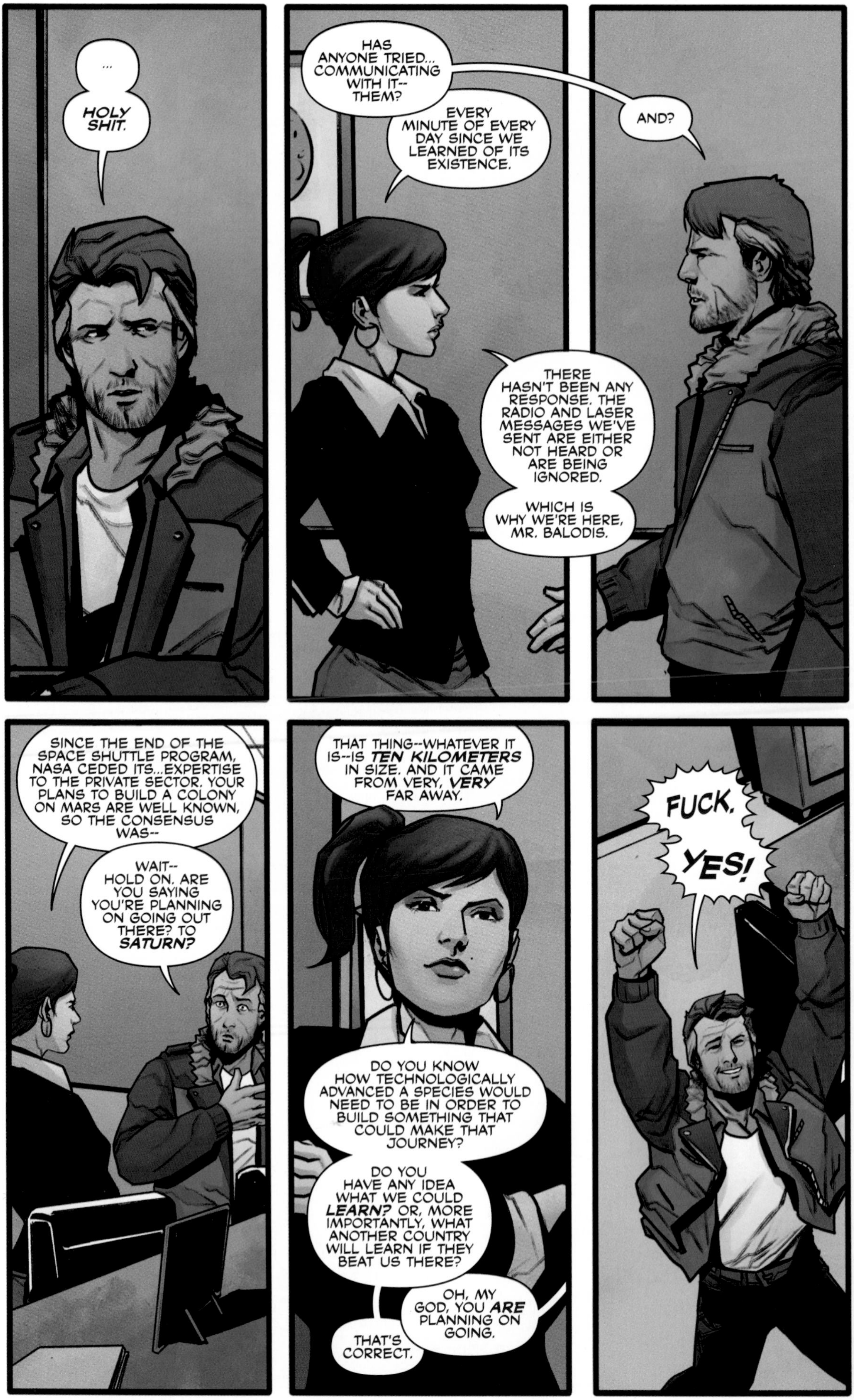

...
HOLY SHIT.
HAS ANYONE TRIED... COMMUNICATING WITH IT--THEM?
EVERY MINUTE OF EVERY DAY SINCE WE LEARNED OF ITS EXISTENCE.
AND?
THERE HASN'T BEEN ANY RESPONSE. THE RADIO AND LASER MESSAGES WE'VE SENT ARE EITHER NOT HEARD OR ARE BEING IGNORED.
WHICH IS WHY WE'RE HERE, MR. BALODIS.
SINCE THE END OF THE SPACE SHUTTLE PROGRAM, NASA CEDED ITS...EXPERTISE TO THE PRIVATE SECTOR. YOUR PLANS TO BUILD A COLONY ON MARS ARE WELL KNOWN, SO THE CONSENSUS WAS--
WAIT-- HOLD ON. ARE YOU SAYING YOU'RE PLANNING ON GOING OUT THERE? TO SATURN?
THAT THING--WHATEVER IT IS--IS TEN KILOMETERS IN SIZE. AND IT CAME FROM VERY, VERY FAR AWAY.
DO YOU KNOW HOW TECHNOLOGICALLY ADVANCED A SPECIES WOULD NEED TO BE IN ORDER TO BUILD SOMETHING THAT COULD MAKE THAT JOURNEY?
DO YOU HAVE ANY IDEA WHAT WE COULD LEARN? OR, MORE IMPORTANTLY, WHAT ANOTHER COUNTRY WILL LEARN IF THEY BEAT US THERE?
OH, MY GOD, YOU ARE PLANNING ON GOING.
THAT'S CORRECT.
FUCK, YES!

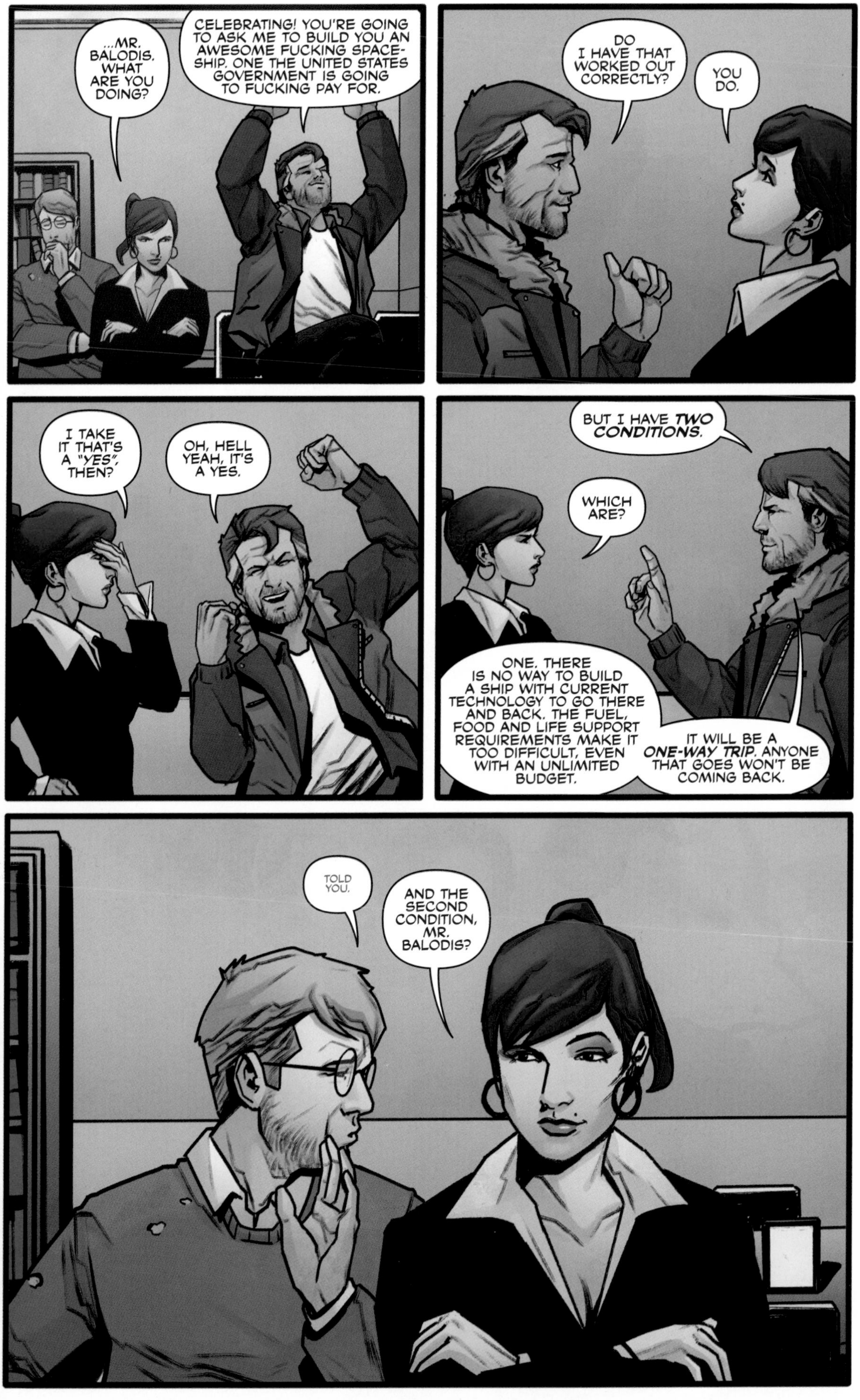
...MR. BALODIS. WHAT ARE YOU DOING?
CELEBRATING! YOU'RE GOING TO ASK ME TO BUILD YOU AN AWESOME FUCKING SPACE-SHIP. ONE THE UNITED STATES GOVERNMENT IS GOING TO FUCKING PAY FOR.
DO I HAVE THAT WORKED OUT CORRECTLY?
YOU DO.
I TAKE IT THAT'S A "YES", THEN?
OH, HELL YEAH, IT'S A YES.
BUT I HAVE TWO CONDITIONS.
WHICH ARE?
ONE. THERE IS NO WAY TO BUILD A SHIP WITH CURRENT TECHNOLOGY TO GO THERE AND BACK. THE FUEL, FOOD AND LIFE SUPPORT REQUIREMENTS MAKE IT TOO DIFFICULT, EVEN WITH AN UNLIMITED BUDGET.
IT WILL BE A ONE-WAY TRIP. ANYONE THAT GOES WON'T BE COMING BACK.
TOLD YOU.
AND THE SECOND CONDITION, MR. BALODIS?

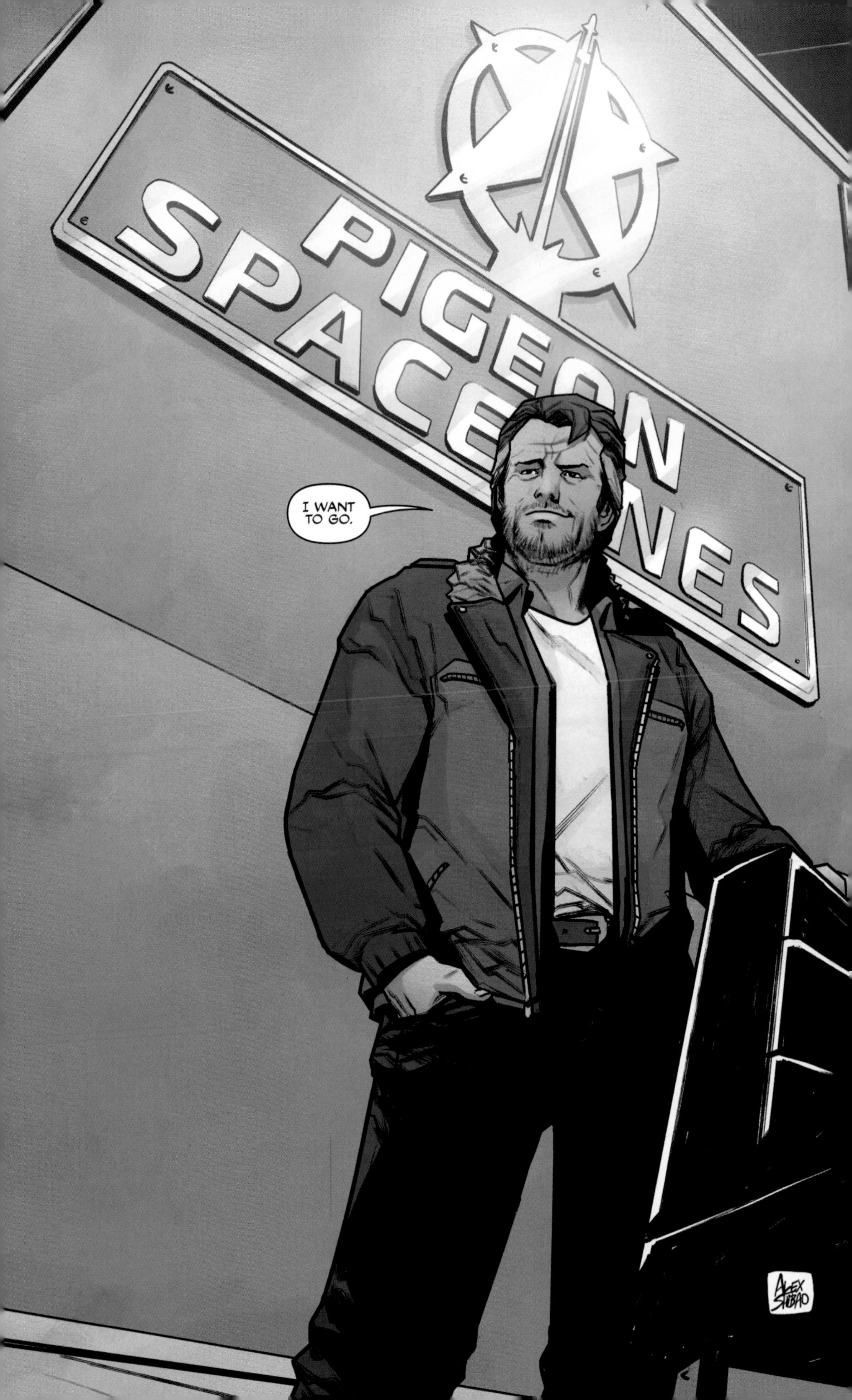
PIGEON
I WANT TO GO.
ALEX SHIBAO

2

PHOSPHOR

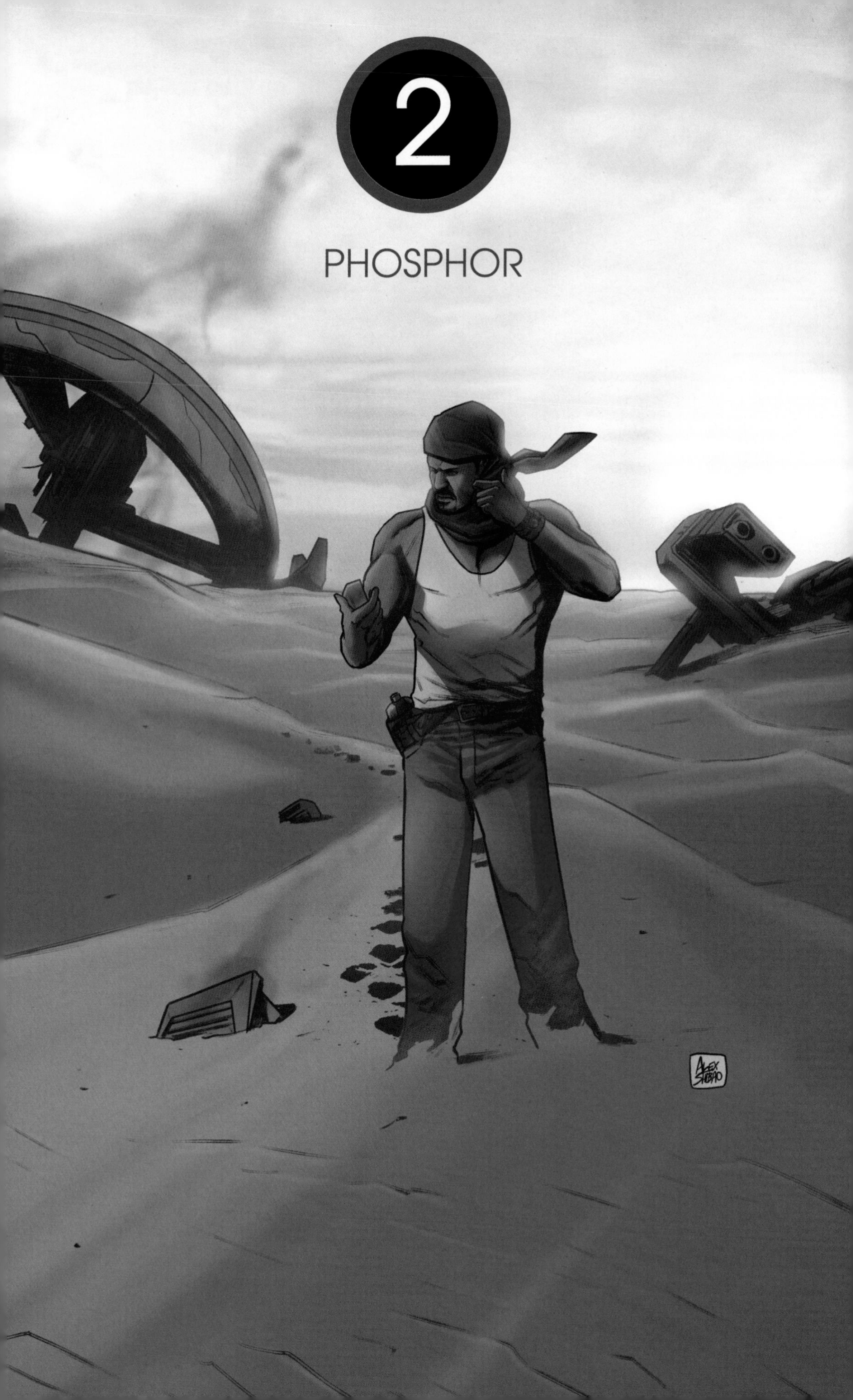
ALEX SHIBAO

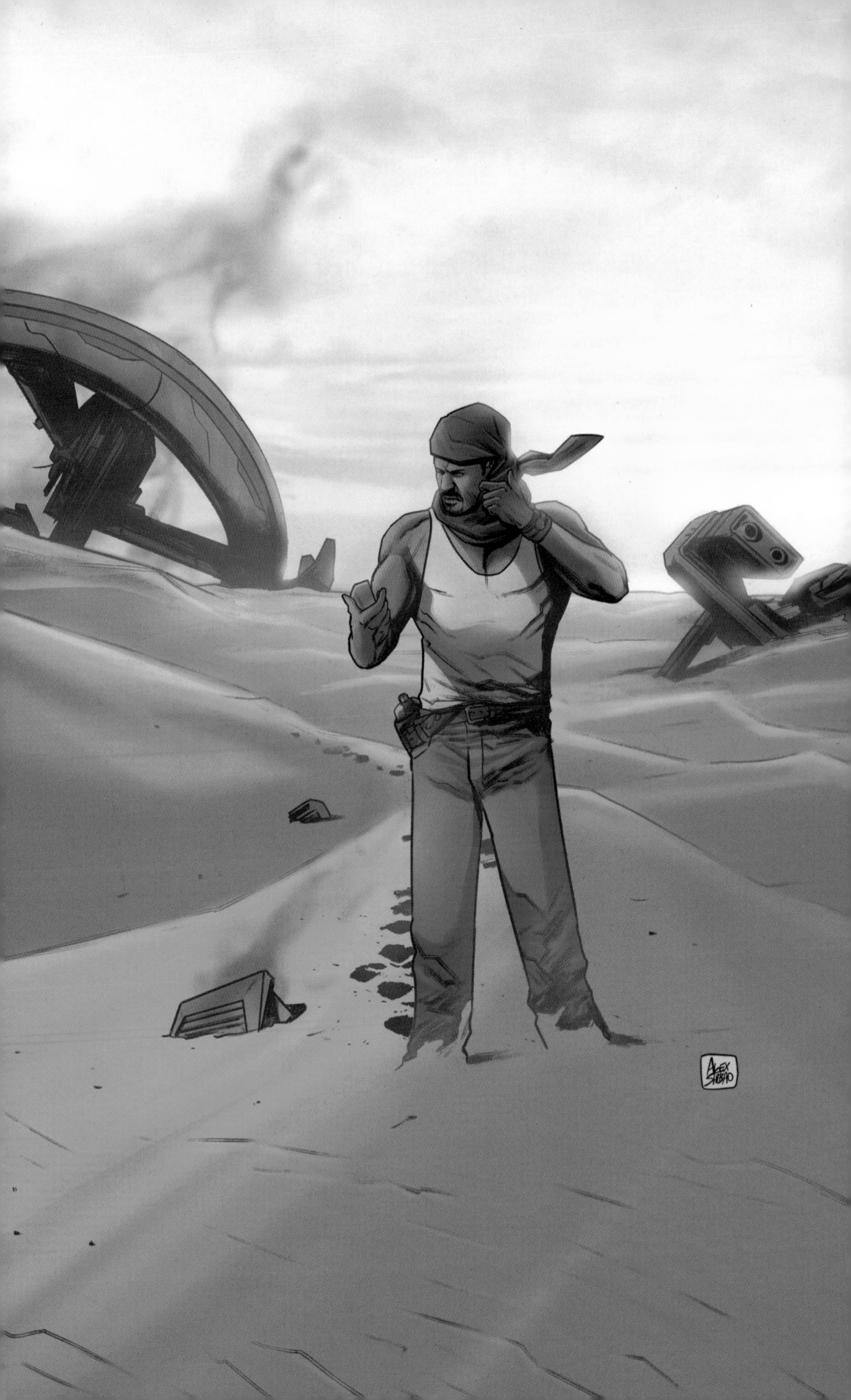

A MINDLESS DREAM OF FLIGHT

-OR-

The Terror of Dying and Not Being Remembered

A Memoir of
ROGER FREEMAN

The tale of a black man trying to succeed
in America and find meaning in his life
despite the color of his skin.

"A life is a story remembered in the mind of God."
- H.L. Williamson

"Stories are tricks. Yes, they are a trick."
- Jep Gambardella

Compton and Song Press

Compton and Song Press

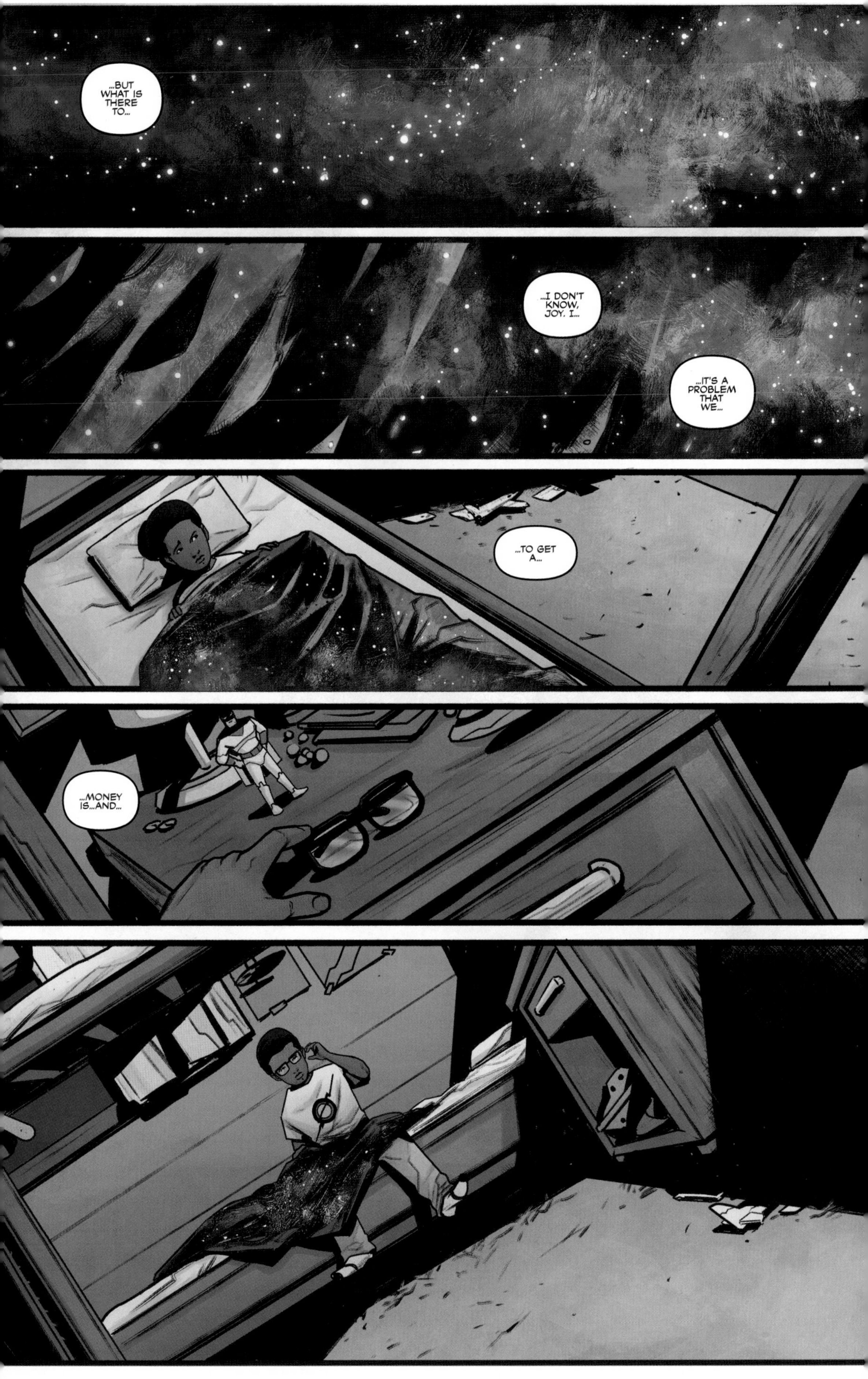
...BUT WHAT IS THERE TO...
...I DON'T KNOW, JOY. I...
...IT'S A PROBLEM THAT WE...
...TO GET A...
...MONEY IS...AND...

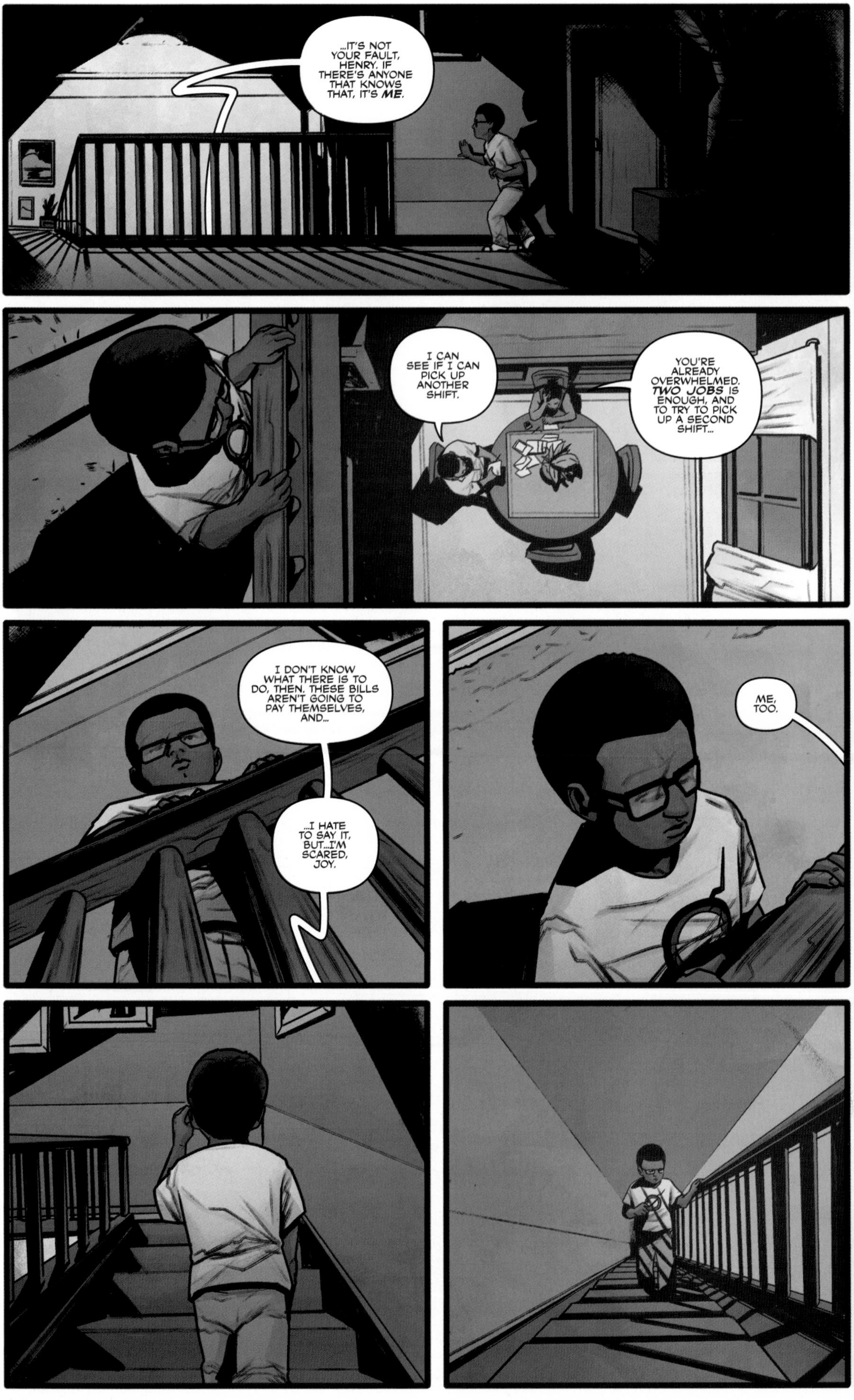
...IT'S NOT YOUR FAULT, HENRY. IF THERE'S ANYONE THAT KNOWS THAT, IT'S ME.
I CAN SEE IF I CAN PICK UP ANOTHER SHIFT.
YOU'RE ALREADY OVERWHELMED. TWO JOBS IS ENOUGH, AND TO TRY TO PICK UP A SECOND SHIFT...
I DON'T KNOW WHAT THERE IS TO DO, THEN. THESE BILLS AREN'T GOING TO PAY THEMSELVES, AND...
...I HATE TO SAY IT, BUT...I'M SCARED, JOY.
ME, TOO.

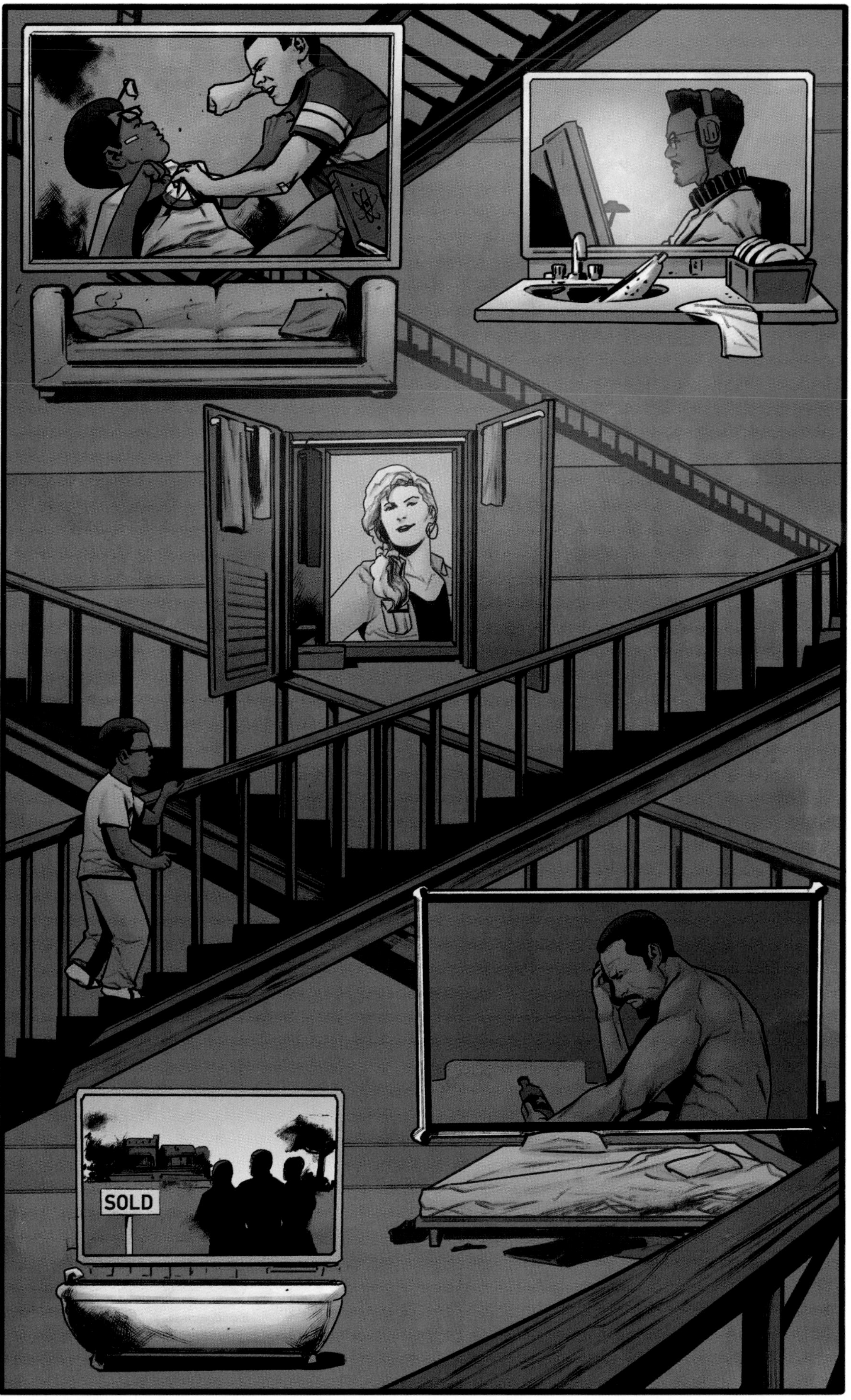
SOLD

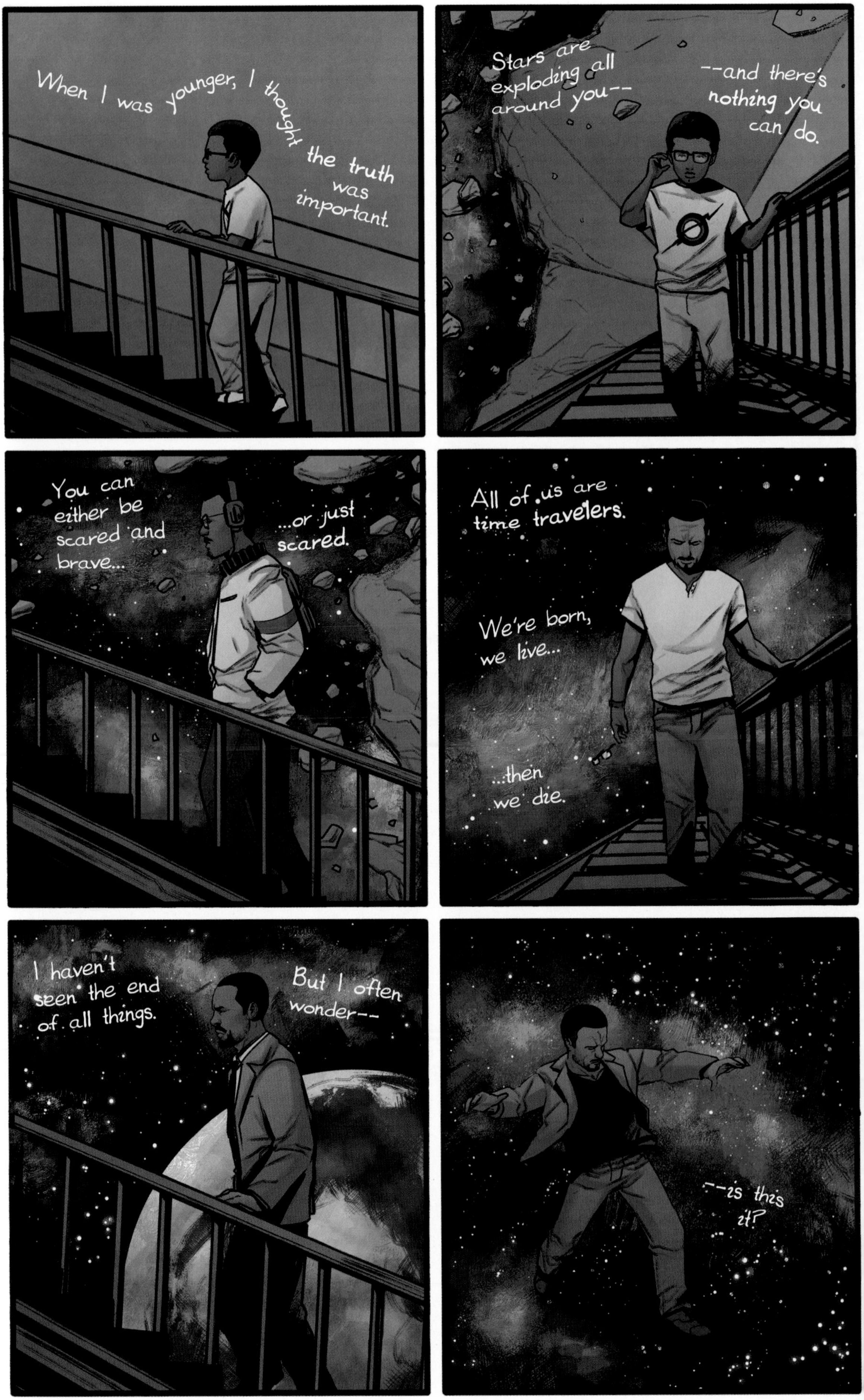
When I was younger, I thought the truth was important.
Stars are exploding all around you--
--and there's nothing you can do.
You can either be scared and brave...
...or just scared.
All of us are time travelers.
We're born, we live...
...then we die.
I haven't seen the end of all things.
But I often wonder--
--is this it?

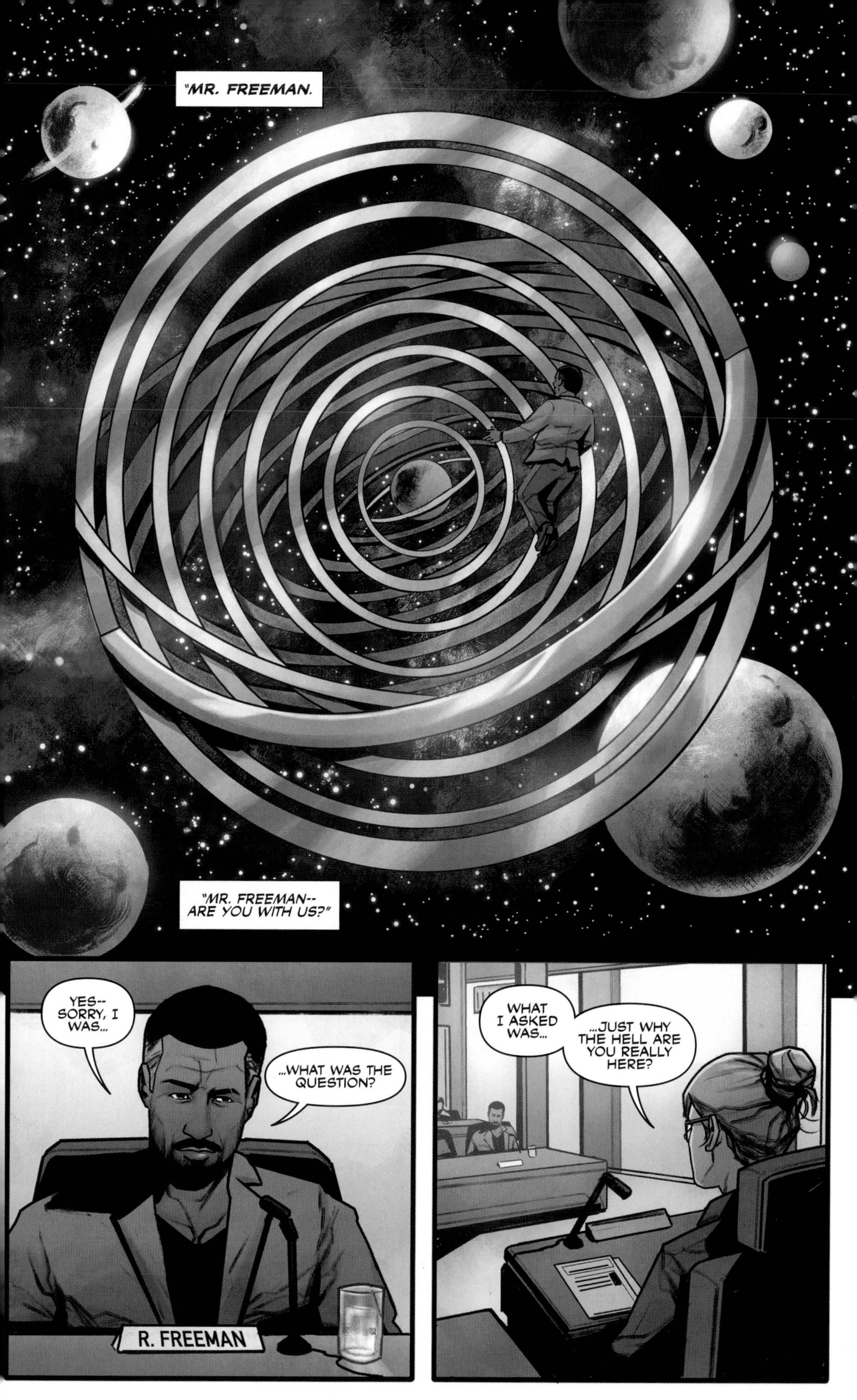
"MR. FREEMAN.
"MR. FREEMAN--
ARE YOU WITH US?"
YES--
SORRY, I
WAS...
...WHAT WAS THE
QUESTION?
R. FREEMAN
WHAT
I ASKED
WAS...
...JUST WHY
THE HELL ARE
YOU REALLY
HERE?

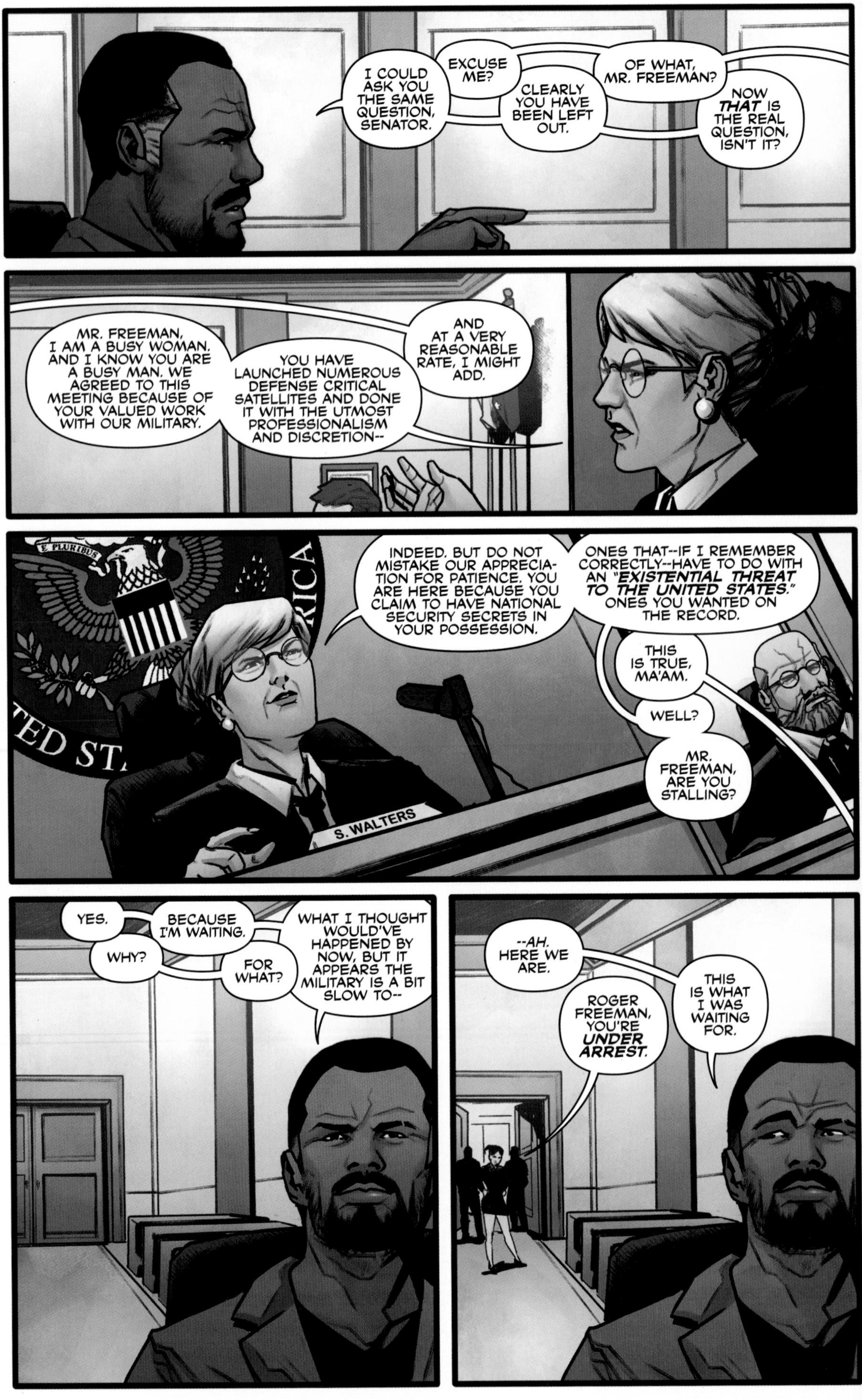
I COULD ASK YOU THE SAME QUESTION, SENATOR.
EXCUSE ME?
CLEARLY YOU HAVE BEEN LEFT OUT.
OF WHAT, MR. FREEMAN?
NOW *THAT* IS THE REAL QUESTION, ISN'T IT?
MR. FREEMAN, I AM A BUSY WOMAN. AND I KNOW YOU ARE A BUSY MAN. WE AGREED TO THIS MEETING BECAUSE OF YOUR VALUED WORK WITH OUR MILITARY.
YOU HAVE LAUNCHED NUMEROUS DEFENSE CRITICAL SATELLITES AND DONE IT WITH THE UTMOST PROFESSIONALISM AND DISCRETION--
AND AT A VERY REASONABLE RATE, I MIGHT ADD.
E PLURIBUS
RICA
TED ST
INDEED. BUT DO NOT MISTAKE OUR APPRECIATION FOR PATIENCE. YOU ARE HERE BECAUSE YOU CLAIM TO HAVE NATIONAL SECURITY SECRETS IN YOUR POSSESSION.
ONES THAT--IF I REMEMBER CORRECTLY--HAVE TO DO WITH AN "*EXISTENTIAL THREAT TO THE UNITED STATES.*" ONES YOU WANTED ON THE RECORD.
THIS IS TRUE, MA'AM.
WELL?
MR. FREEMAN, ARE YOU STALLING?
S. WALTERS
YES.
WHY?
BECAUSE I'M WAITING.
FOR WHAT?
WHAT I THOUGHT WOULD'VE HAPPENED BY NOW, BUT IT APPEARS THE MILITARY IS A BIT SLOW TO--
--*AH.* HERE WE ARE.
THIS IS WHAT I WAS WAITING FOR.
ROGER FREEMAN, YOU'RE ***UNDER ARREST.***

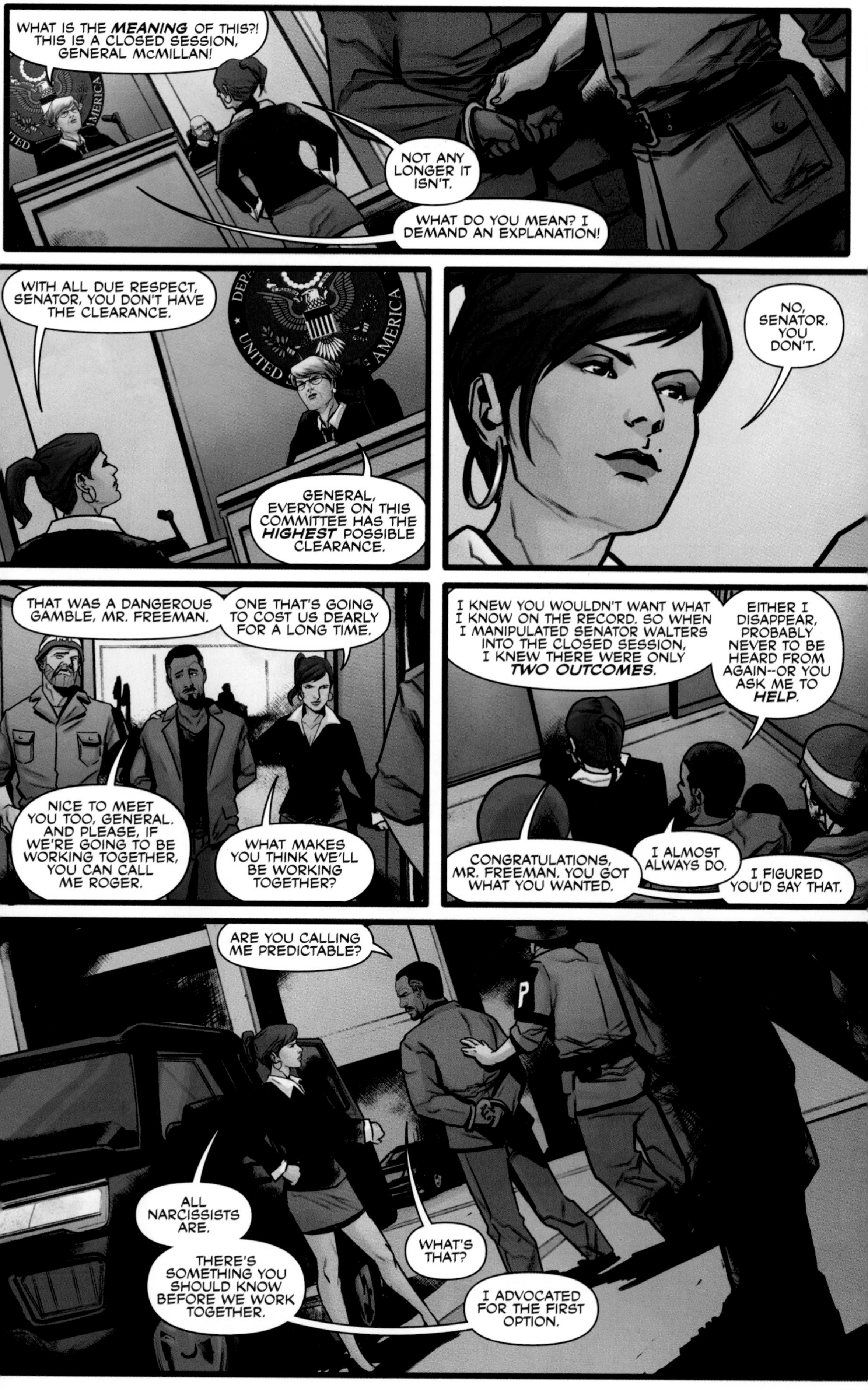
WHAT IS THE MEANING OF THIS?! THIS IS A CLOSED SESSION, GENERAL McMILLAN!
NOT ANY LONGER IT ISN'T.
WHAT DO YOU MEAN? I DEMAND AN EXPLANATION!
WITH ALL DUE RESPECT, SENATOR, YOU DON'T HAVE THE CLEARANCE.
GENERAL, EVERYONE ON THIS COMMITTEE HAS THE HIGHEST POSSIBLE CLEARANCE.
NO, SENATOR. YOU DON'T.
THAT WAS A DANGEROUS GAMBLE, MR. FREEMAN.
ONE THAT'S GOING TO COST US DEARLY FOR A LONG TIME.
NICE TO MEET YOU TOO, GENERAL. AND PLEASE, IF WE'RE GOING TO BE WORKING TOGETHER, YOU CAN CALL ME ROGER.
WHAT MAKES YOU THINK WE'LL BE WORKING TOGETHER?
I KNEW YOU WOULDN'T WANT WHAT I KNOW ON THE RECORD. SO WHEN I MANIPULATED SENATOR WALTERS INTO THE CLOSED SESSION, I KNEW THERE WERE ONLY TWO OUTCOMES.
EITHER I DISAPPEAR, PROBABLY NEVER TO BE HEARD FROM AGAIN--OR YOU ASK ME TO HELP.
CONGRATULATIONS, MR. FREEMAN. YOU GOT WHAT YOU WANTED.
I ALMOST ALWAYS DO.
I FIGURED YOU'D SAY THAT.
ARE YOU CALLING ME PREDICTABLE?
ALL NARCISSISTS ARE.
THERE'S SOMETHING YOU SHOULD KNOW BEFORE WE WORK TOGETHER.
WHAT'S THAT?
I ADVOCATED FOR THE FIRST OPTION.

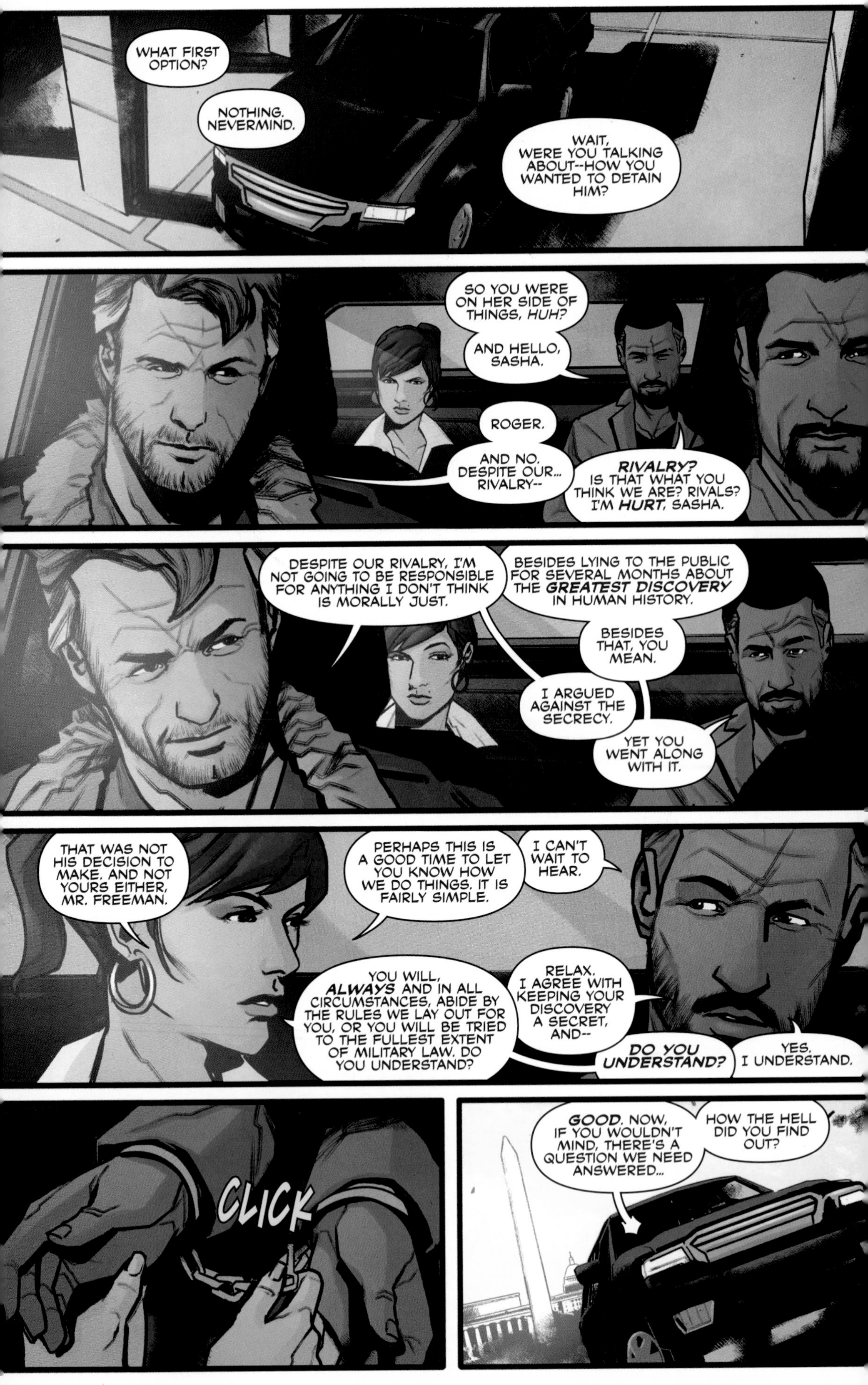
WHAT FIRST OPTION?
NOTHING. NEVERMIND.
WAIT, WERE YOU TALKING ABOUT--HOW YOU WANTED TO DETAIN HIM?
SO YOU WERE ON HER SIDE OF THINGS, HUH?
AND HELLO, SASHA.
ROGER.
AND NO. DESPITE OUR... RIVALRY--
RIVALRY? IS THAT WHAT YOU THINK WE ARE? RIVALS? I'M HURT, SASHA.
DESPITE OUR RIVALRY, I'M NOT GOING TO BE RESPONSIBLE FOR ANYTHING I DON'T THINK IS MORALLY JUST.
BESIDES LYING TO THE PUBLIC FOR SEVERAL MONTHS ABOUT THE GREATEST DISCOVERY IN HUMAN HISTORY.
BESIDES THAT, YOU MEAN.
I ARGUED AGAINST THE SECRECY.
YET YOU WENT ALONG WITH IT.
THAT WAS NOT HIS DECISION TO MAKE. AND NOT YOURS EITHER, MR. FREEMAN.
PERHAPS THIS IS A GOOD TIME TO LET YOU KNOW HOW WE DO THINGS. IT IS FAIRLY SIMPLE.
I CAN'T WAIT TO HEAR.
YOU WILL, ALWAYS AND IN ALL CIRCUMSTANCES, ABIDE BY THE RULES WE LAY OUT FOR YOU, OR YOU WILL BE TRIED TO THE FULLEST EXTENT OF MILITARY LAW. DO YOU UNDERSTAND?
RELAX. I AGREE WITH KEEPING YOUR DISCOVERY A SECRET, AND--
DO YOU UNDERSTAND?
YES. I UNDERSTAND.
CLICK
GOOD. NOW, IF YOU WOULDN'T MIND, THERE'S A QUESTION WE NEED ANSWERED...
HOW THE HELL DID YOU FIND OUT?

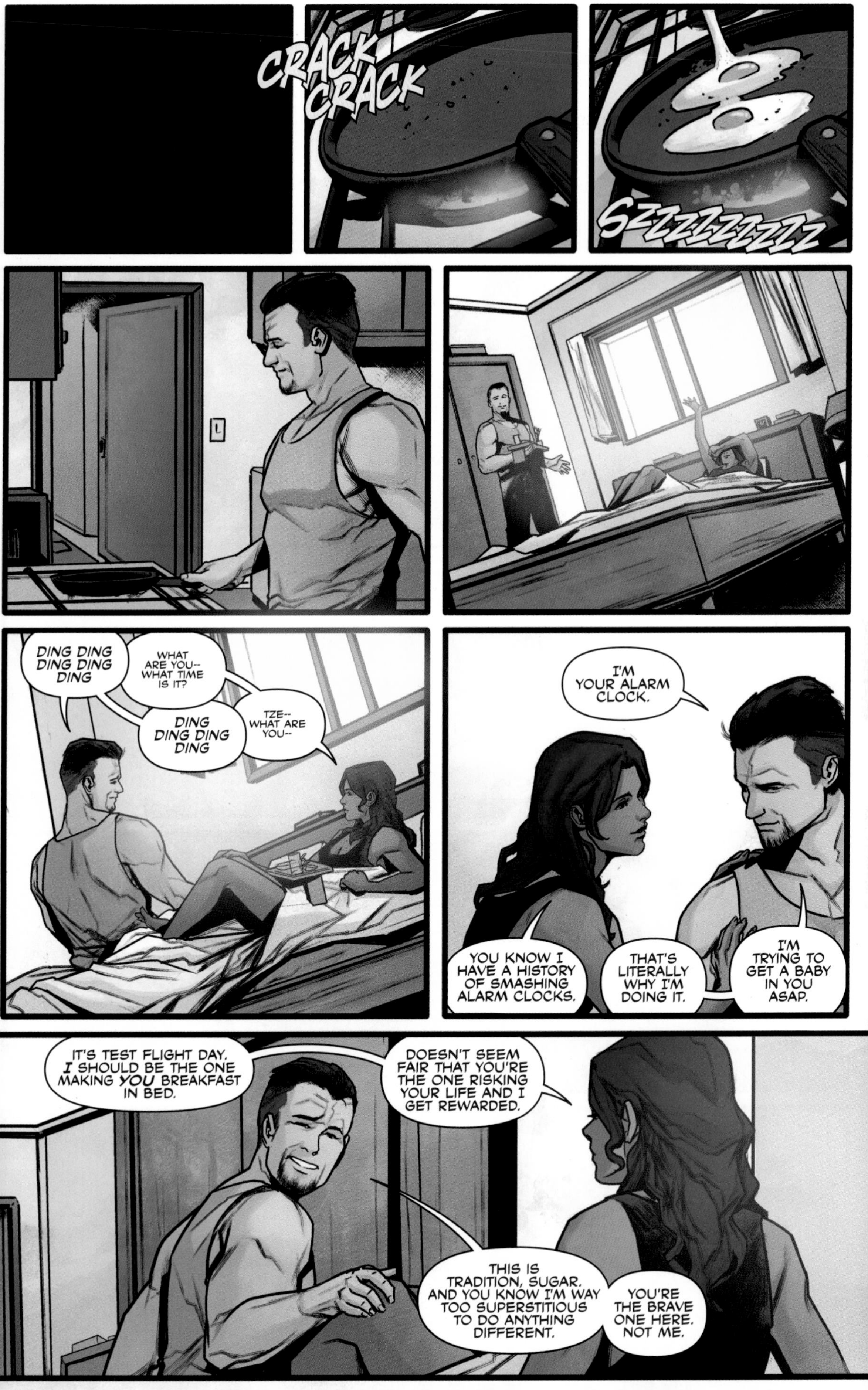
CRACK
CRACK
SZZZZZZZZZZ
DING DING DING DING DING
WHAT ARE YOU-- WHAT TIME IS IT?
DING DING DING DING
TZE-- WHAT ARE YOU--
I'M YOUR ALARM CLOCK.
YOU KNOW I HAVE A HISTORY OF SMASHING ALARM CLOCKS.
THAT'S LITERALLY WHY I'M DOING IT.
I'M TRYING TO GET A BABY IN YOU ASAP.
IT'S TEST FLIGHT DAY. I SHOULD BE THE ONE MAKING YOU BREAKFAST IN BED.
DOESN'T SEEM FAIR THAT YOU'RE THE ONE RISKING YOUR LIFE AND I GET REWARDED.
THIS IS TRADITION, SUGAR. AND YOU KNOW I'M WAY TOO SUPERSTITIOUS TO DO ANYTHING DIFFERENT.
YOU'RE THE BRAVE ONE HERE. NOT ME.

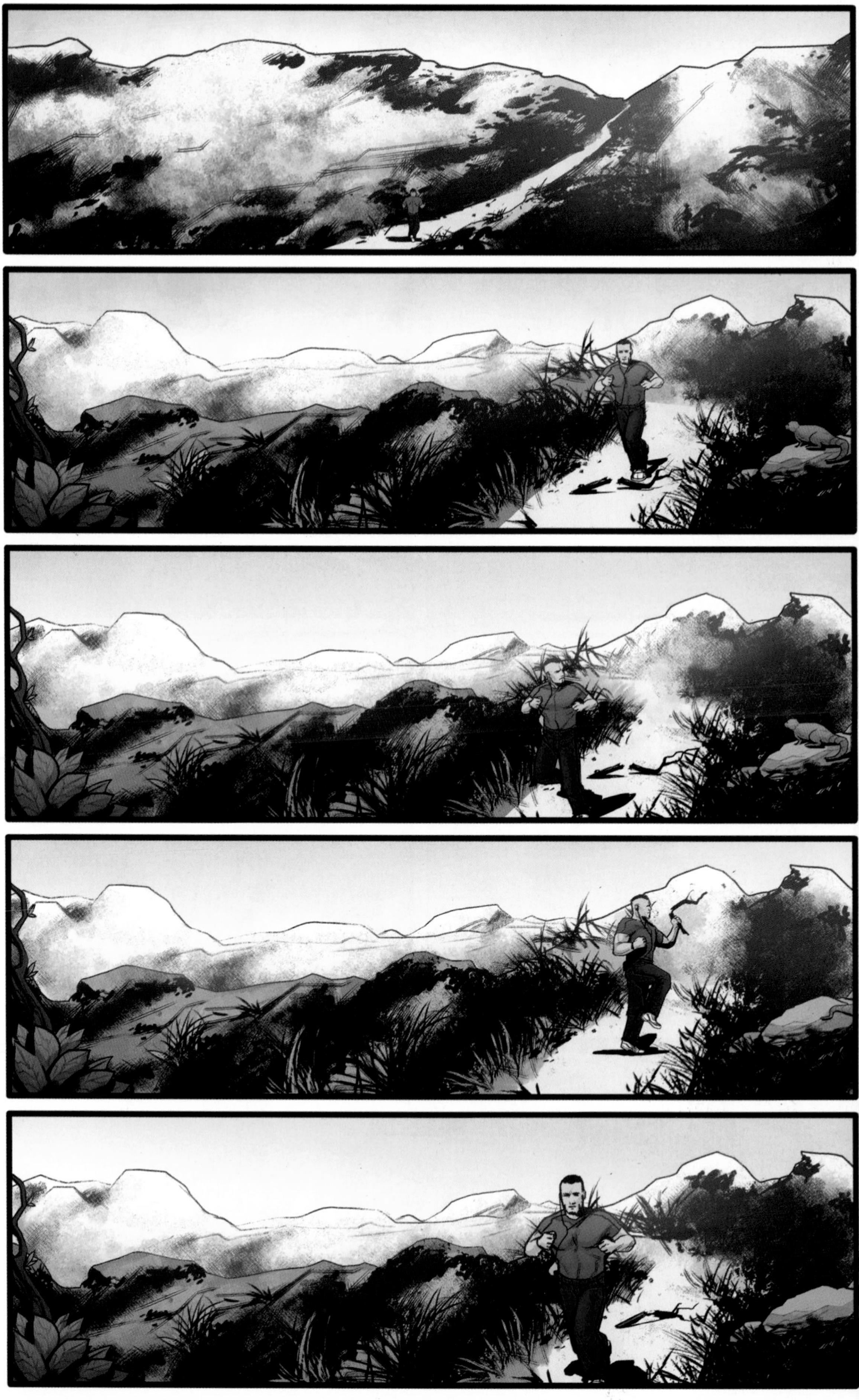

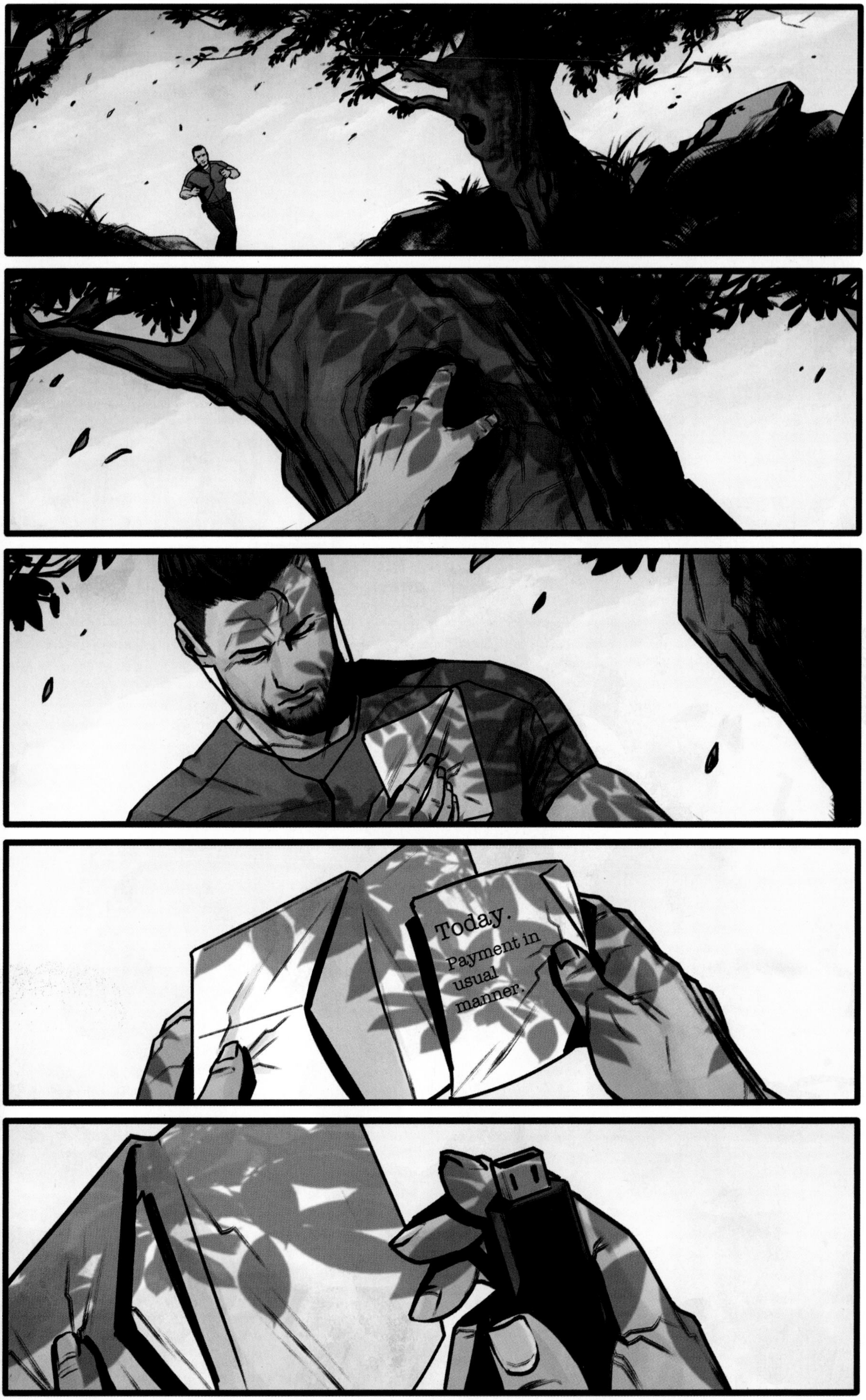
Today.
Payment in usual manner.

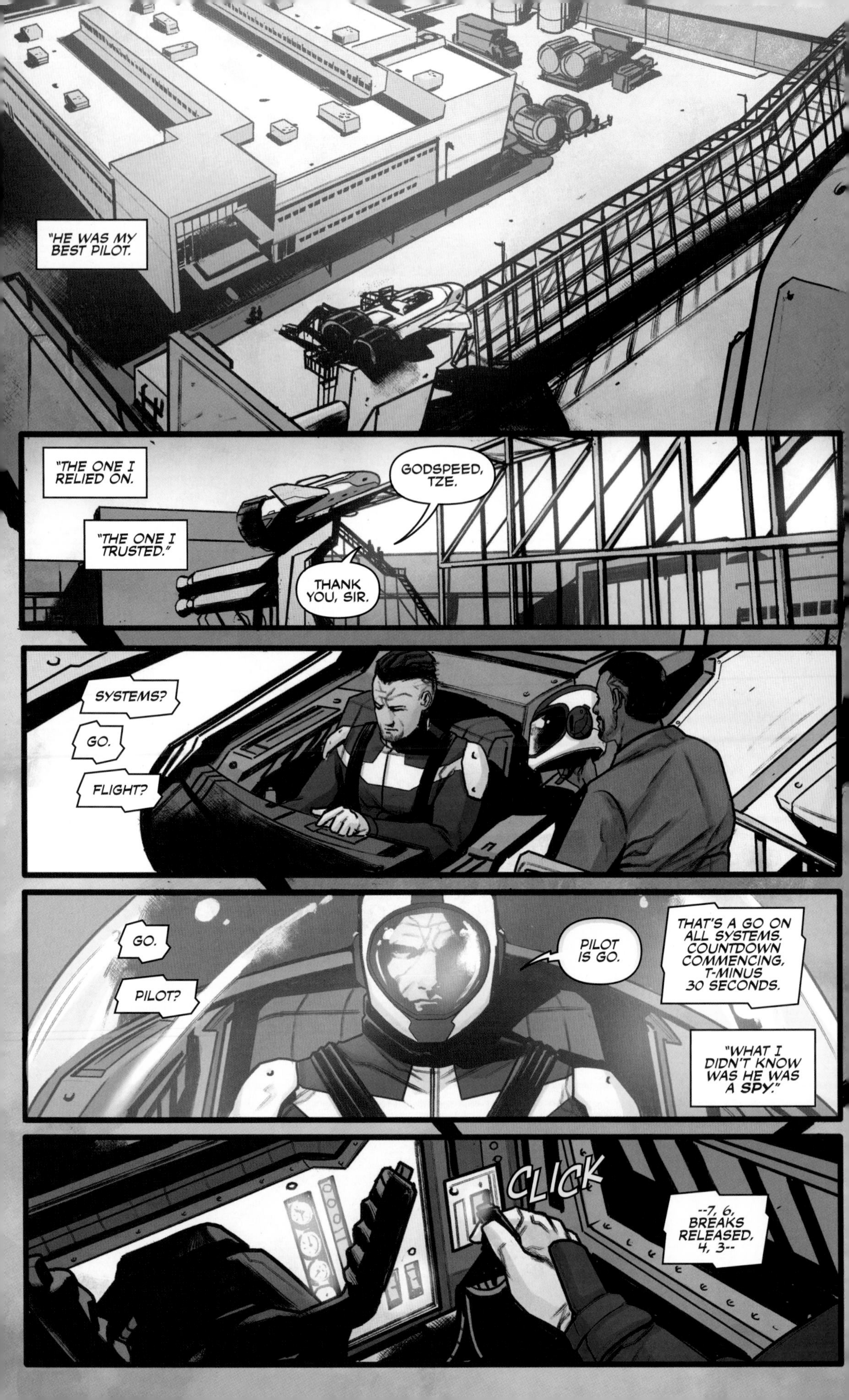
"HE WAS MY BEST PILOT.
"THE ONE I RELIED ON.
GODSPEED, TZE.
"THE ONE I TRUSTED."
THANK YOU, SIR.
SYSTEMS?
GO.
FLIGHT?
GO.
PILOT?
PILOT IS GO.
THAT'S A GO ON ALL SYSTEMS. COUNTDOWN COMMENCING, T-MINUS 30 SECONDS.
"WHAT I DIDN'T KNOW WAS HE WAS A SPY."
CLICK
--7, 6, BREAKS RELEASED, 4, 3--

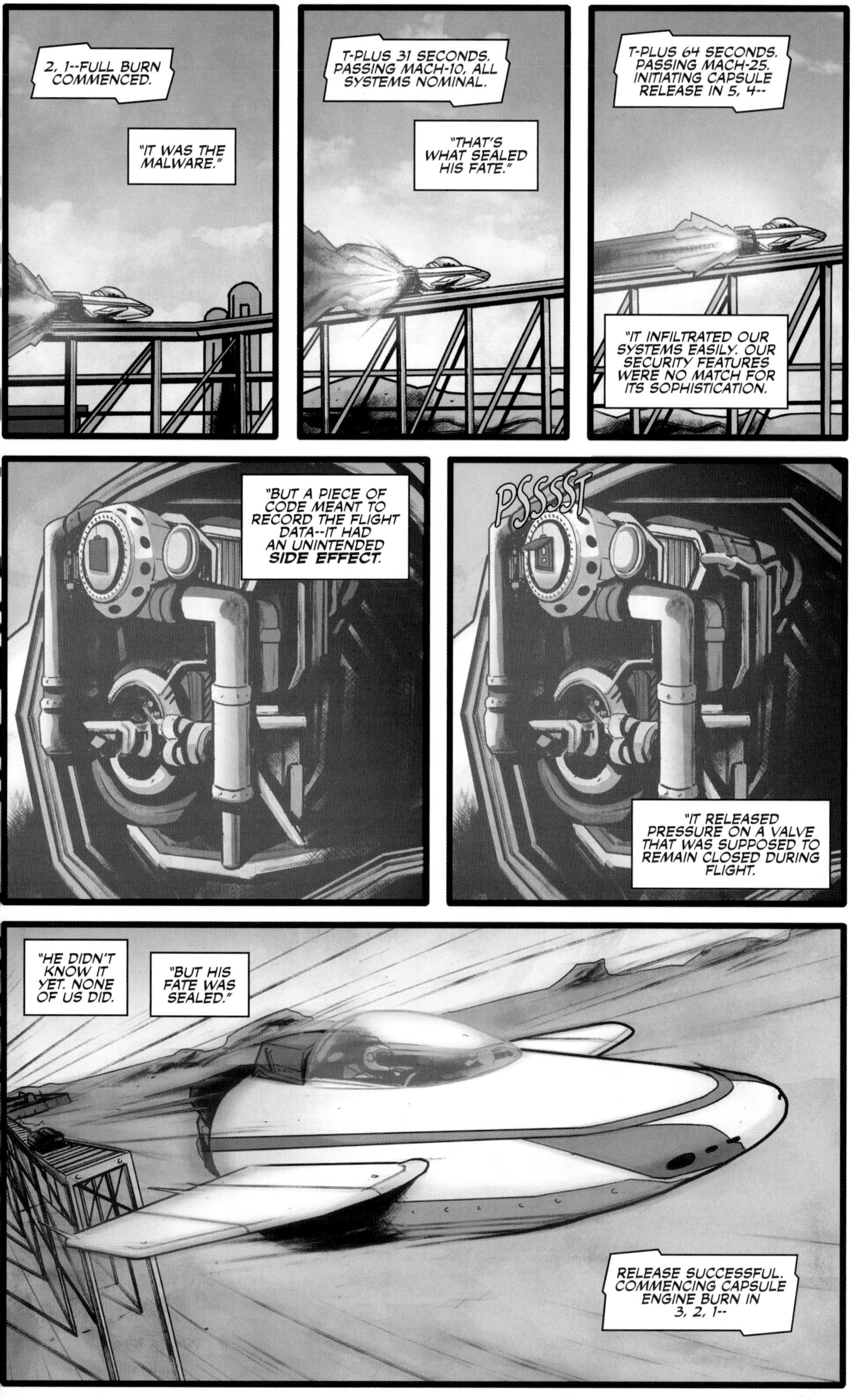
2, 1--FULL BURN COMMENCED.
"IT WAS THE MALWARE."
T-PLUS 31 SECONDS. PASSING MACH-10, ALL SYSTEMS NOMINAL.
"THAT'S WHAT SEALED HIS FATE."
T-PLUS 64 SECONDS. PASSING MACH-25. INITIATING CAPSULE RELEASE IN 5, 4--
"IT INFILTRATED OUR SYSTEMS EASILY. OUR SECURITY FEATURES WERE NO MATCH FOR ITS SOPHISTICATION.
"BUT A PIECE OF CODE MEANT TO RECORD THE FLIGHT DATA--IT HAD AN UNINTENDED **SIDE EFFECT**.
PSSSST
"IT RELEASED PRESSURE ON A VALVE THAT WAS SUPPOSED TO REMAIN CLOSED DURING FLIGHT.
"HE DIDN'T KNOW IT YET. NONE OF US DID.
"BUT HIS FATE WAS SEALED."
RELEASE SUCCESSFUL. COMMENCING CAPSULE ENGINE BURN IN 3, 2, 1--

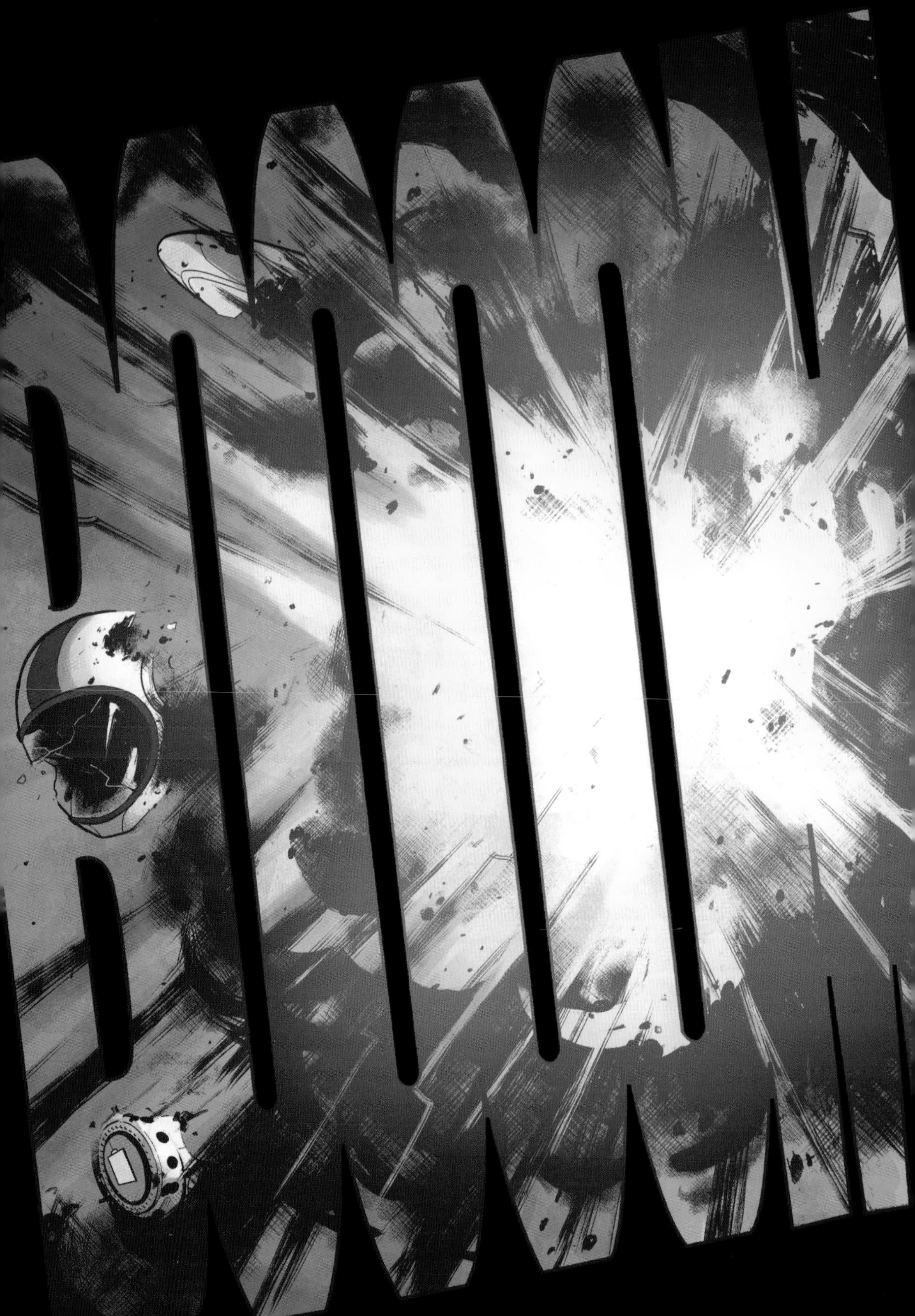

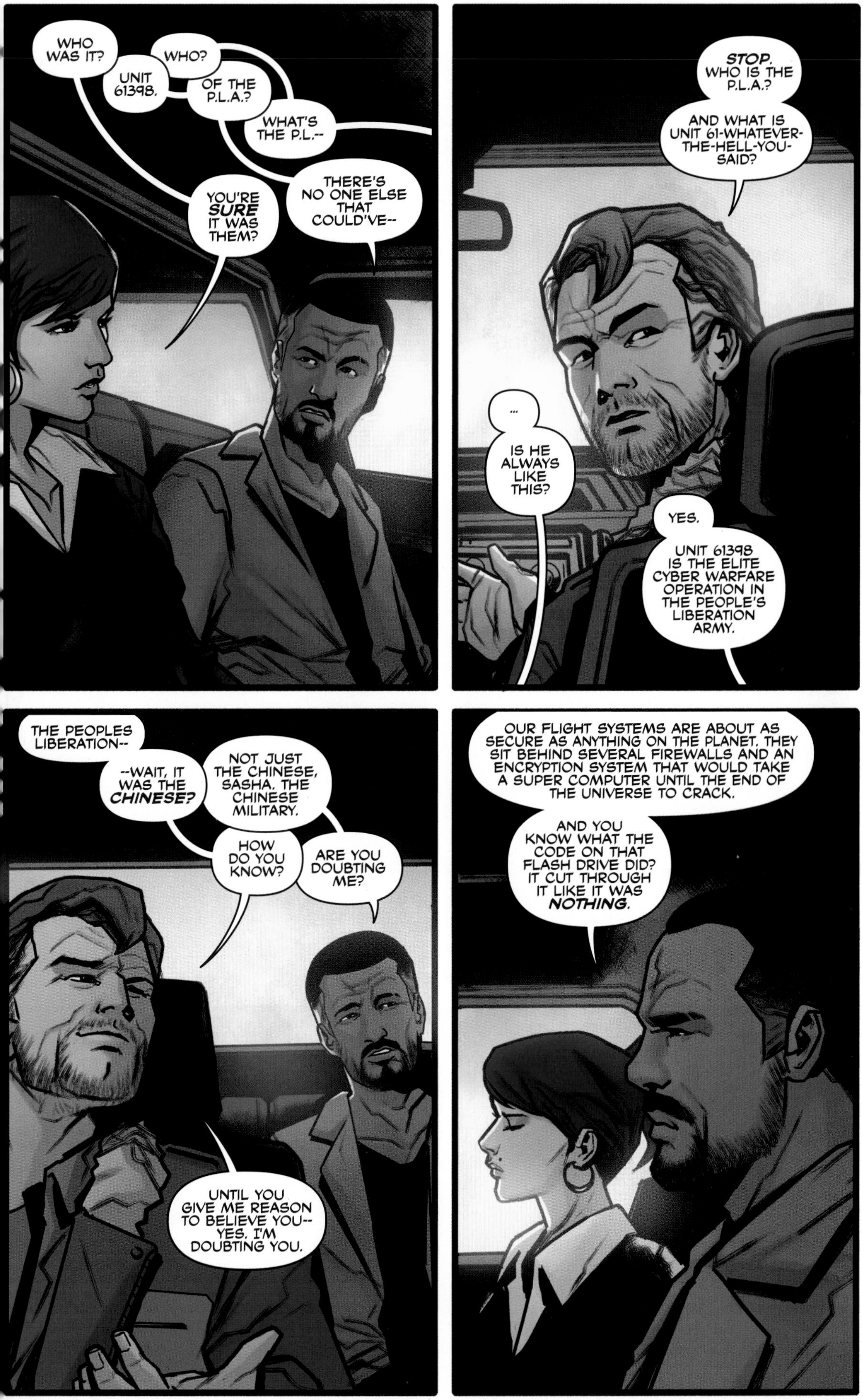
WHO WAS IT?
UNIT 61398.
WHO?
OF THE P.L.A.?
WHAT'S THE P.L.--
YOU'RE SURE IT WAS THEM?
THERE'S NO ONE ELSE THAT COULD'VE--
STOP. WHO IS THE P.L.A.?
AND WHAT IS UNIT 61-WHATEVER-THE-HELL-YOU-SAID?
...
IS HE ALWAYS LIKE THIS?
YES.
UNIT 61398 IS THE ELITE CYBER WARFARE OPERATION IN THE PEOPLE'S LIBERATION ARMY.
THE PEOPLES LIBERATION--
--WAIT, IT WAS THE CHINESE?
NOT JUST THE CHINESE, SASHA. THE CHINESE MILITARY.
HOW DO YOU KNOW?
ARE YOU DOUBTING ME?
UNTIL YOU GIVE ME REASON TO BELIEVE YOU-- YES. I'M DOUBTING YOU.
OUR FLIGHT SYSTEMS ARE ABOUT AS SECURE AS ANYTHING ON THE PLANET. THEY SIT BEHIND SEVERAL FIREWALLS AND AN ENCRYPTION SYSTEM THAT WOULD TAKE A SUPER COMPUTER UNTIL THE END OF THE UNIVERSE TO CRACK.
AND YOU KNOW WHAT THE CODE ON THAT FLASH DRIVE DID? IT CUT THROUGH IT LIKE IT WAS NOTHING.

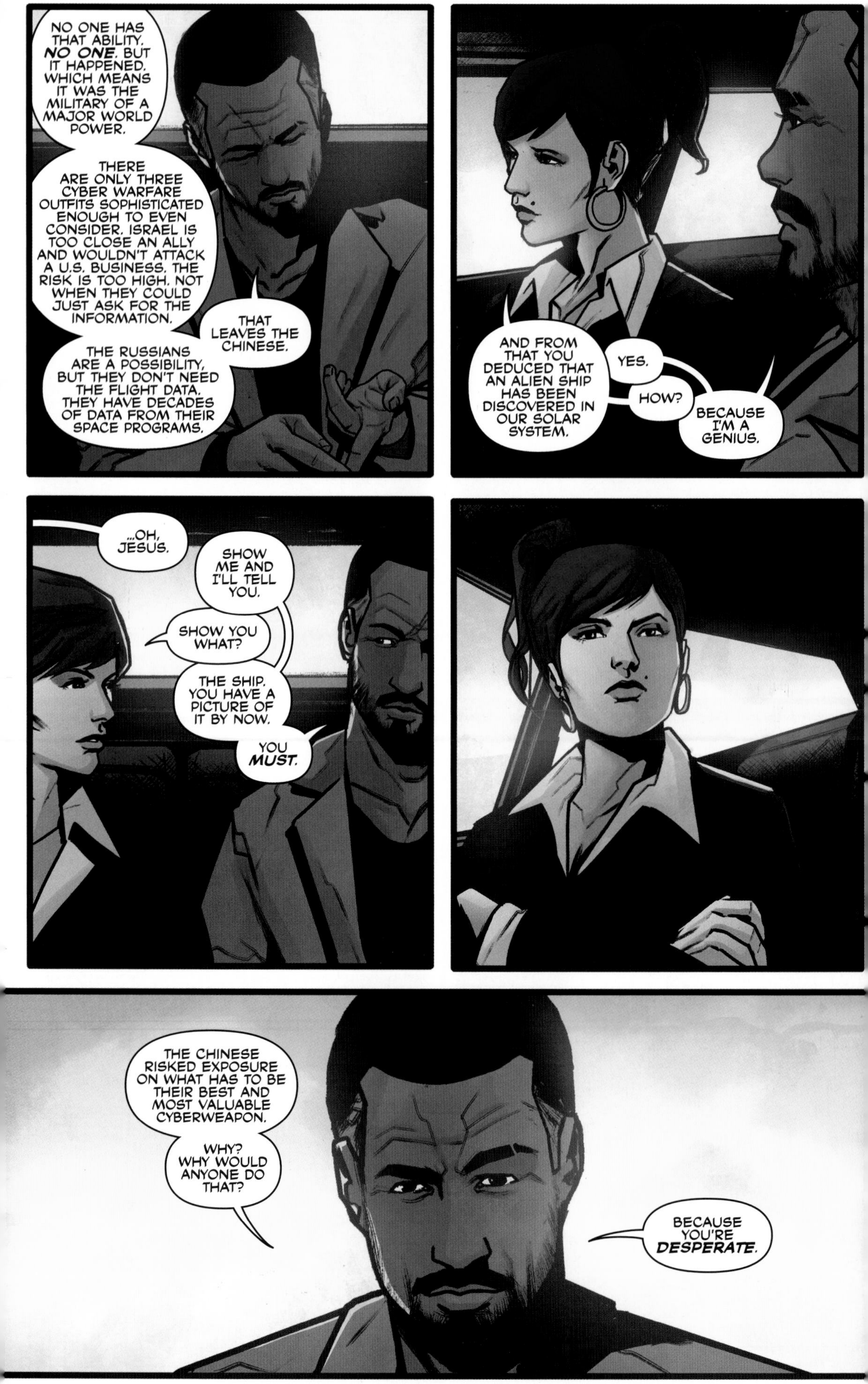
NO ONE HAS THAT ABILITY. NO ONE. BUT IT HAPPENED. WHICH MEANS IT WAS THE MILITARY OF A MAJOR WORLD POWER.
THERE ARE ONLY THREE CYBER WARFARE OUTFITS SOPHISTICATED ENOUGH TO EVEN CONSIDER. ISRAEL IS TOO CLOSE AN ALLY AND WOULDN'T ATTACK A U.S. BUSINESS. THE RISK IS TOO HIGH. NOT WHEN THEY COULD JUST ASK FOR THE INFORMATION.
THE RUSSIANS ARE A POSSIBILITY, BUT THEY DON'T NEED THE FLIGHT DATA. THEY HAVE DECADES OF DATA FROM THEIR SPACE PROGRAMS.
THAT LEAVES THE CHINESE.
AND FROM THAT YOU DEDUCED THAT AN ALIEN SHIP HAS BEEN DISCOVERED IN OUR SOLAR SYSTEM.
YES.
HOW?
BECAUSE I'M A GENIUS.
...OH, JESUS.
SHOW ME AND I'LL TELL YOU.
SHOW YOU WHAT?
THE SHIP. YOU HAVE A PICTURE OF IT BY NOW.
YOU MUST.
THE CHINESE RISKED EXPOSURE ON WHAT HAS TO BE THEIR BEST AND MOST VALUABLE CYBERWEAPON.
WHY? WHY WOULD ANYONE DO THAT?
BECAUSE YOU'RE DESPERATE.

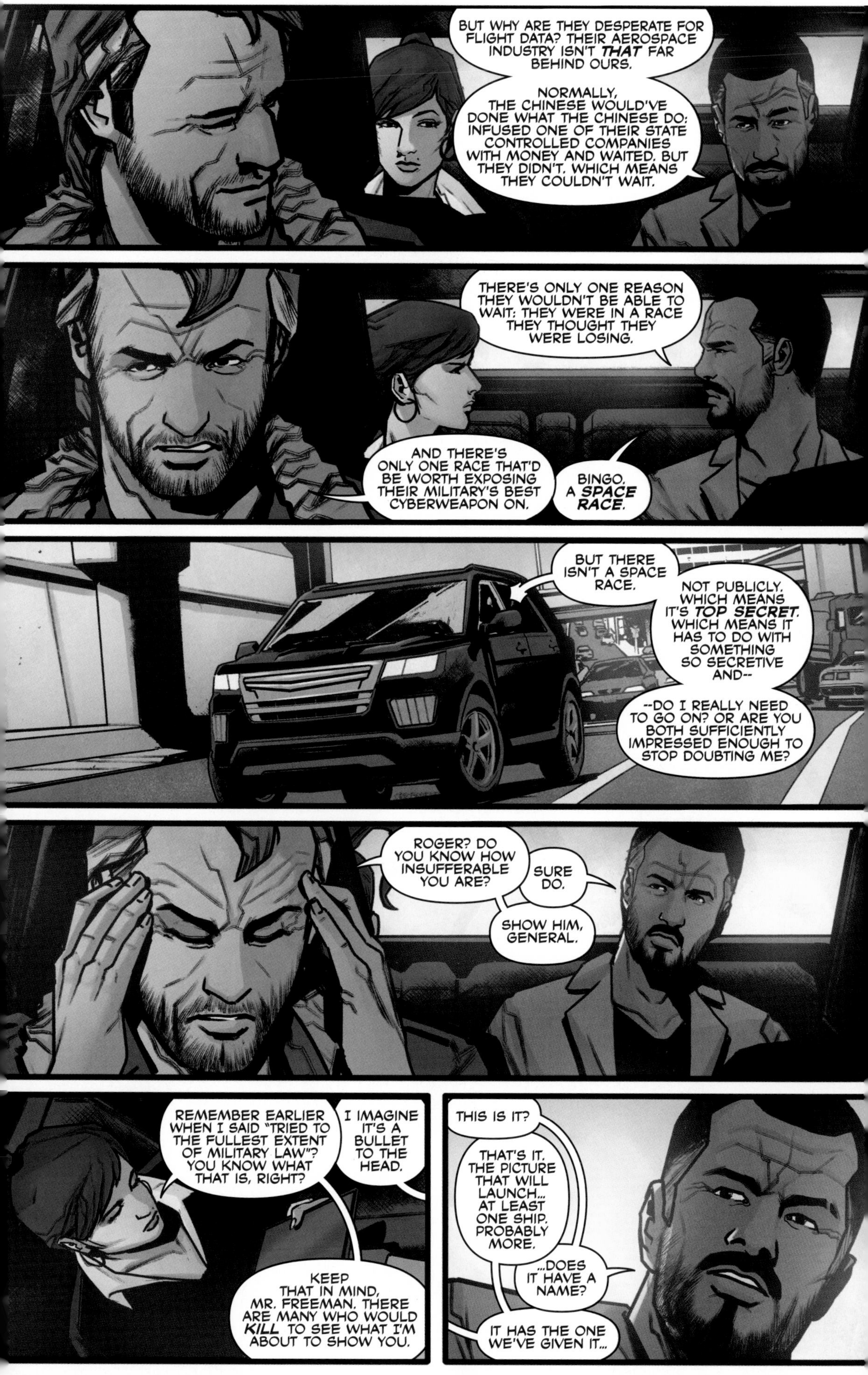
BUT WHY ARE THEY DESPERATE FOR FLIGHT DATA? THEIR AEROSPACE INDUSTRY ISN'T THAT FAR BEHIND OURS.
NORMALLY, THE CHINESE WOULD'VE DONE WHAT THE CHINESE DO: INFUSED ONE OF THEIR STATE CONTROLLED COMPANIES WITH MONEY AND WAITED. BUT THEY DIDN'T. WHICH MEANS THEY COULDN'T WAIT.
THERE'S ONLY ONE REASON THEY WOULDN'T BE ABLE TO WAIT: THEY WERE IN A RACE THEY THOUGHT THEY WERE LOSING.
AND THERE'S ONLY ONE RACE THAT'D BE WORTH EXPOSING THEIR MILITARY'S BEST CYBERWEAPON ON.
BINGO. A SPACE RACE.
BUT THERE ISN'T A SPACE RACE.
NOT PUBLICLY. WHICH MEANS IT'S TOP SECRET. WHICH MEANS IT HAS TO DO WITH SOMETHING SO SECRETIVE AND--
--DO I REALLY NEED TO GO ON? OR ARE YOU BOTH SUFFICIENTLY IMPRESSED ENOUGH TO STOP DOUBTING ME?
ROGER? DO YOU KNOW HOW INSUFFERABLE YOU ARE?
SURE DO.
SHOW HIM, GENERAL.
REMEMBER EARLIER WHEN I SAID "TRIED TO THE FULLEST EXTENT OF MILITARY LAW"? YOU KNOW WHAT THAT IS, RIGHT?
I IMAGINE IT'S A BULLET TO THE HEAD.
KEEP THAT IN MIND, MR. FREEMAN. THERE ARE MANY WHO WOULD KILL TO SEE WHAT I'M ABOUT TO SHOW YOU.
THIS IS IT?
THAT'S IT. THE PICTURE THAT WILL LAUNCH... AT LEAST ONE SHIP. PROBABLY MORE.
...DOES IT HAVE A NAME?
IT HAS THE ONE WE'VE GIVEN IT...

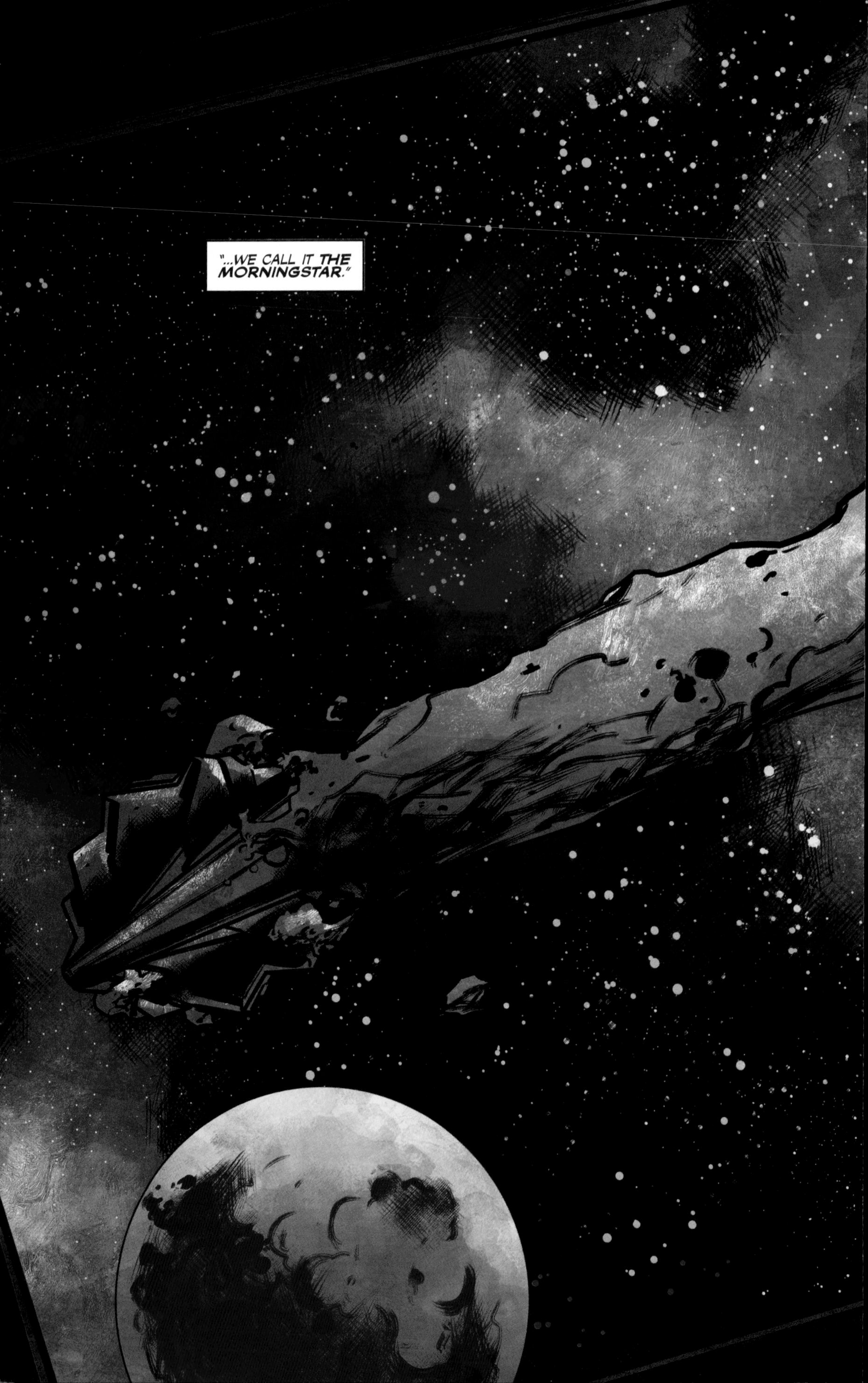
"...WE CALL IT THE MORNINGSTAR."

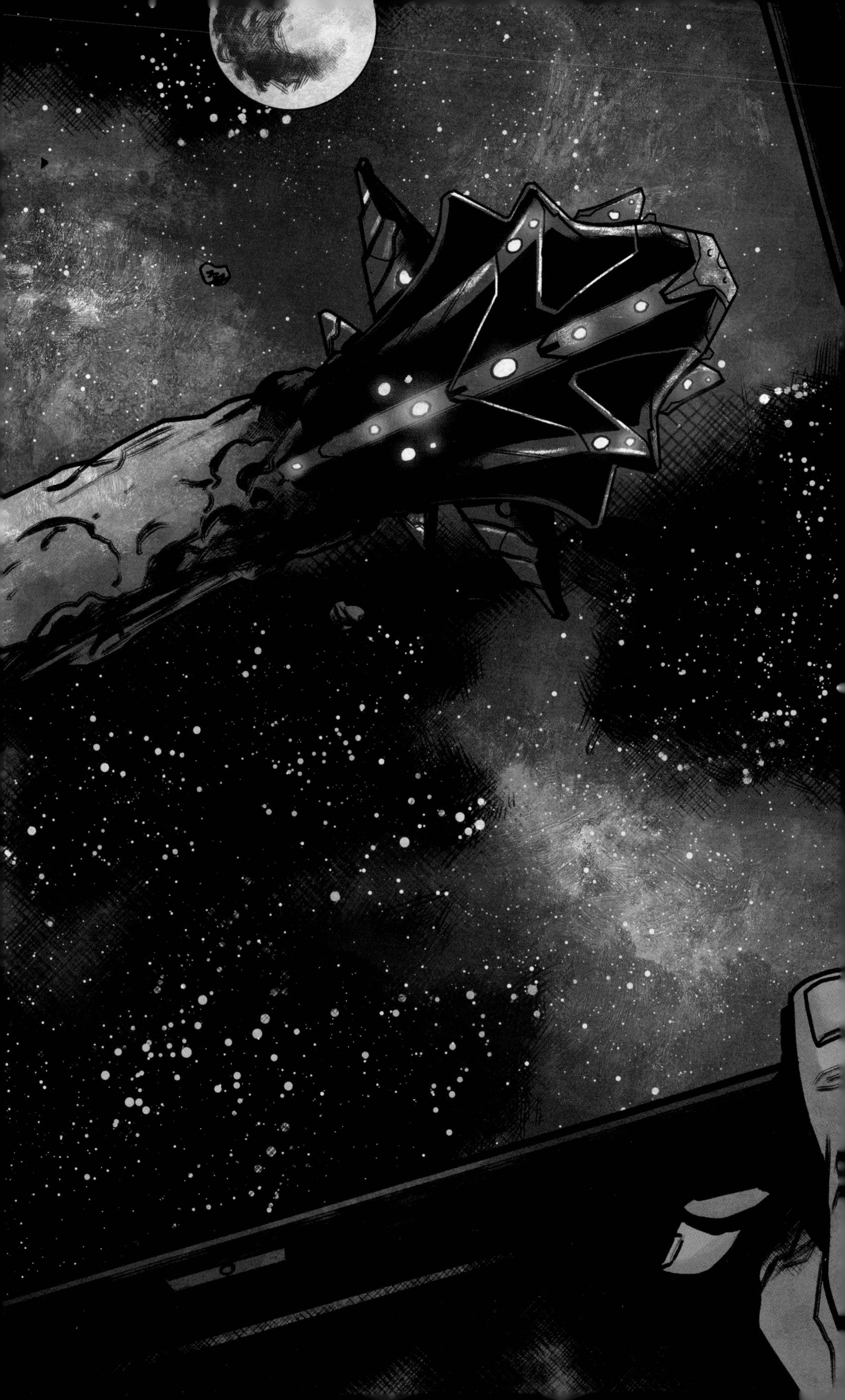

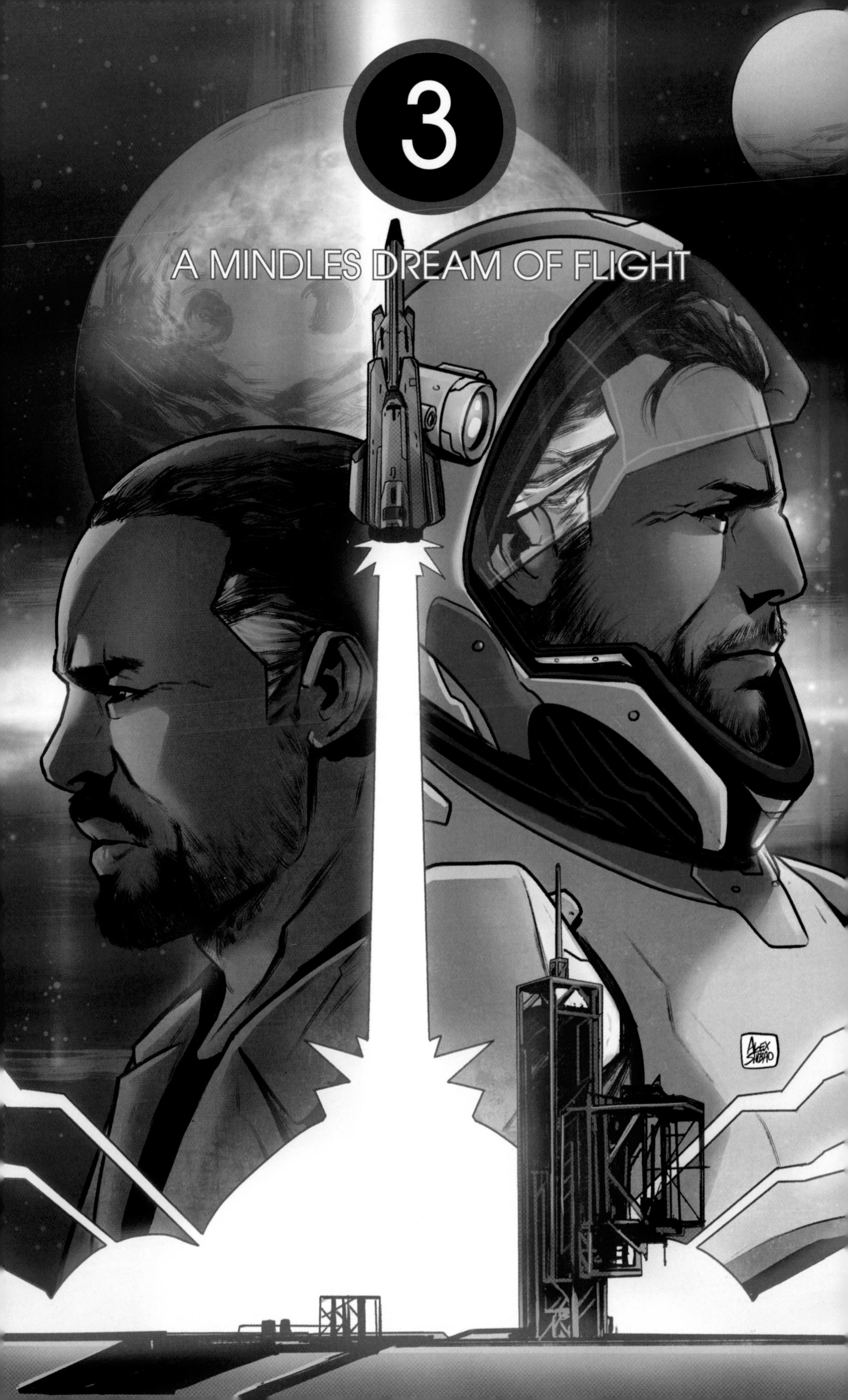
3
A MINDLES DREAM OF FLIGHT
ALEX SHIBAO

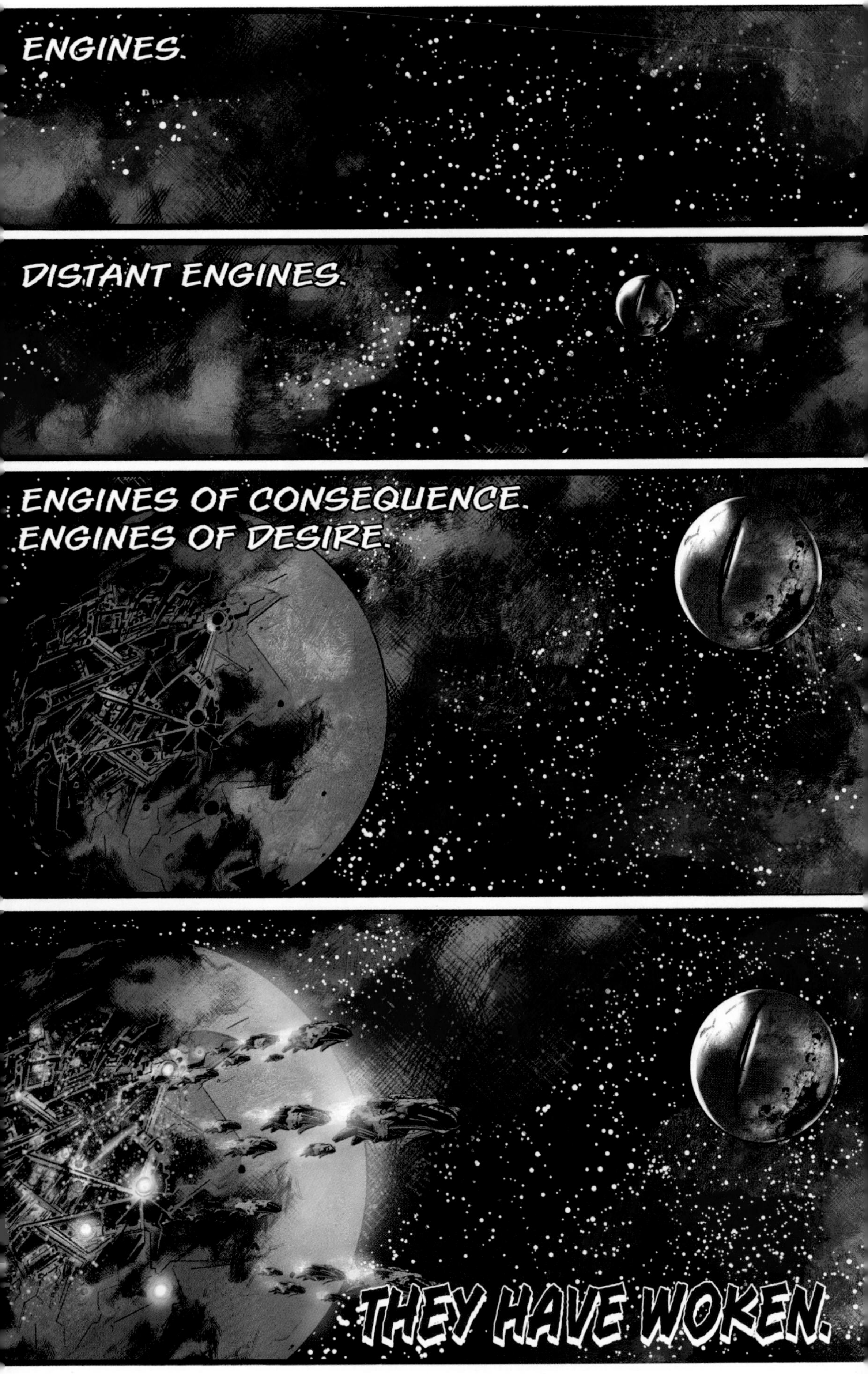
ENGINES.
DISTANT ENGINES.
ENGINES OF CONSEQUENCE.
ENGINES OF DESIRE.
THEY HAVE WOKEN.

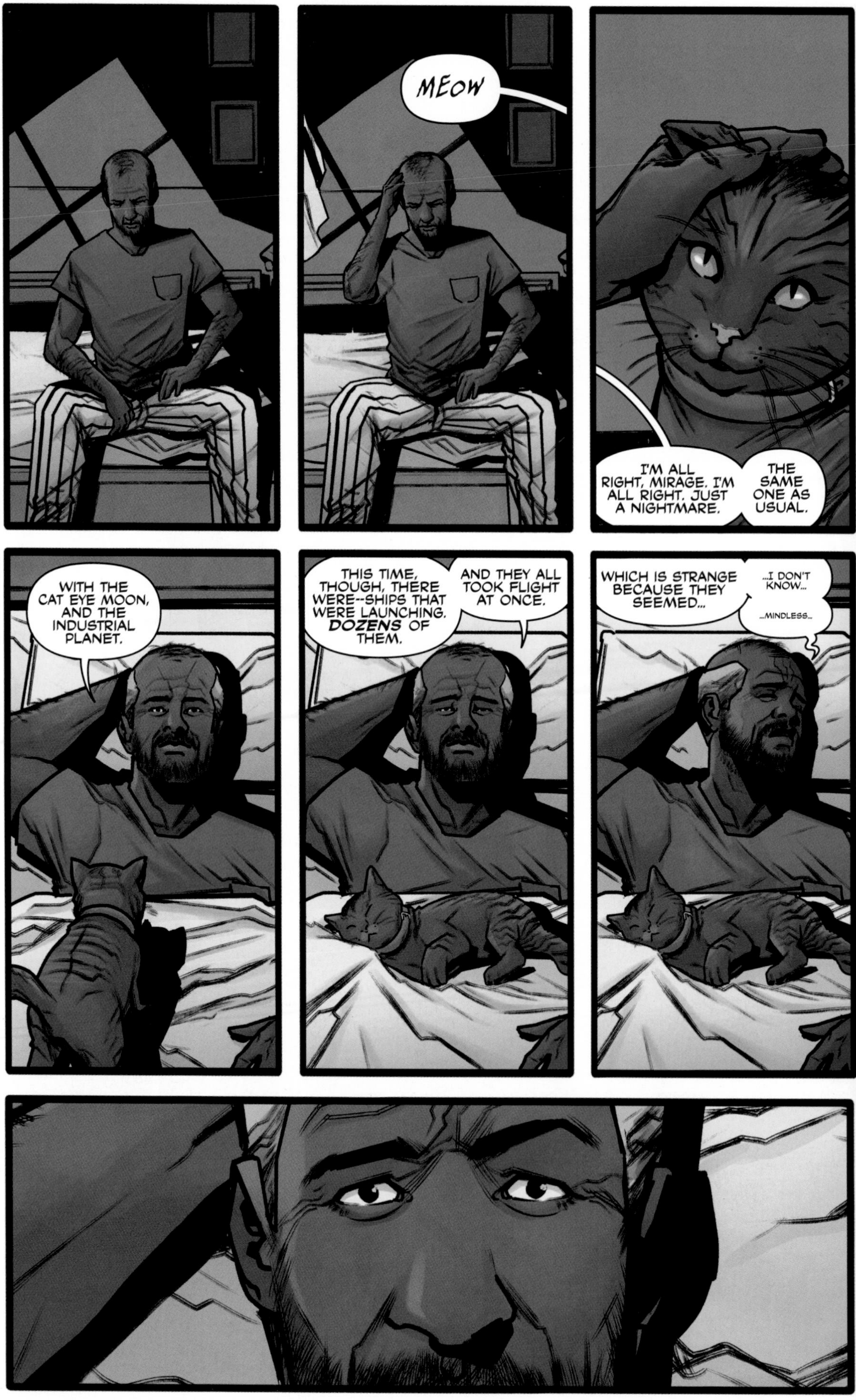
MEOW
I'M ALL RIGHT, MIRAGE. I'M ALL RIGHT. JUST A NIGHTMARE.
THE SAME ONE AS USUAL.
WITH THE CAT EYE MOON, AND THE INDUSTRIAL PLANET.
THIS TIME, THOUGH, THERE WERE--SHIPS THAT WERE LAUNCHING. **DOZENS** OF THEM.
AND THEY ALL TOOK FLIGHT AT ONCE.
WHICH IS STRANGE BECAUSE THEY SEEMED...
...I DON'T KNOW...
...MINDLESS...

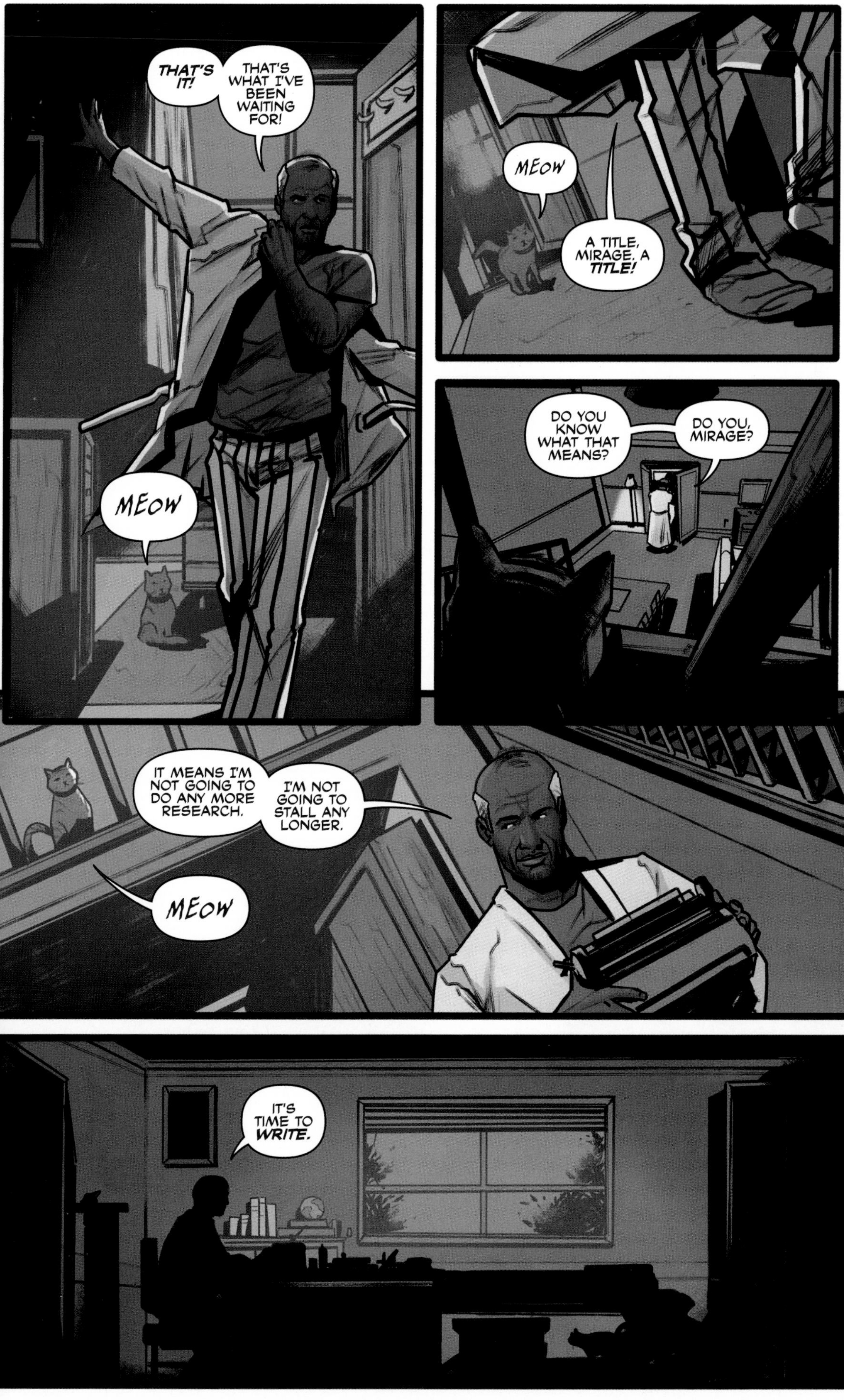
THAT'S IT!
THAT'S WHAT I'VE BEEN WAITING FOR!
MEOW
MEOW
A TITLE, MIRAGE, A TITLE!
DO YOU KNOW WHAT THAT MEANS?
DO YOU, MIRAGE?
IT MEANS I'M NOT GOING TO DO ANY MORE RESEARCH.
I'M NOT GOING TO STALL ANY LONGER.
MEOW
IT'S TIME TO WRITE.

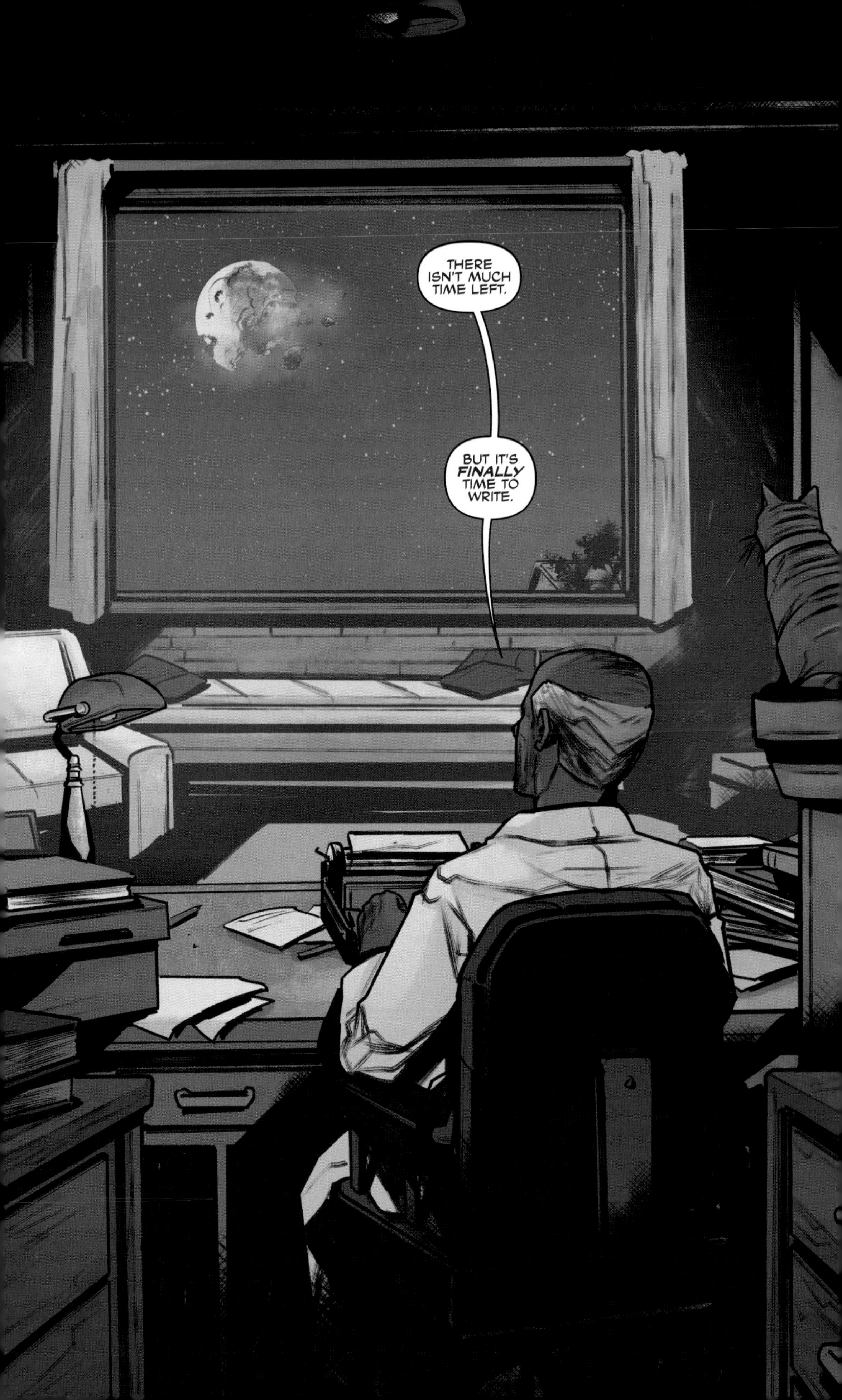
THERE ISN'T MUCH TIME LEFT.
BUT IT'S *FINALLY* TIME TO WRITE.

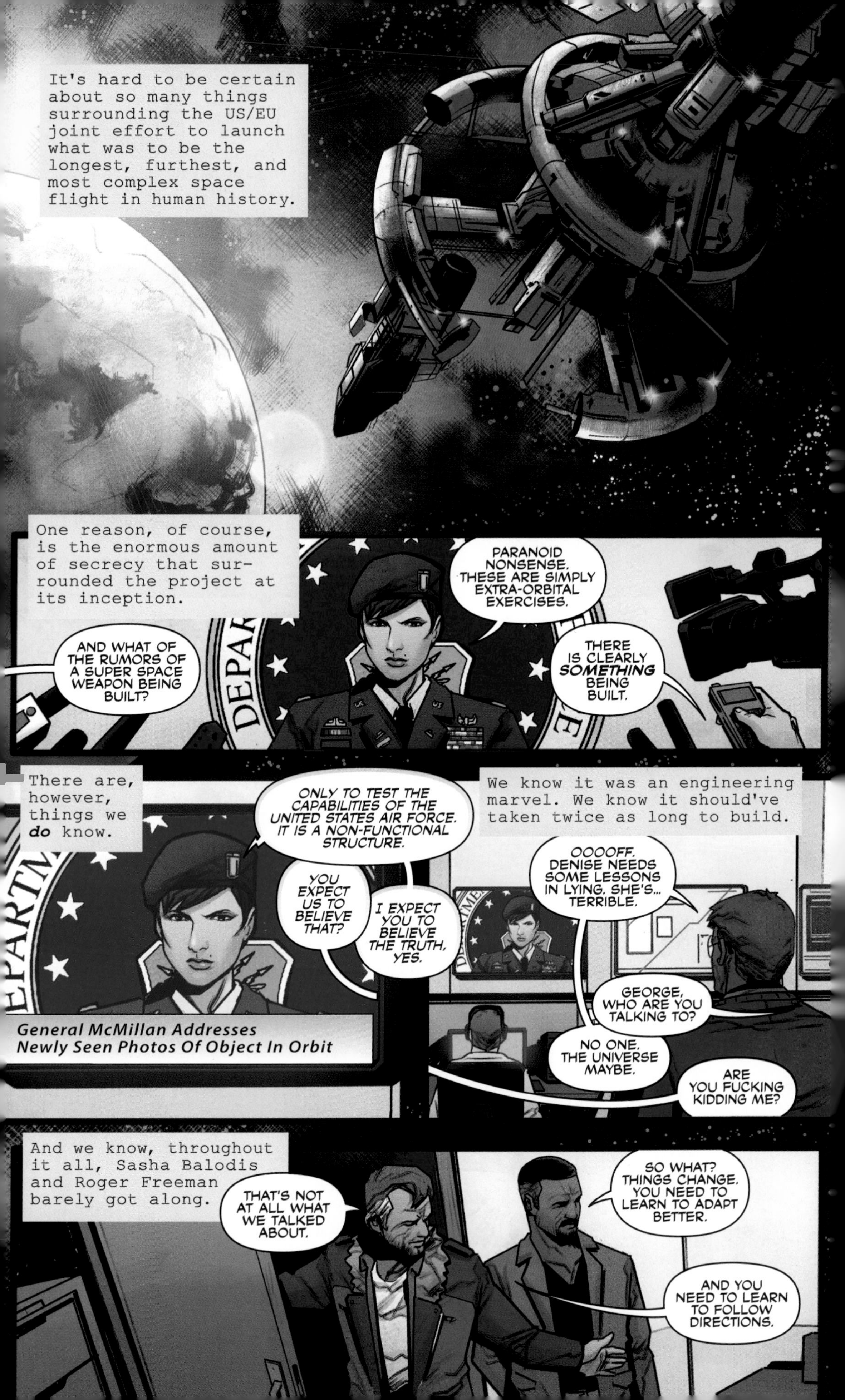
It's hard to be certain about so many things surrounding the US/EU joint effort to launch what was to be the longest, furthest, and most complex space flight in human history.
One reason, of course, is the enormous amount of secrecy that surrounded the project at its inception.
AND WHAT OF THE RUMORS OF A SUPER SPACE WEAPON BEING BUILT?
PARANOID NONSENSE. THESE ARE SIMPLY EXTRA-ORBITAL EXERCISES.
THERE IS CLEARLY SOMETHING BEING BUILT.
There are, however, things we do know.
ONLY TO TEST THE CAPABILITIES OF THE UNITED STATES AIR FORCE. IT IS A NON-FUNCTIONAL STRUCTURE.
YOU EXPECT US TO BELIEVE THAT?
I EXPECT YOU TO BELIEVE THE TRUTH, YES.
General McMillan Addresses Newly Seen Photos Of Object In Orbit
We know it was an engineering marvel. We know it should've taken twice as long to build.
OOOOFF. DENISE NEEDS SOME LESSONS IN LYING. SHE'S... TERRIBLE.
GEORGE, WHO ARE YOU TALKING TO?
NO ONE. THE UNIVERSE MAYBE.
ARE YOU FUCKING KIDDING ME?
And we know, throughout it all, Sasha Balodis and Roger Freeman barely got along.
THAT'S NOT AT ALL WHAT WE TALKED ABOUT.
SO WHAT? THINGS CHANGE. YOU NEED TO LEARN TO ADAPT BETTER.
AND YOU NEED TO LEARN TO FOLLOW DIRECTIONS.

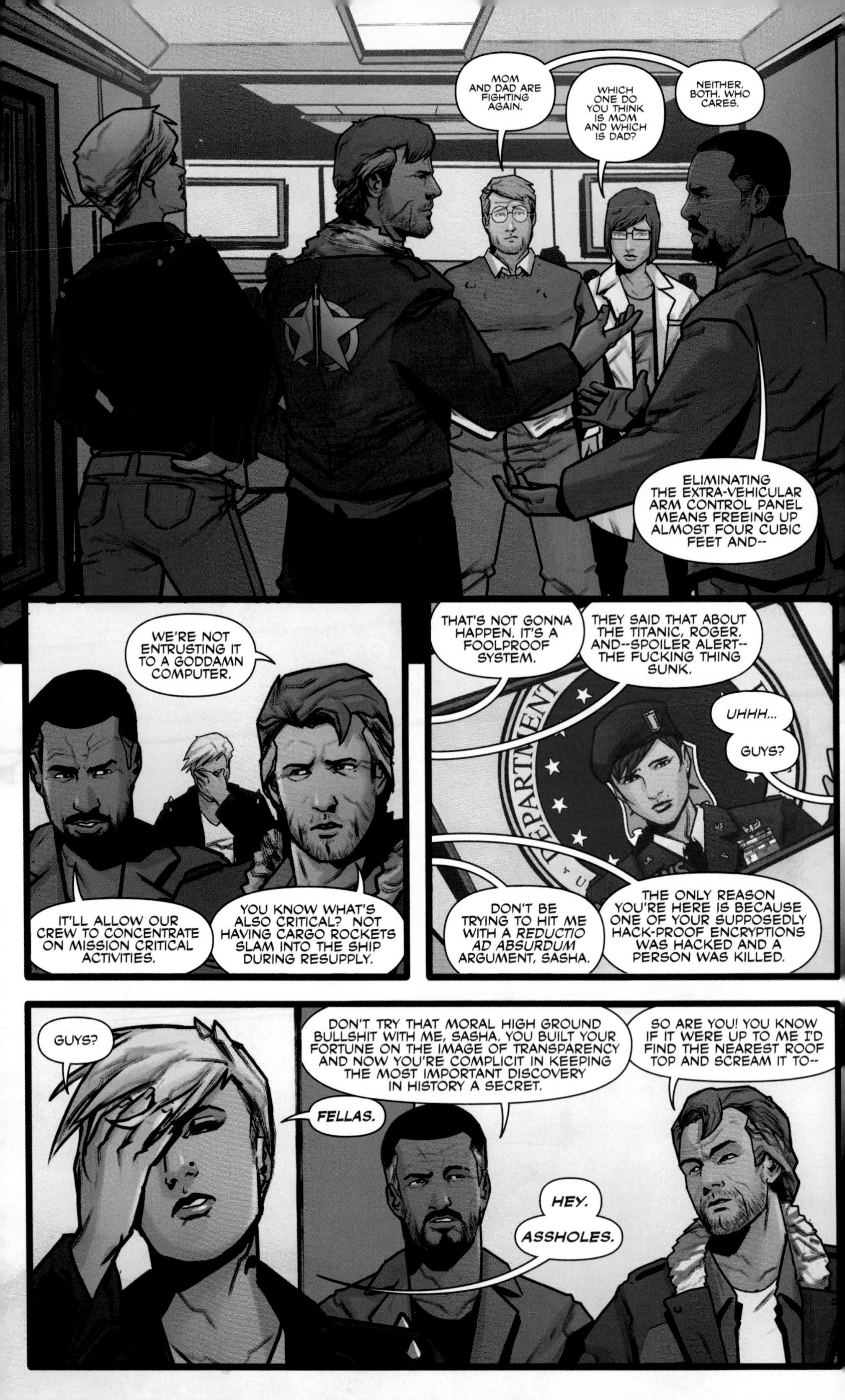
MOM AND DAD ARE FIGHTING AGAIN.
WHICH ONE DO YOU THINK IS MOM AND WHICH IS DAD?
NEITHER. BOTH. WHO CARES.
ELIMINATING THE EXTRA-VEHICULAR ARM CONTROL PANEL MEANS FREEING UP ALMOST FOUR CUBIC FEET AND--
WE'RE NOT ENTRUSTING IT TO A GODDAMN COMPUTER.
IT'LL ALLOW OUR CREW TO CONCENTRATE ON MISSION CRITICAL ACTIVITIES.
YOU KNOW WHAT'S ALSO CRITICAL? NOT HAVING CARGO ROCKETS SLAM INTO THE SHIP DURING RESUPPLY.
THAT'S NOT GONNA HAPPEN. IT'S A FOOLPROOF SYSTEM.
THEY SAID THAT ABOUT THE TITANIC, ROGER. AND--SPOILER ALERT--THE FUCKING THING SUNK.
UHHH...
GUYS?
DON'T BE TRYING TO HIT ME WITH A *REDUCTIO AD ABSURDUM* ARGUMENT, SASHA.
THE ONLY REASON YOU'RE HERE IS BECAUSE ONE OF YOUR SUPPOSEDLY HACK-PROOF ENCRYPTIONS WAS HACKED AND A PERSON WAS KILLED.
GUYS?
DON'T TRY THAT MORAL HIGH GROUND BULLSHIT WITH ME, SASHA. YOU BUILT YOUR FORTUNE ON THE IMAGE OF TRANSPARENCY AND NOW YOU'RE COMPLICIT IN KEEPING THE MOST IMPORTANT DISCOVERY IN HISTORY A SECRET.
SO ARE YOU! YOU KNOW IF IT WERE UP TO ME I'D FIND THE NEAREST ROOF TOP AND SCREAM IT TO--
FELLAS.
HEY.
ASSHOLES.

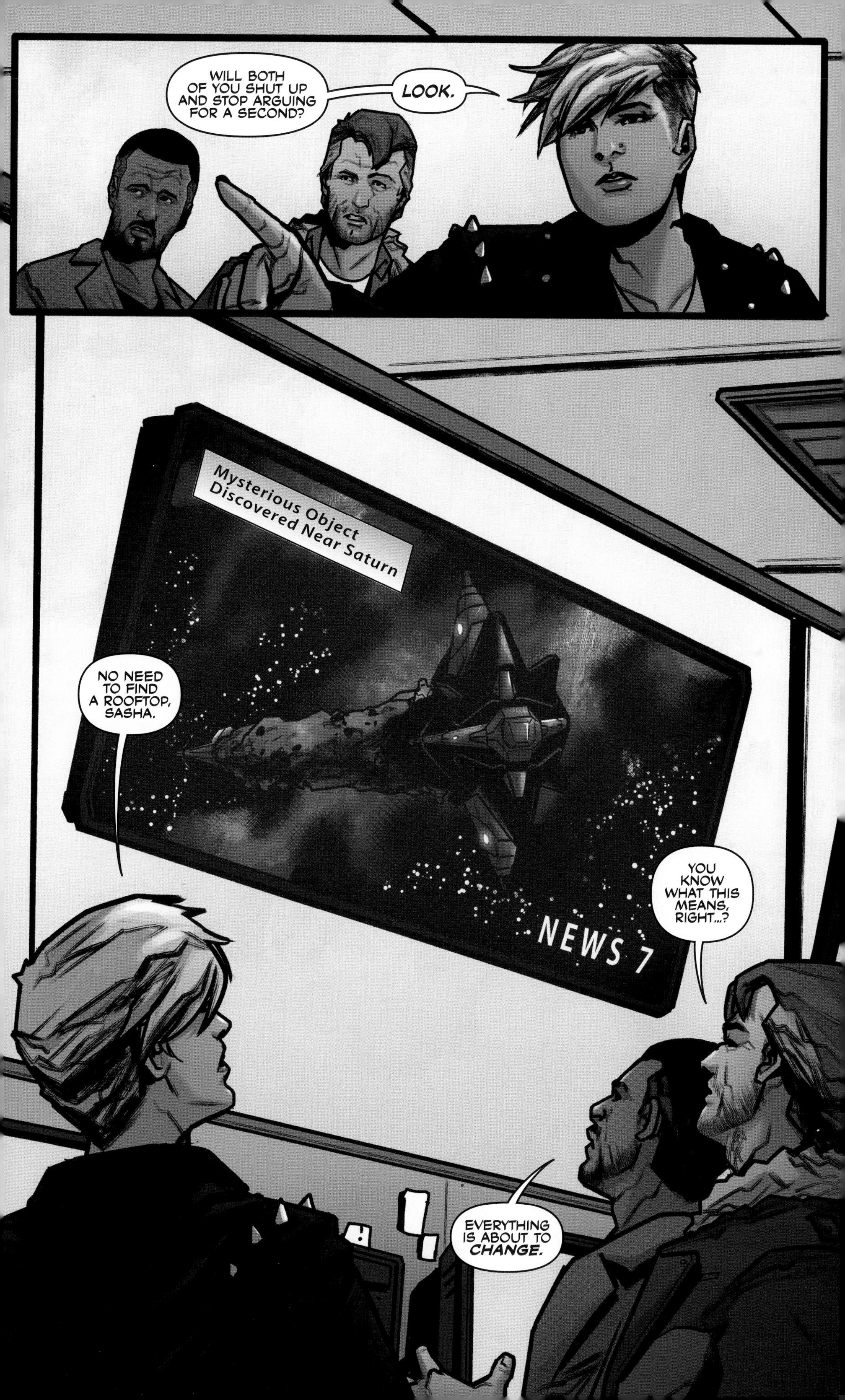
WILL BOTH OF YOU SHUT UP AND STOP ARGUING FOR A SECOND?
LOOK.
Mysterious Object Discovered Near Saturn
NO NEED TO FIND A ROOFTOP, SASHA.
NEWS 7
YOU KNOW WHAT THIS MEANS, RIGHT...?
EVERYTHING IS ABOUT TO CHANGE.

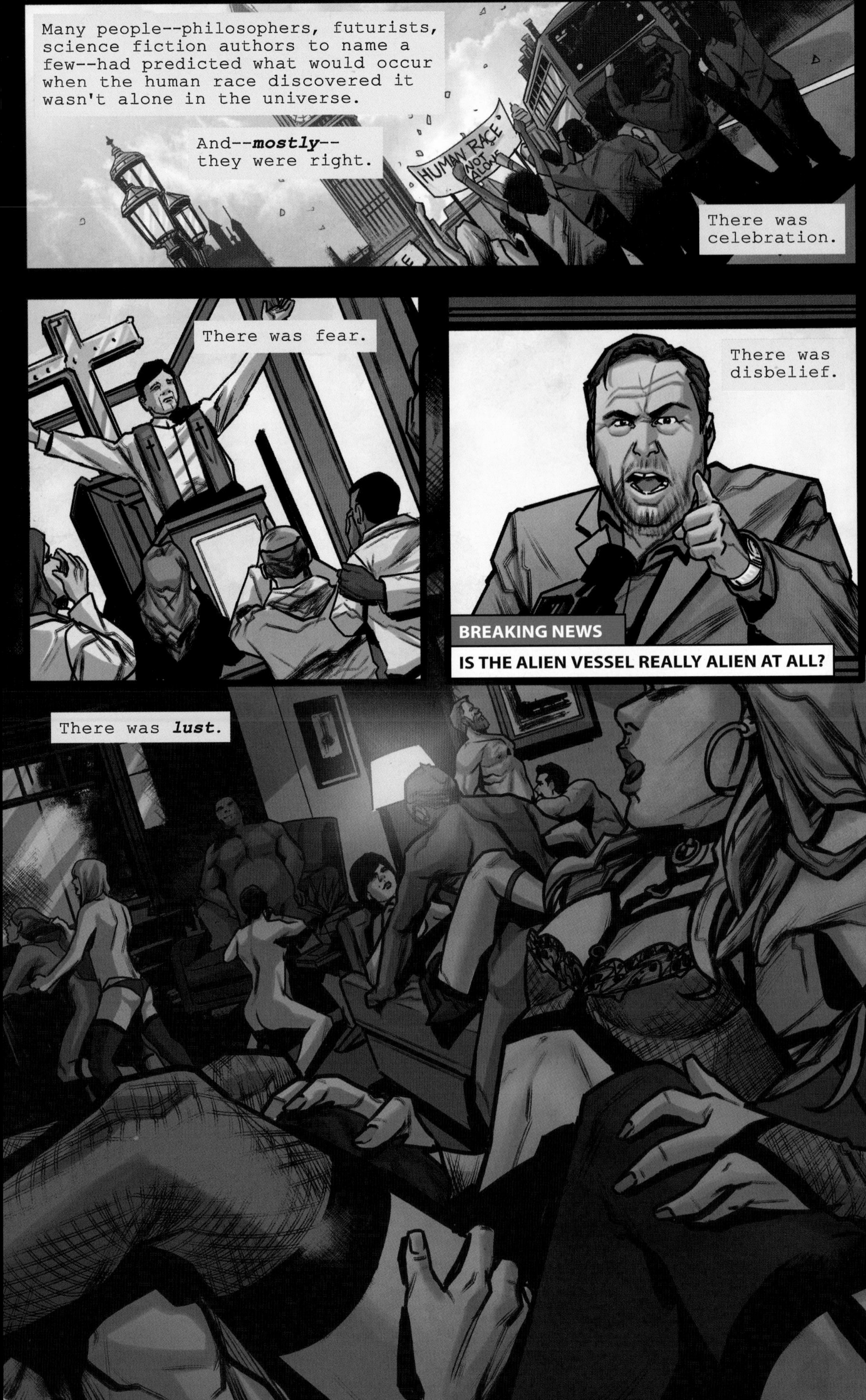
Many people--philosophers, futurists, science fiction authors to name a few--had predicted what would occur when the human race discovered it wasn't alone in the universe.
And--***mostly***--they were right.
HUMAN RACE NOT ALONE
There was celebration.
There was fear.
There was disbelief.
BREAKING NEWS
IS THE ALIEN VESSEL REALLY ALIEN AT ALL?
There was ***lust.***

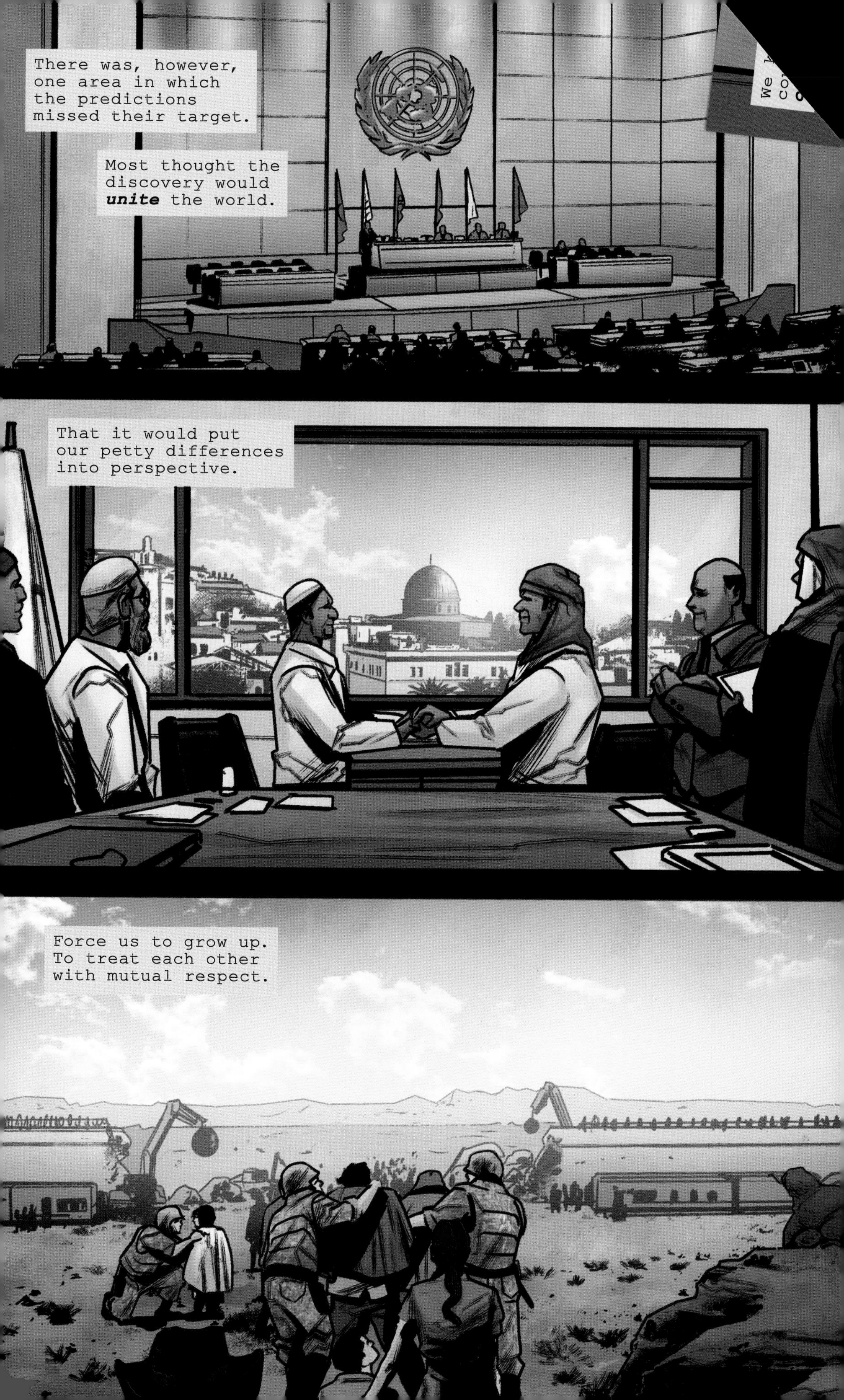
There was, however, one area in which the predictions missed their target.
Most thought the discovery would ***unite*** the world.
That it would put our petty differences into perspective.
Force us to grow up. To treat each other with mutual respect.

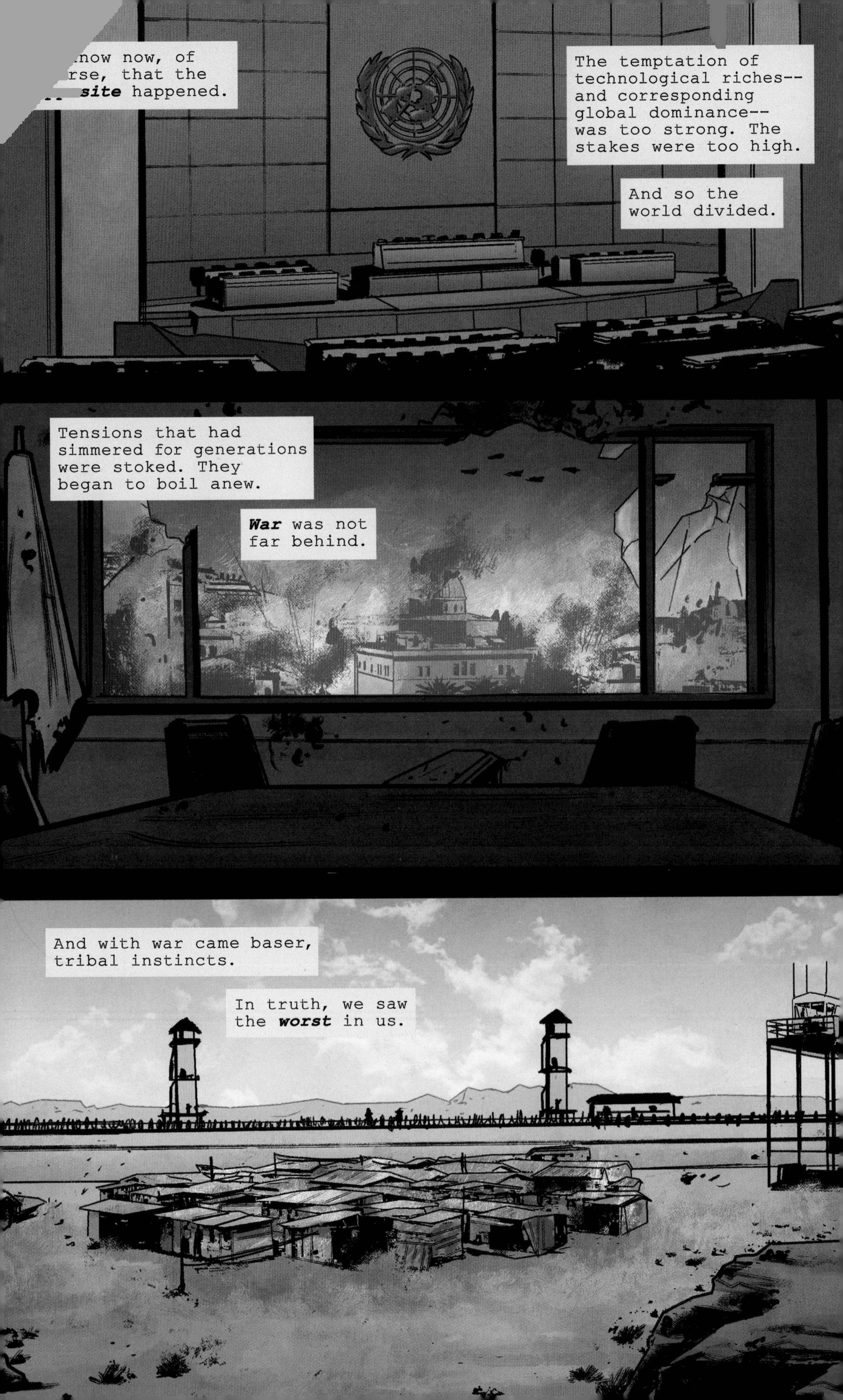
now now, of
rse, that the
site happened.
The temptation of technological riches--and corresponding global dominance--was too strong. The stakes were too high.
And so the world divided.
Tensions that had simmered for generations were stoked. They began to boil anew.
War was not far behind.
And with war came baser, tribal instincts.
In truth, we saw the worst in us.

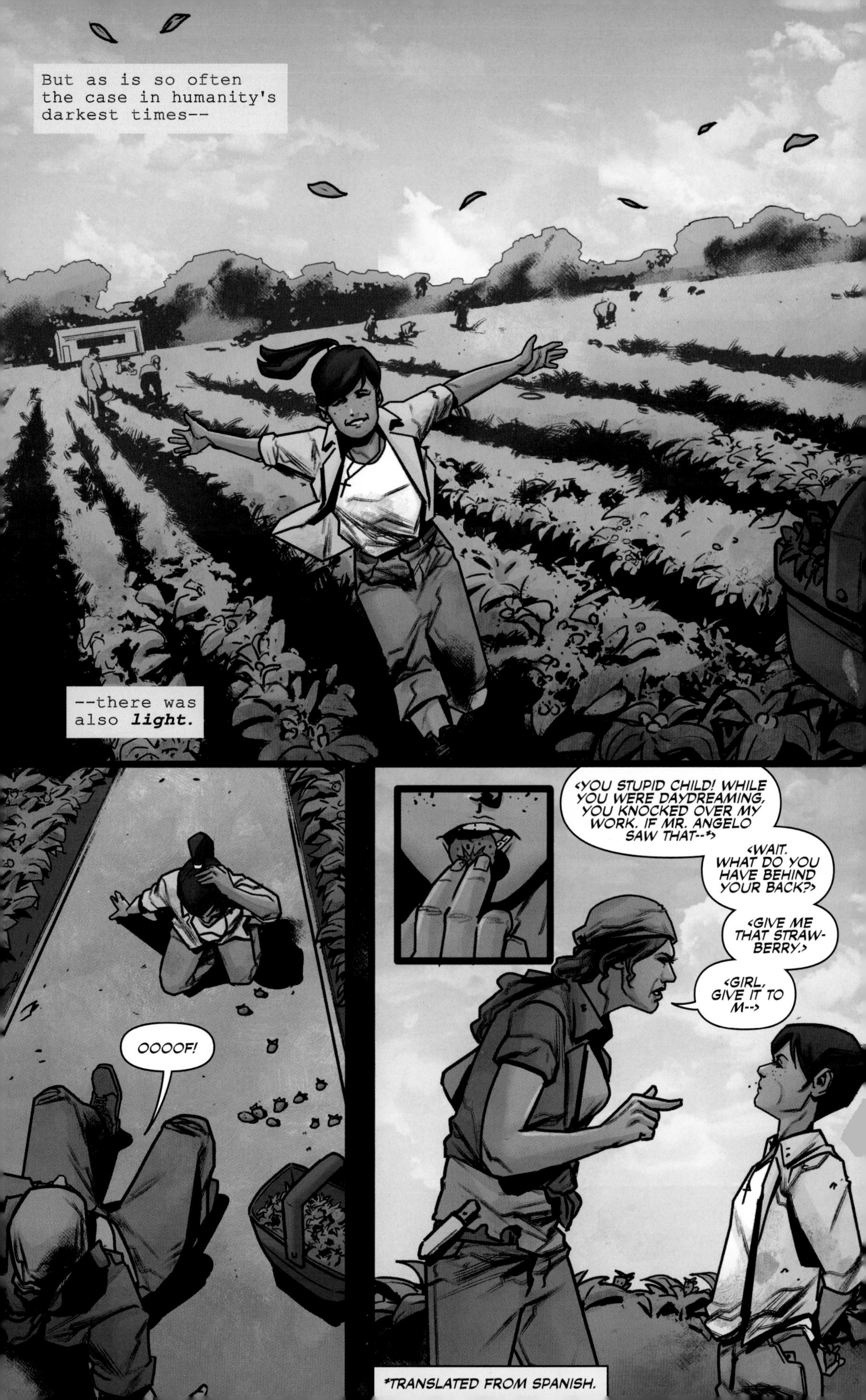

But as is so often the case in humanity's darkest times--
--there was also *light.*
OOOOF!
<YOU STUPID CHILD! WHILE YOU WERE DAYDREAMING, YOU KNOCKED OVER MY WORK. IF MR. ANGELO SAW THAT--*>
<WAIT. WHAT DO YOU HAVE BEHIND YOUR BACK?>
<GIVE ME THAT STRAW-BERRY.>
<GIRL, GIVE IT TO M-->
*TRANSLATED FROM SPANISH.

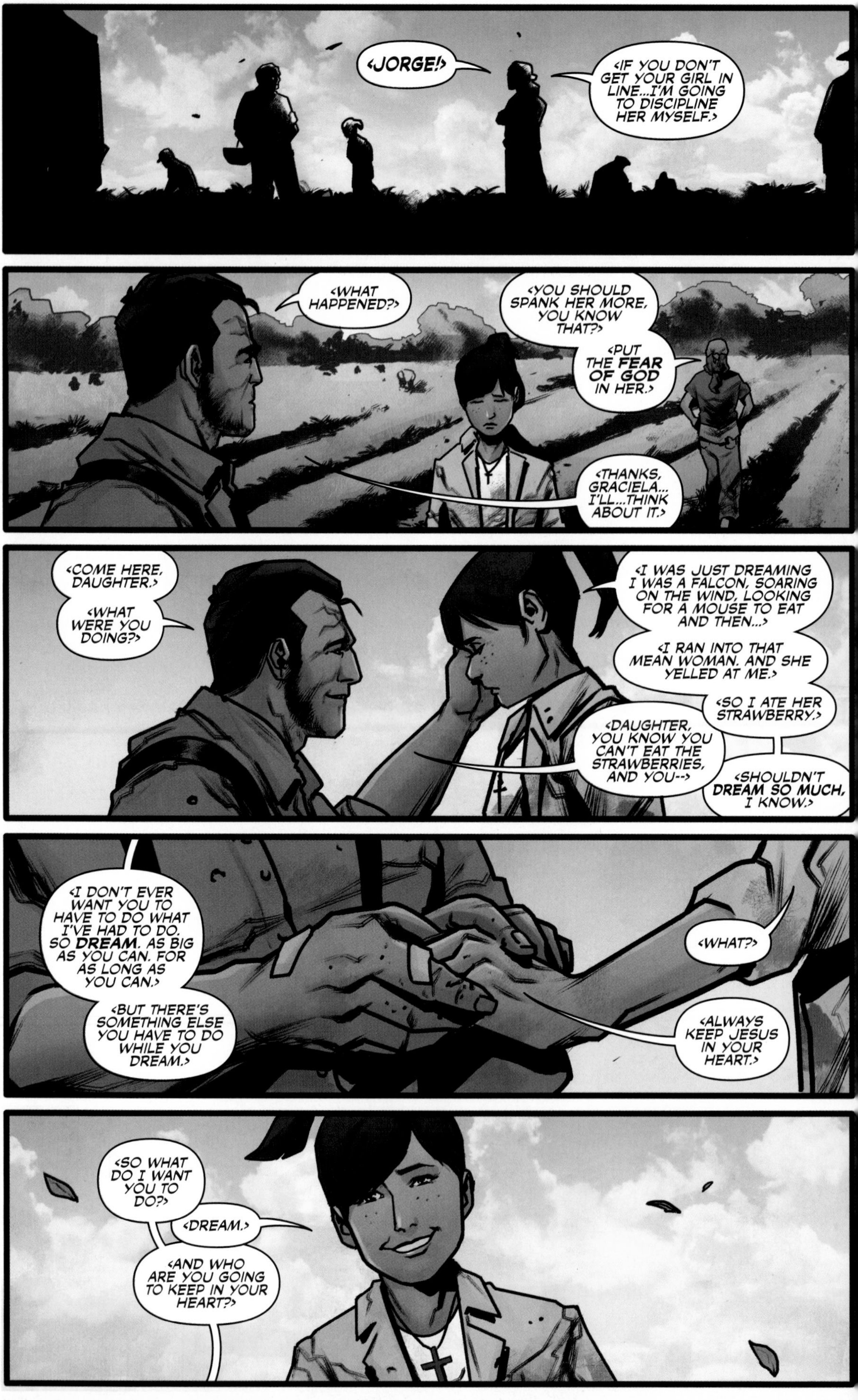
‹JORGE!›
‹IF YOU DON'T GET YOUR GIRL IN LINE...I'M GOING TO DISCIPLINE HER MYSELF.›
‹WHAT HAPPENED?›
‹YOU SHOULD SPANK HER MORE, YOU KNOW THAT?›
‹PUT THE **FEAR OF GOD** IN HER.›
‹THANKS, GRACIELA... I'LL...THINK ABOUT IT.›
‹COME HERE, DAUGHTER.›
‹WHAT WERE YOU DOING?›
‹I WAS JUST DREAMING I WAS A FALCON, SOARING ON THE WIND, LOOKING FOR A MOUSE TO EAT AND THEN...›
‹I RAN INTO THAT MEAN WOMAN. AND SHE YELLED AT ME.›
‹SO I ATE HER STRAWBERRY.›
‹DAUGHTER, YOU KNOW YOU CAN'T EAT THE STRAWBERRIES, AND YOU--›
‹SHOULDN'T **DREAM SO MUCH**, I KNOW.›
‹I DON'T EVER WANT YOU TO HAVE TO DO WHAT I'VE HAD TO DO. SO **DREAM**. AS BIG AS YOU CAN. FOR AS LONG AS YOU CAN.›
‹BUT THERE'S SOMETHING ELSE YOU HAVE TO DO WHILE YOU DREAM.›
‹WHAT?›
‹ALWAYS KEEP JESUS IN YOUR HEART.›
‹SO WHAT DO I WANT YOU TO DO?›
‹DREAM.›
‹AND WHO ARE YOU GOING TO KEEP IN YOUR HEART?›

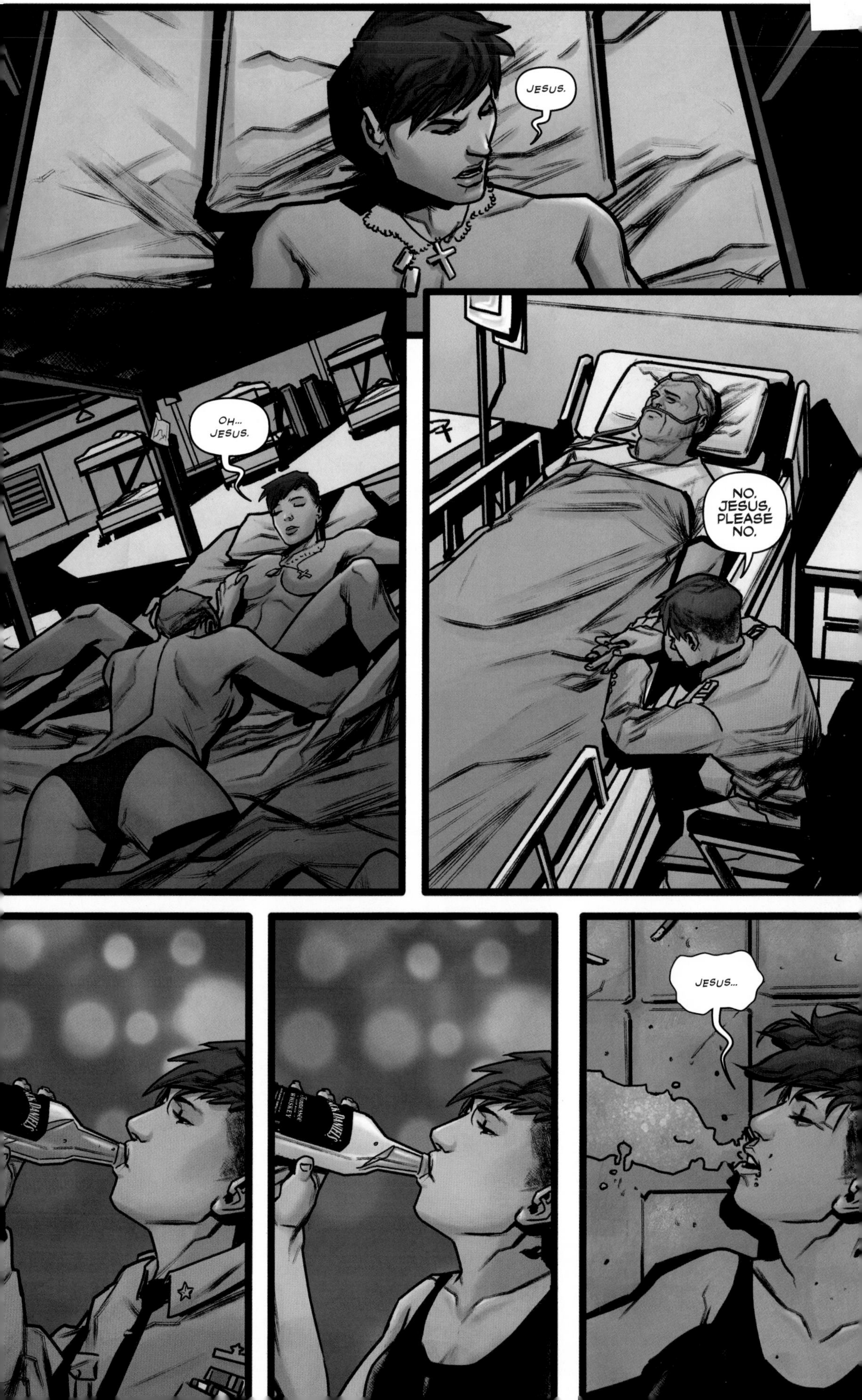
JESUS.
OH... JESUS.
NO, JESUS, PLEASE NO.
JESUS...

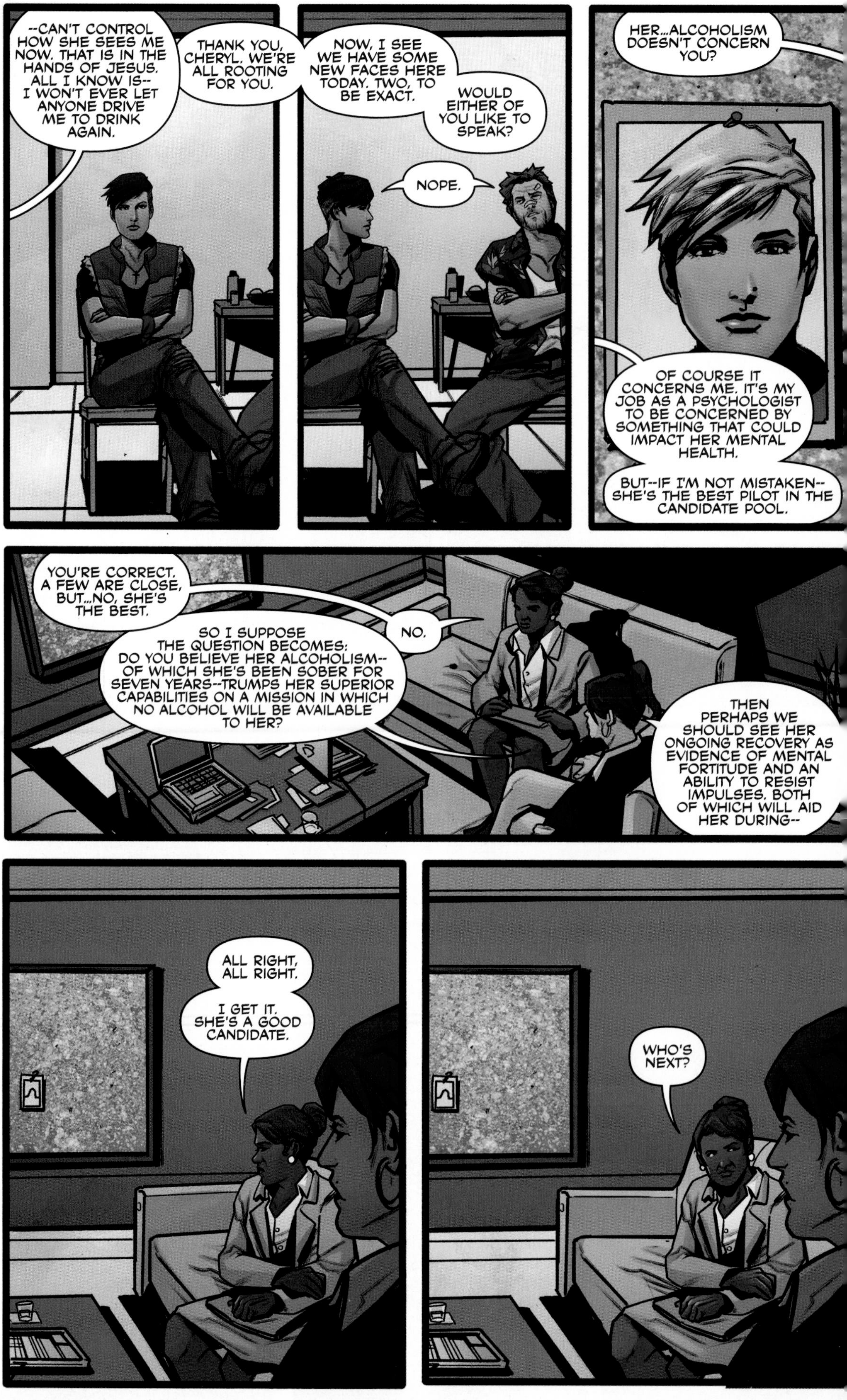
--CAN'T CONTROL HOW SHE SEES ME NOW. THAT IS IN THE HANDS OF JESUS. ALL I KNOW IS-- I WON'T EVER LET ANYONE DRIVE ME TO DRINK AGAIN.
THANK YOU, CHERYL. WE'RE ALL ROOTING FOR YOU.
NOW, I SEE WE HAVE SOME NEW FACES HERE TODAY. TWO, TO BE EXACT.
WOULD EITHER OF YOU LIKE TO SPEAK?
NOPE.
HER...ALCOHOLISM DOESN'T CONCERN YOU?
OF COURSE IT CONCERNS ME. IT'S MY JOB AS A PSYCHOLOGIST TO BE CONCERNED BY SOMETHING THAT COULD IMPACT HER MENTAL HEALTH.
BUT--IF I'M NOT MISTAKEN-- SHE'S THE BEST PILOT IN THE CANDIDATE POOL.
YOU'RE CORRECT. A FEW ARE CLOSE, BUT...NO, SHE'S THE BEST.
NO.
SO I SUPPOSE THE QUESTION BECOMES: DO YOU BELIEVE HER ALCOHOLISM-- OF WHICH SHE'S BEEN SOBER FOR SEVEN YEARS--TRUMPS HER SUPERIOR CAPABILITIES ON A MISSION IN WHICH NO ALCOHOL WILL BE AVAILABLE TO HER?
THEN PERHAPS WE SHOULD SEE HER ONGOING RECOVERY AS EVIDENCE OF MENTAL FORTITUDE AND AN ABILITY TO RESIST IMPULSES. BOTH OF WHICH WILL AID HER DURING--
ALL RIGHT, ALL RIGHT.
I GET IT. SHE'S A GOOD CANDIDATE.
WHO'S NEXT?

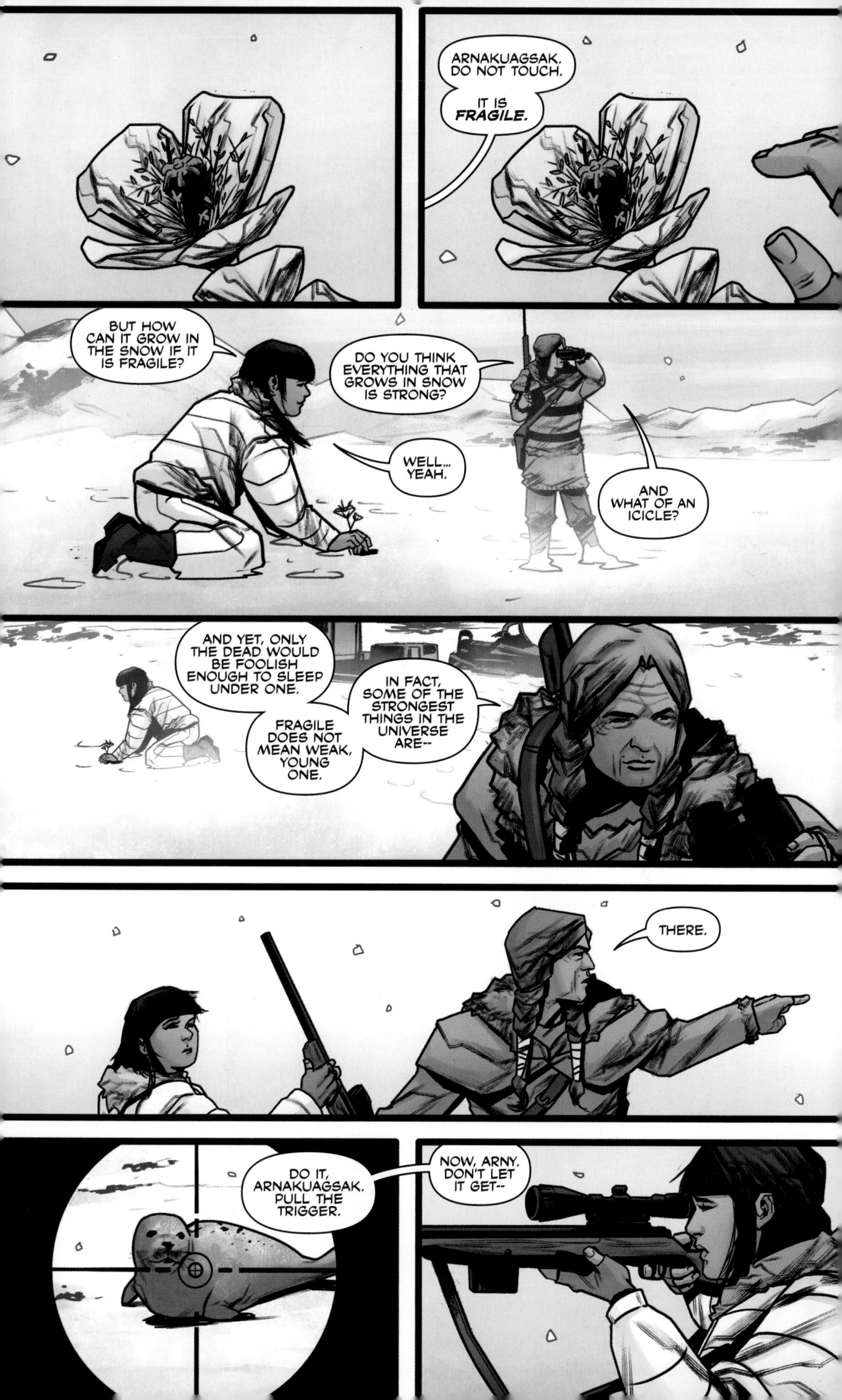
ARNAKUAGSAK. DO NOT TOUCH.
IT IS *FRAGILE.*
BUT HOW CAN IT GROW IN THE SNOW IF IT IS FRAGILE?
DO YOU THINK EVERYTHING THAT GROWS IN SNOW IS STRONG?
WELL... YEAH.
AND WHAT OF AN ICICLE?
AND YET, ONLY THE DEAD WOULD BE FOOLISH ENOUGH TO SLEEP UNDER ONE.
FRAGILE DOES NOT MEAN WEAK, YOUNG ONE.
IN FACT, SOME OF THE STRONGEST THINGS IN THE UNIVERSE ARE--
THERE.
DO IT, ARNAKUAGSAK. PULL THE TRIGGER.
NOW, ARNY. DON'T LET IT GET--

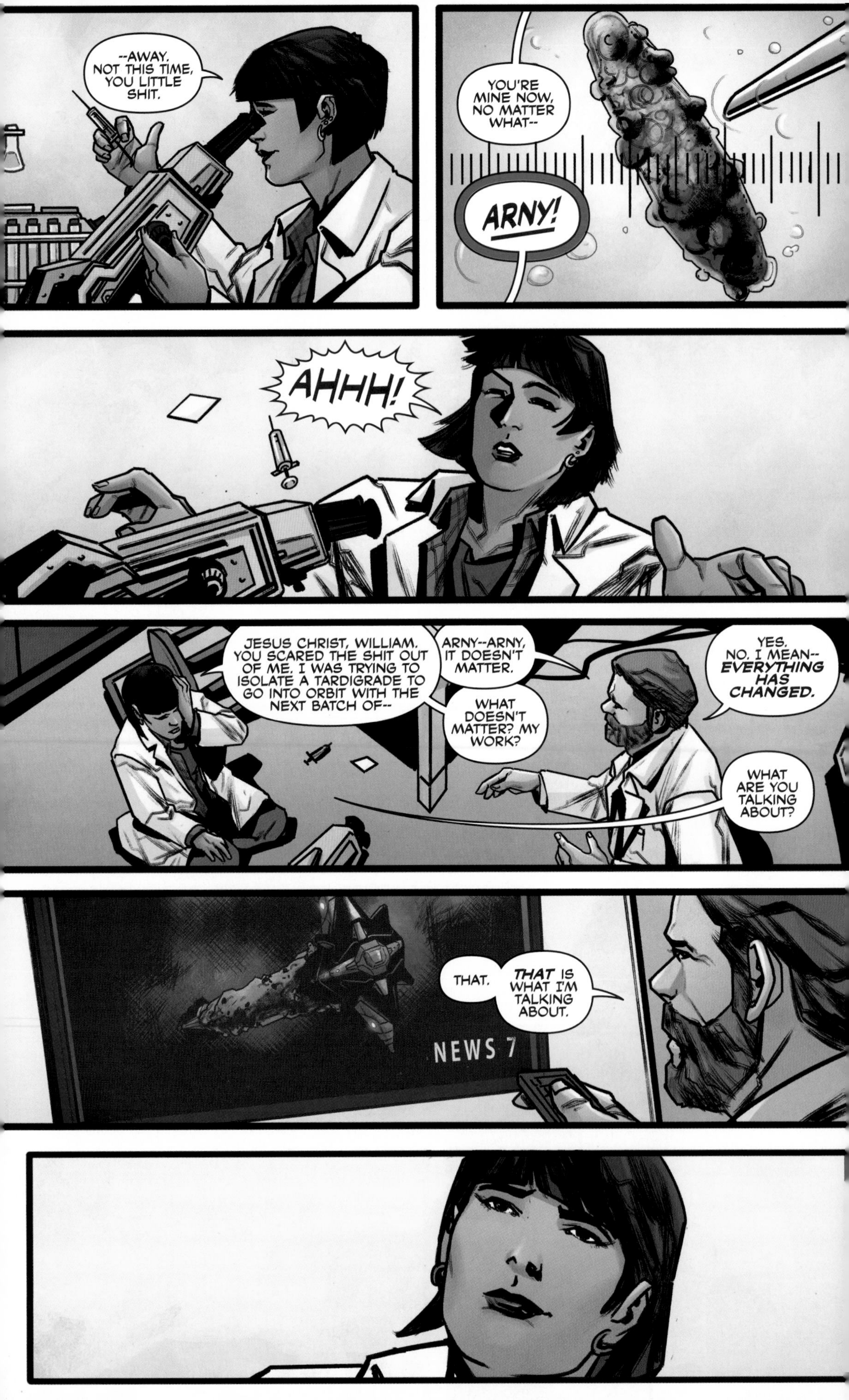
--AWAY. NOT THIS TIME, YOU LITTLE SHIT.
YOU'RE MINE NOW, NO MATTER WHAT--
ARNY!
AHHH!
JESUS CHRIST, WILLIAM. YOU SCARED THE SHIT OUT OF ME. I WAS TRYING TO ISOLATE A TARDIGRADE TO GO INTO ORBIT WITH THE NEXT BATCH OF--
ARNY--ARNY, IT DOESN'T MATTER.
WHAT DOESN'T MATTER? MY WORK?
YES. NO. I MEAN-- EVERYTHING HAS CHANGED.
WHAT ARE YOU TALKING ABOUT?
NEWS 7
THAT.
THAT IS WHAT I'M TALKING ABOUT.

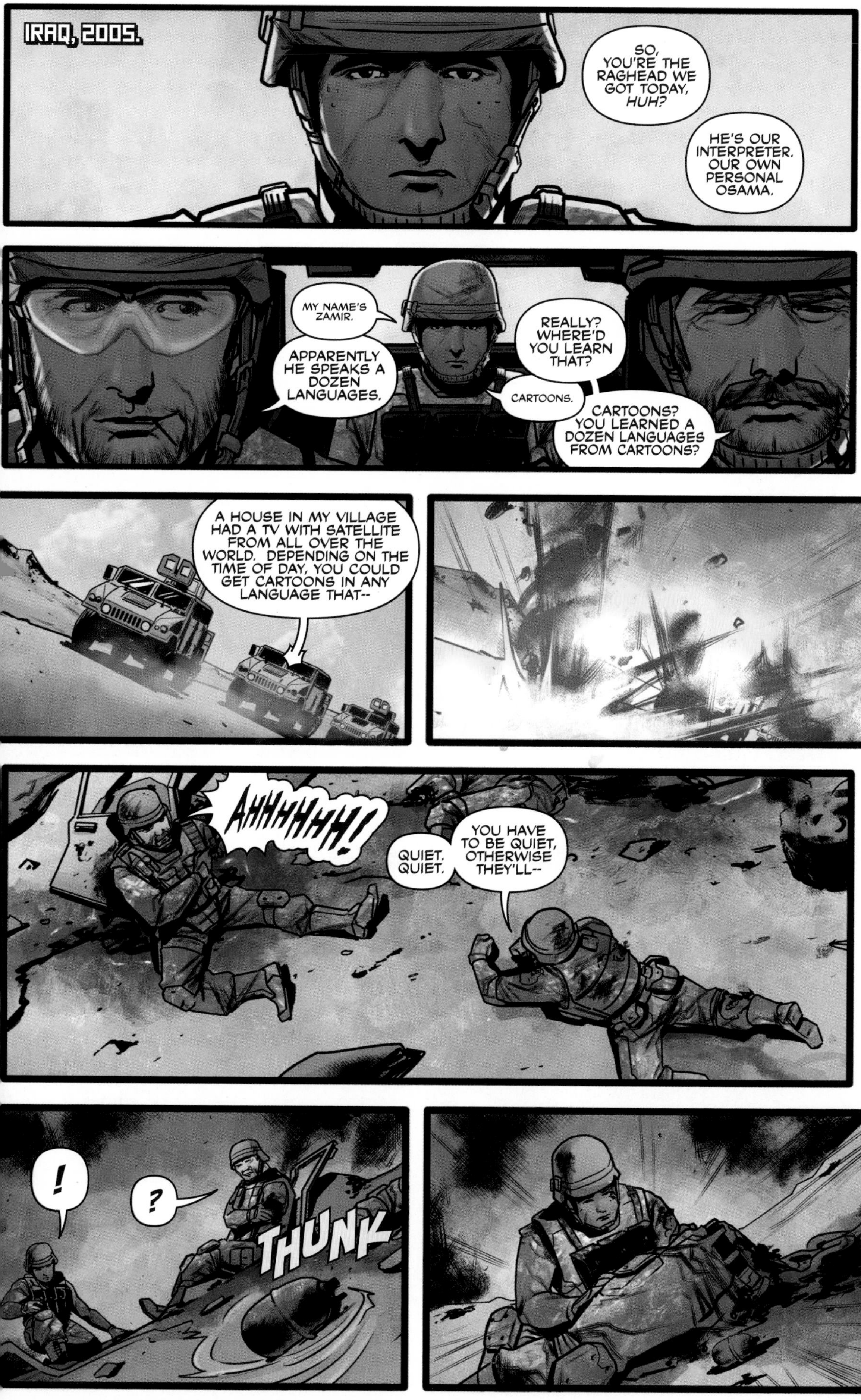
IRAQ, 2005.
SO, YOU'RE THE RAGHEAD WE GOT TODAY, HUH?
HE'S OUR INTERPRETER. OUR OWN PERSONAL OSAMA.
MY NAME'S ZAMIR.
APPARENTLY HE SPEAKS A DOZEN LANGUAGES.
REALLY? WHERE'D YOU LEARN THAT?
CARTOONS.
CARTOONS? YOU LEARNED A DOZEN LANGUAGES FROM CARTOONS?
A HOUSE IN MY VILLAGE HAD A TV WITH SATELLITE FROM ALL OVER THE WORLD. DEPENDING ON THE TIME OF DAY, YOU COULD GET CARTOONS IN ANY LANGUAGE THAT--
AHHHHHH!
QUIET. QUIET.
YOU HAVE TO BE QUIET, OTHERWISE THEY'LL--
!
?
THUNK

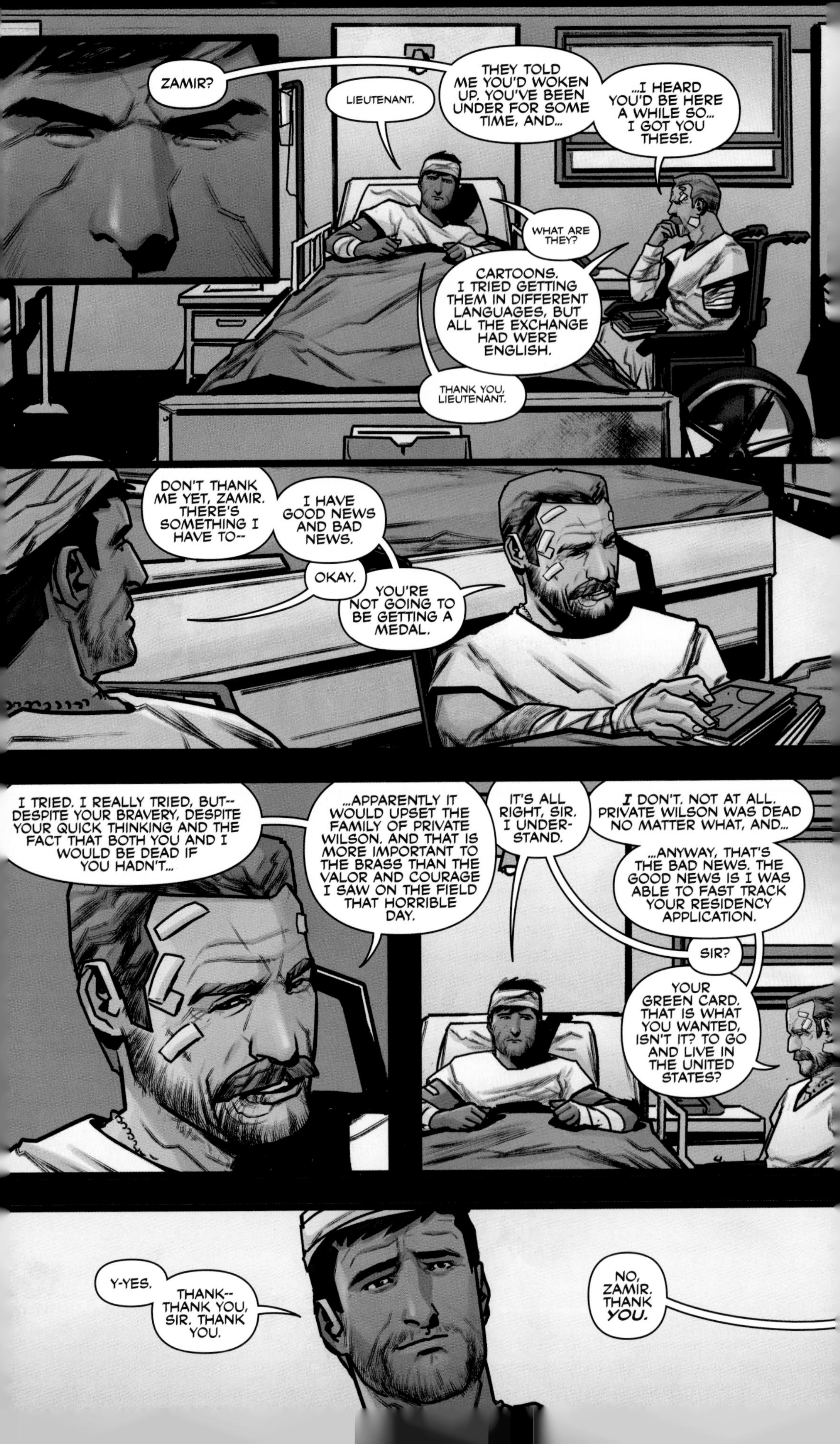
ZAMIR?
LIEUTENANT.
THEY TOLD ME YOU'D WOKEN UP. YOU'VE BEEN UNDER FOR SOME TIME, AND...
...I HEARD YOU'D BE HERE A WHILE SO... I GOT YOU THESE.
WHAT ARE THEY?
CARTOONS. I TRIED GETTING THEM IN DIFFERENT LANGUAGES, BUT ALL THE EXCHANGE HAD WERE ENGLISH.
THANK YOU, LIEUTENANT.
DON'T THANK ME YET, ZAMIR. THERE'S SOMETHING I HAVE TO--
I HAVE GOOD NEWS AND BAD NEWS.
OKAY.
YOU'RE NOT GOING TO BE GETTING A MEDAL.
I TRIED. I REALLY TRIED, BUT-- DESPITE YOUR BRAVERY, DESPITE YOUR QUICK THINKING AND THE FACT THAT BOTH YOU AND I WOULD BE DEAD IF YOU HADN'T...
...APPARENTLY IT WOULD UPSET THE FAMILY OF PRIVATE WILSON, AND THAT IS MORE IMPORTANT TO THE BRASS THAN THE VALOR AND COURAGE I SAW ON THE FIELD THAT HORRIBLE DAY.
IT'S ALL RIGHT, SIR. I UNDERSTAND.
I DON'T. NOT AT ALL. PRIVATE WILSON WAS DEAD NO MATTER WHAT, AND...
...ANYWAY, THAT'S THE BAD NEWS. THE GOOD NEWS IS I WAS ABLE TO FAST TRACK YOUR RESIDENCY APPLICATION.
SIR?
YOUR GREEN CARD. THAT IS WHAT YOU WANTED, ISN'T IT? TO GO AND LIVE IN THE UNITED STATES?
Y-YES.
THANK-- THANK YOU, SIR. THANK YOU.
NO, ZAMIR. THANK *YOU*.

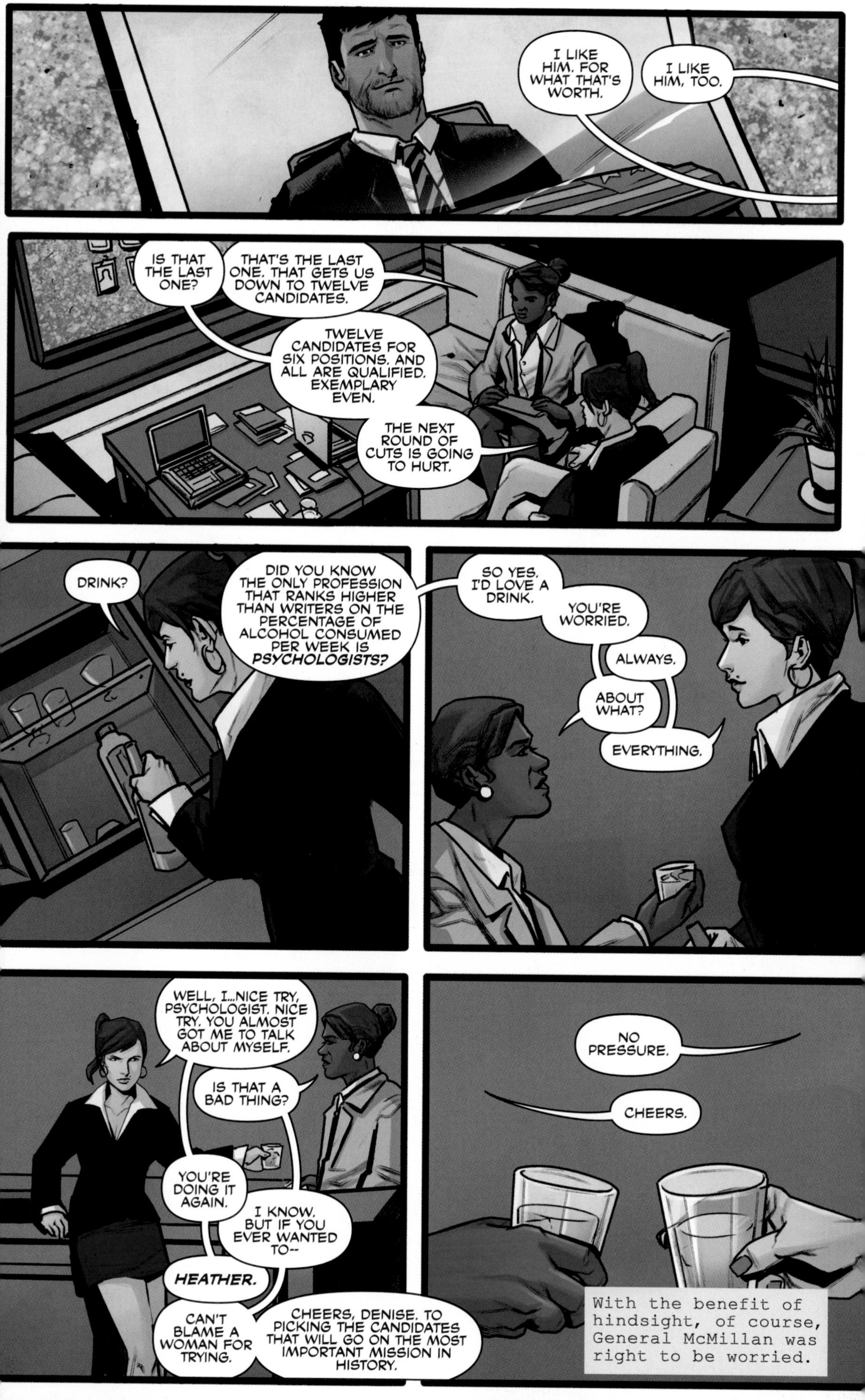
I LIKE HIM. FOR WHAT THAT'S WORTH.
I LIKE HIM, TOO.
IS THAT THE LAST ONE?
THAT'S THE LAST ONE. THAT GETS US DOWN TO TWELVE CANDIDATES.
TWELVE CANDIDATES FOR SIX POSITIONS. AND ALL ARE QUALIFIED. EXEMPLARY EVEN.
THE NEXT ROUND OF CUTS IS GOING TO HURT.
DRINK?
DID YOU KNOW THE ONLY PROFESSION THAT RANKS HIGHER THAN WRITERS ON THE PERCENTAGE OF ALCOHOL CONSUMED PER WEEK IS *PSYCHOLOGISTS?*
SO YES. I'D LOVE A DRINK.
YOU'RE WORRIED.
ALWAYS.
ABOUT WHAT?
EVERYTHING.
WELL, I...NICE TRY, PSYCHOLOGIST. NICE TRY. YOU ALMOST GOT ME TO TALK ABOUT MYSELF.
IS THAT A BAD THING?
YOU'RE DOING IT AGAIN.
I KNOW. BUT IF YOU EVER WANTED TO--
HEATHER.
CAN'T BLAME A WOMAN FOR TRYING.
CHEERS, DENISE. TO PICKING THE CANDIDATES THAT WILL GO ON THE MOST IMPORTANT MISSION IN HISTORY.
NO PRESSURE.
CHEERS.
With the benefit of hindsight, of course, General McMillan was right to be worried.

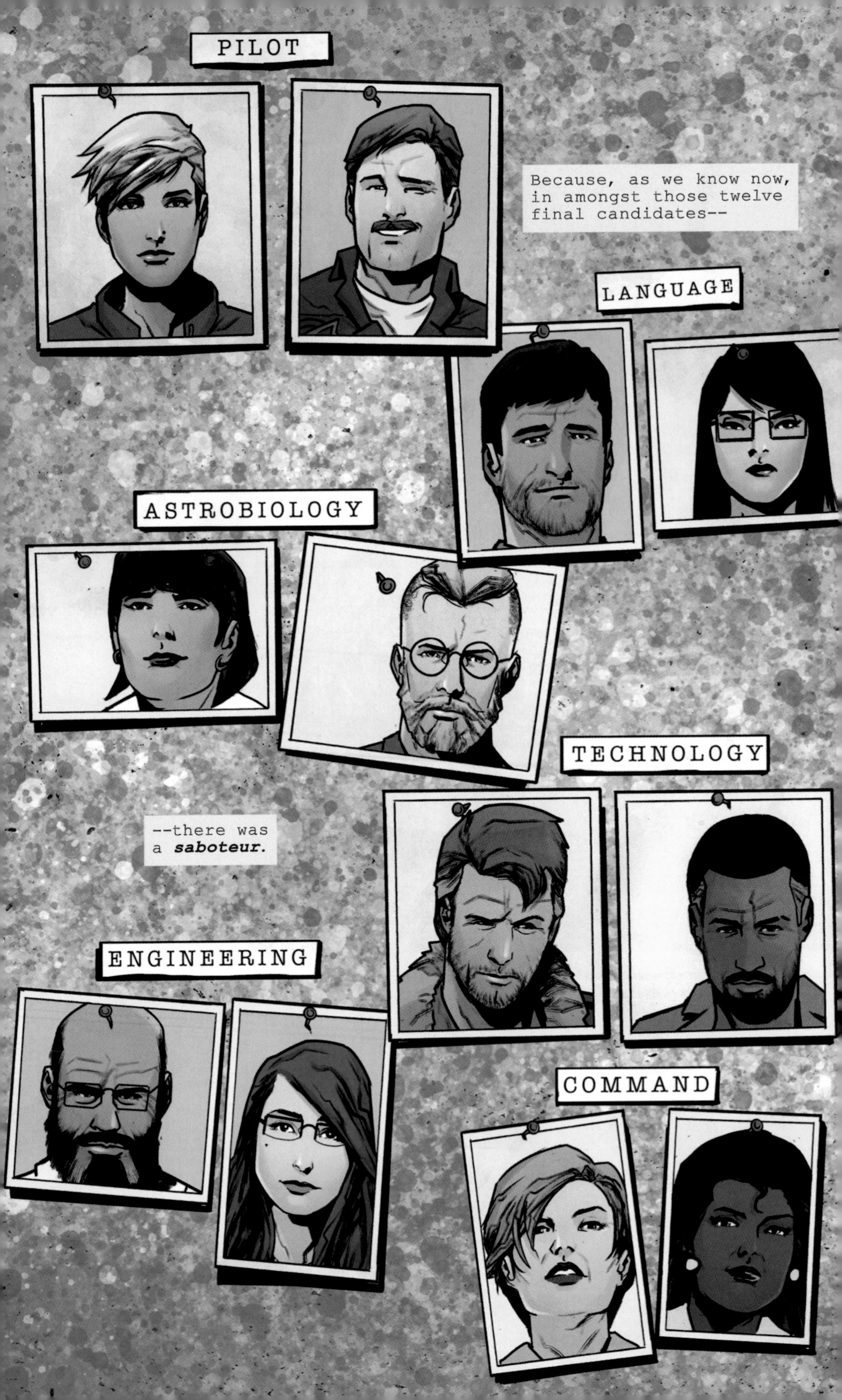

PILOT
Because, as we know now, in amongst those twelve final candidates--
LANGUAGE
ASTROBIOLOGY
TECHNOLOGY
--there was a *saboteur*.
ENGINEERING
COMMAND

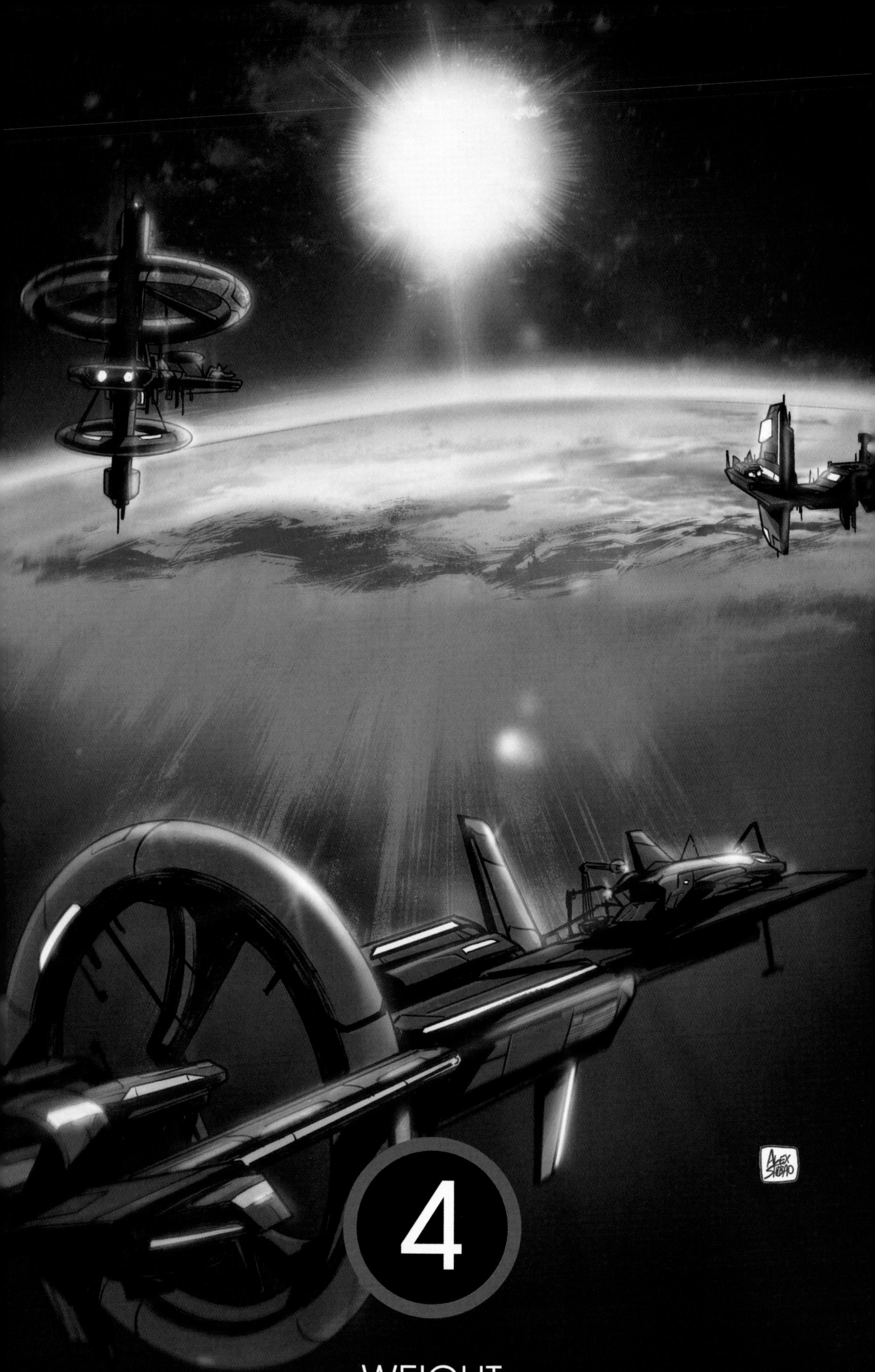

4

WEIGHT

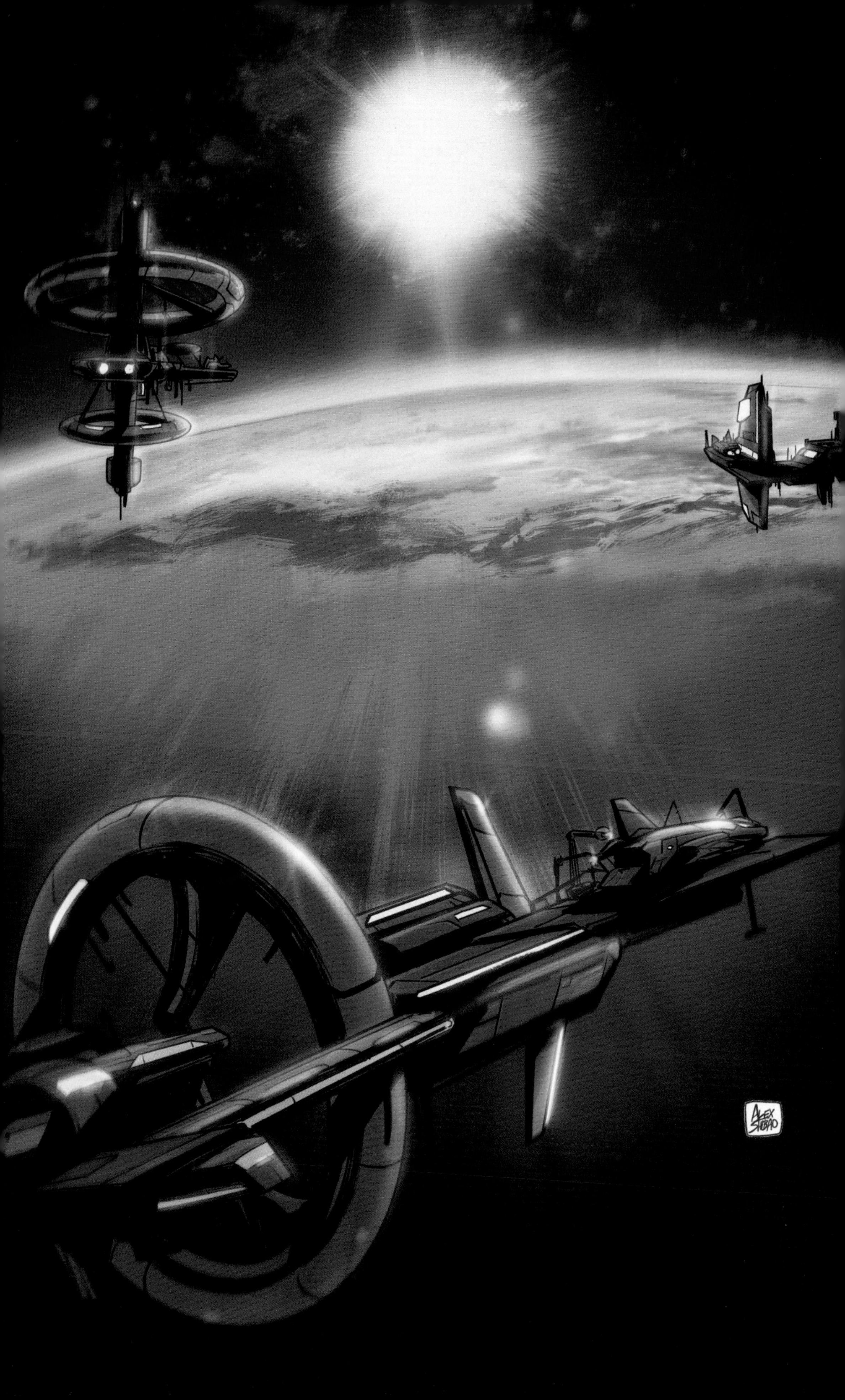

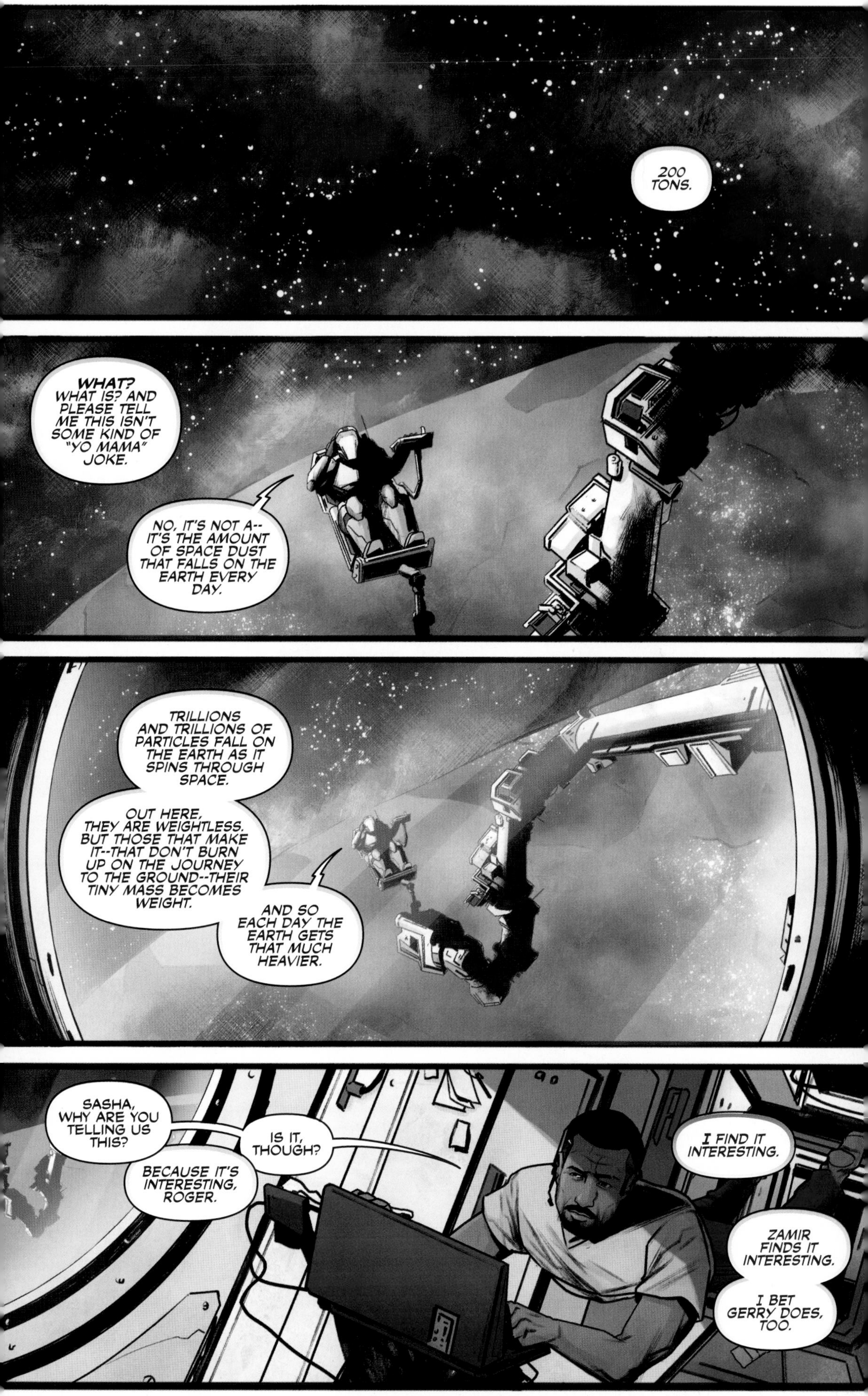
200 TONS.
WHAT? WHAT IS? AND PLEASE TELL ME THIS ISN'T SOME KIND OF "YO MAMA" JOKE.
NO, IT'S NOT A-- IT'S THE AMOUNT OF SPACE DUST THAT FALLS ON THE EARTH EVERY DAY.
TRILLIONS AND TRILLIONS OF PARTICLES FALL ON THE EARTH AS IT SPINS THROUGH SPACE.
OUT HERE, THEY ARE WEIGHTLESS. BUT THOSE THAT MAKE IT--THAT DON'T BURN UP ON THE JOURNEY TO THE GROUND--THEIR TINY MASS BECOMES WEIGHT.
AND SO EACH DAY THE EARTH GETS THAT MUCH HEAVIER.
SASHA, WHY ARE YOU TELLING US THIS?
BECAUSE IT'S INTERESTING, ROGER.
IS IT, THOUGH?
I FIND IT INTERESTING.
ZAMIR FINDS IT INTERESTING.
I BET GERRY DOES, TOO.

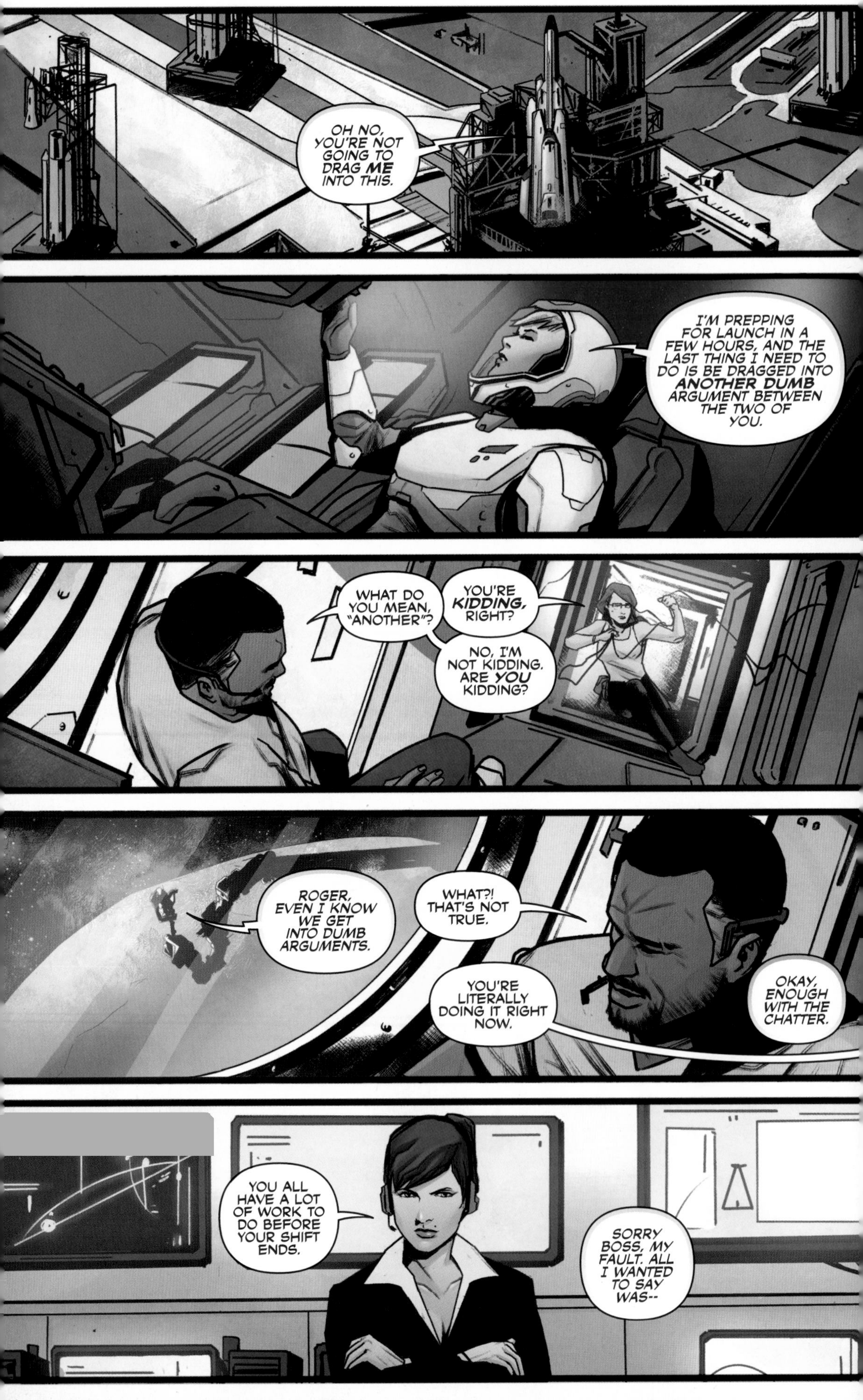
OH NO, YOU'RE NOT GOING TO DRAG ME INTO THIS.
I'M PREPPING FOR LAUNCH IN A FEW HOURS, AND THE LAST THING I NEED TO DO IS BE DRAGGED INTO ANOTHER DUMB ARGUMENT BETWEEN THE TWO OF YOU.
WHAT DO YOU MEAN, "ANOTHER"?
YOU'RE KIDDING, RIGHT?
NO, I'M NOT KIDDING. ARE YOU KIDDING?
ROGER, EVEN I KNOW WE GET INTO DUMB ARGUMENTS.
WHAT?! THAT'S NOT TRUE.
YOU'RE LITERALLY DOING IT RIGHT NOW.
OKAY, ENOUGH WITH THE CHATTER.
YOU ALL HAVE A LOT OF WORK TO DO BEFORE YOUR SHIFT ENDS.
SORRY BOSS, MY FAULT. ALL I WANTED TO SAY WAS--

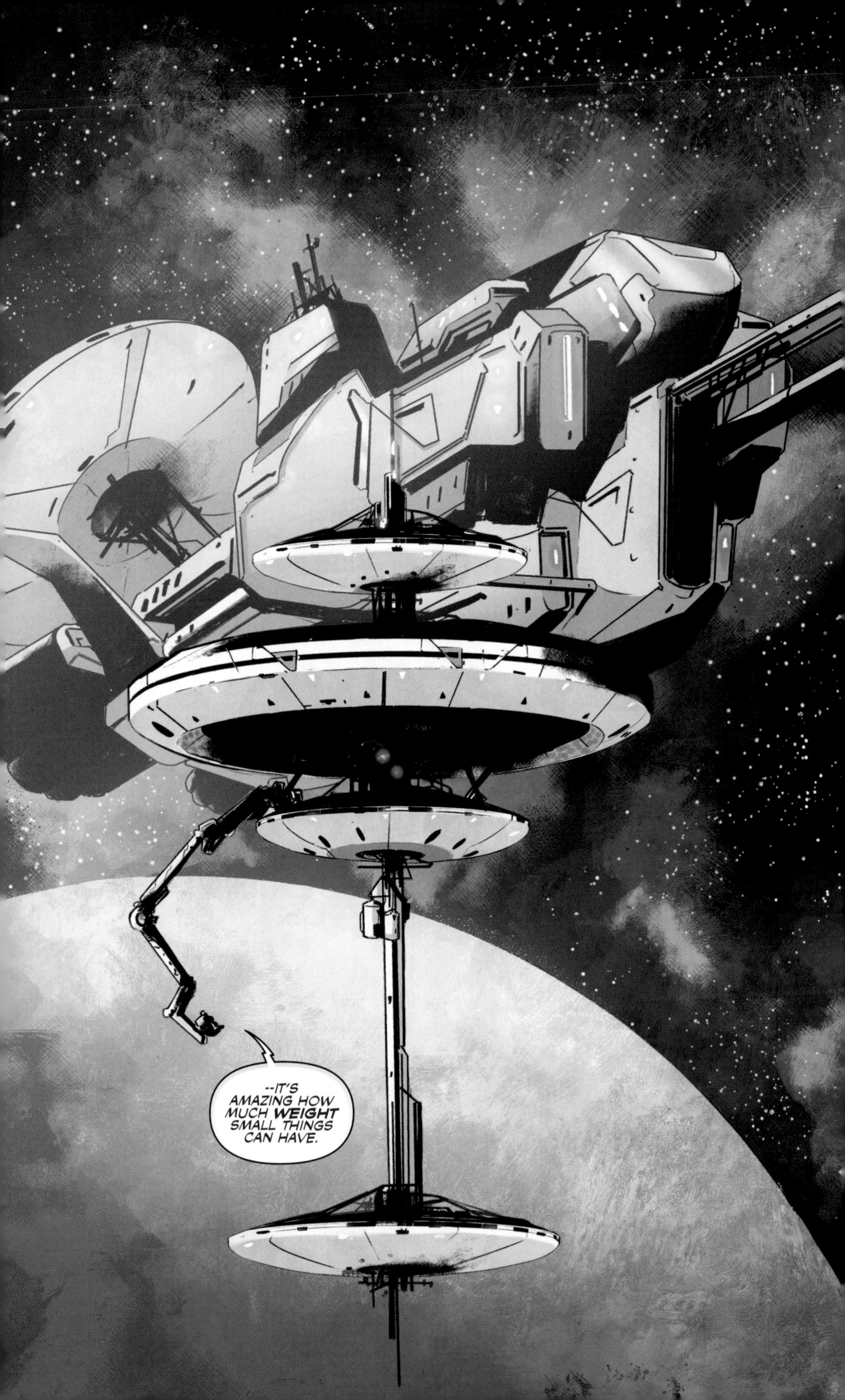
--IT'S AMAZING HOW MUCH WEIGHT SMALL THINGS CAN HAVE.

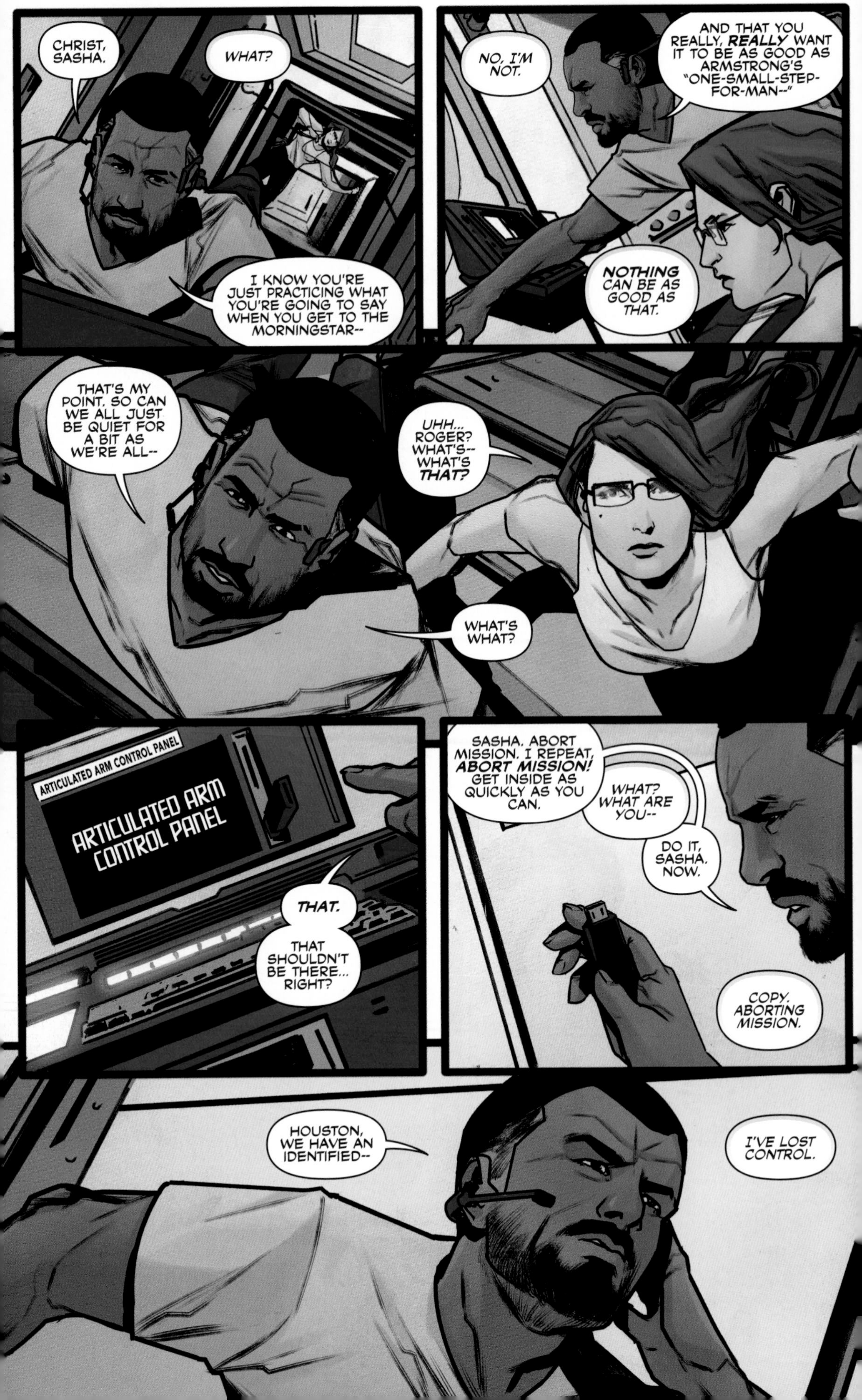
CHRIST, SASHA.
WHAT?
I KNOW YOU'RE JUST PRACTICING WHAT YOU'RE GOING TO SAY WHEN YOU GET TO THE MORNINGSTAR--
NO, I'M NOT.
AND THAT YOU REALLY, REALLY WANT IT TO BE AS GOOD AS ARMSTRONG'S "ONE-SMALL-STEP-FOR-MAN--"
NOTHING CAN BE AS GOOD AS THAT.
THAT'S MY POINT. SO CAN WE ALL JUST BE QUIET FOR A BIT AS WE'RE ALL--
UHH... ROGER? WHAT'S-- WHAT'S THAT?
WHAT'S WHAT?
ARTICULATED ARM CONTROL PANEL
ARTICULATED ARM CONTROL PANEL
THAT.
THAT SHOULDN'T BE THERE... RIGHT?
SASHA. ABORT MISSION. I REPEAT, ABORT MISSION! GET INSIDE AS QUICKLY AS YOU CAN.
WHAT? WHAT ARE YOU--
DO IT, SASHA. NOW.
COPY. ABORTING MISSION.
HOUSTON, WE HAVE AN IDENTIFIED--
I'VE LOST CONTROL.

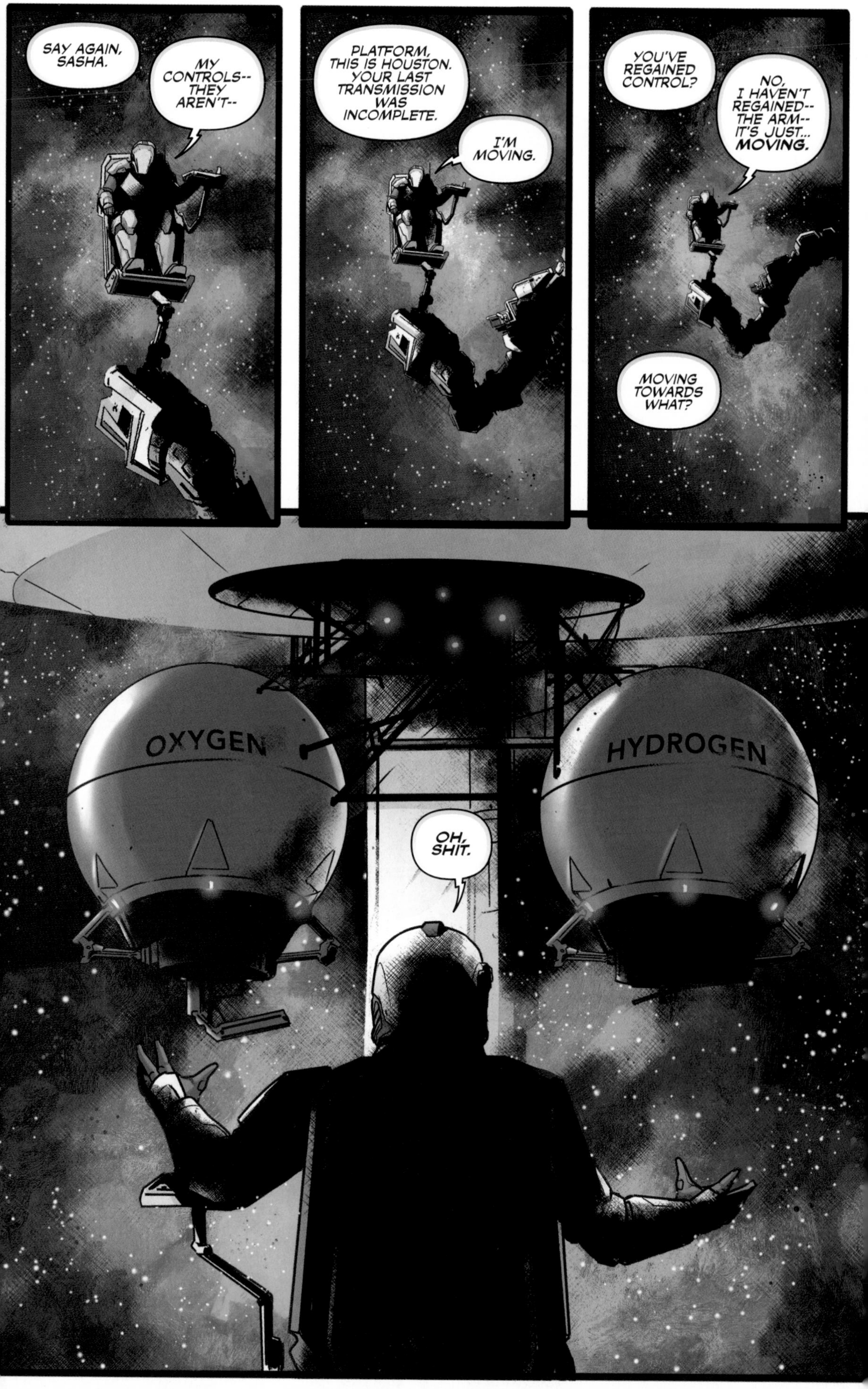
SAY AGAIN, SASHA.
MY CONTROLS-- THEY AREN'T--
PLATFORM, THIS IS HOUSTON. YOUR LAST TRANSMISSION WAS INCOMPLETE.
I'M MOVING.
YOU'VE REGAINED CONTROL?
NO, I HAVEN'T REGAINED-- THE ARM-- IT'S JUST... MOVING.
MOVING TOWARDS WHAT?
OXYGEN
HYDROGEN
OH, SHIT.

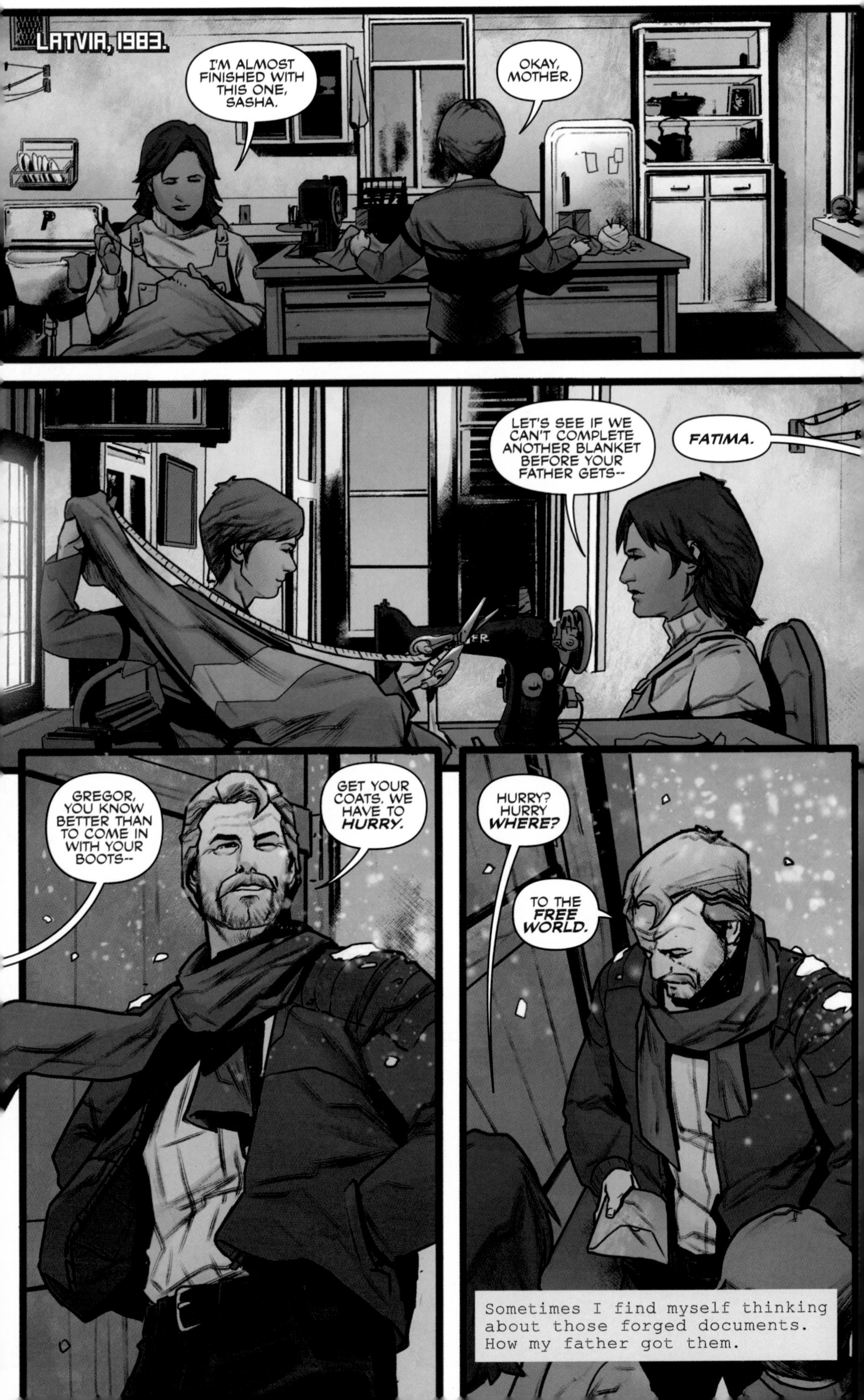
LATVIA, 1983.
I'M ALMOST FINISHED WITH THIS ONE, SASHA.
OKAY, MOTHER.
LET'S SEE IF WE CAN'T COMPLETE ANOTHER BLANKET BEFORE YOUR FATHER GETS--
FATIMA.
GREGOR, YOU KNOW BETTER THAN TO COME IN WITH YOUR BOOTS--
GET YOUR COATS. WE HAVE TO HURRY.
HURRY? HURRY WHERE?
TO THE FREE WORLD.
Sometimes I find myself thinking about those forged documents. How my father got them.

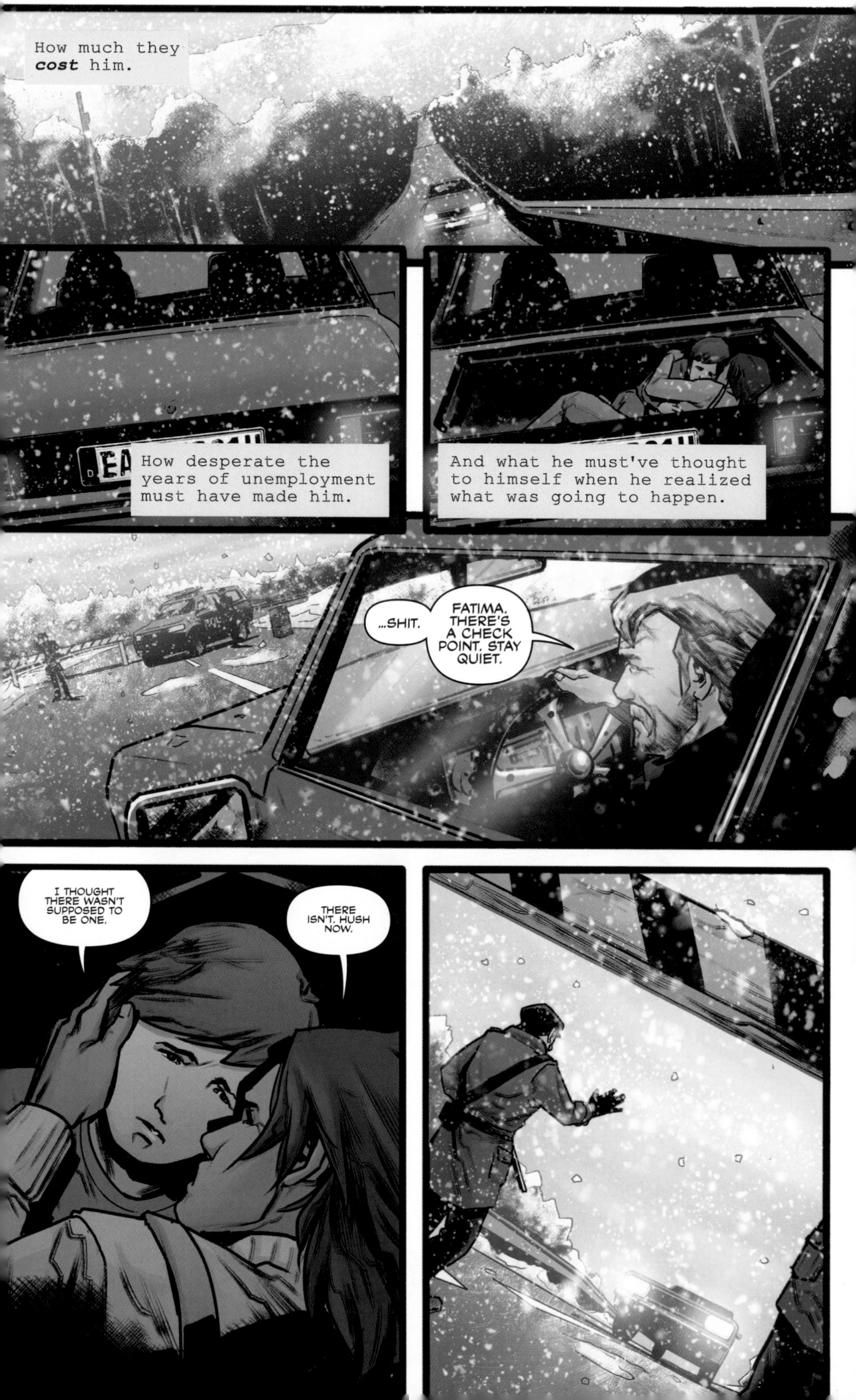

How much they *cost* him.
How desperate the years of unemployment must have made him.
And what he must've thought to himself when he realized what was going to happen.
...SHIT.
FATIMA. THERE'S A CHECK POINT. STAY QUIET.
I THOUGHT THERE WASN'T SUPPOSED TO BE ONE.
THERE ISN'T. HUSH NOW.

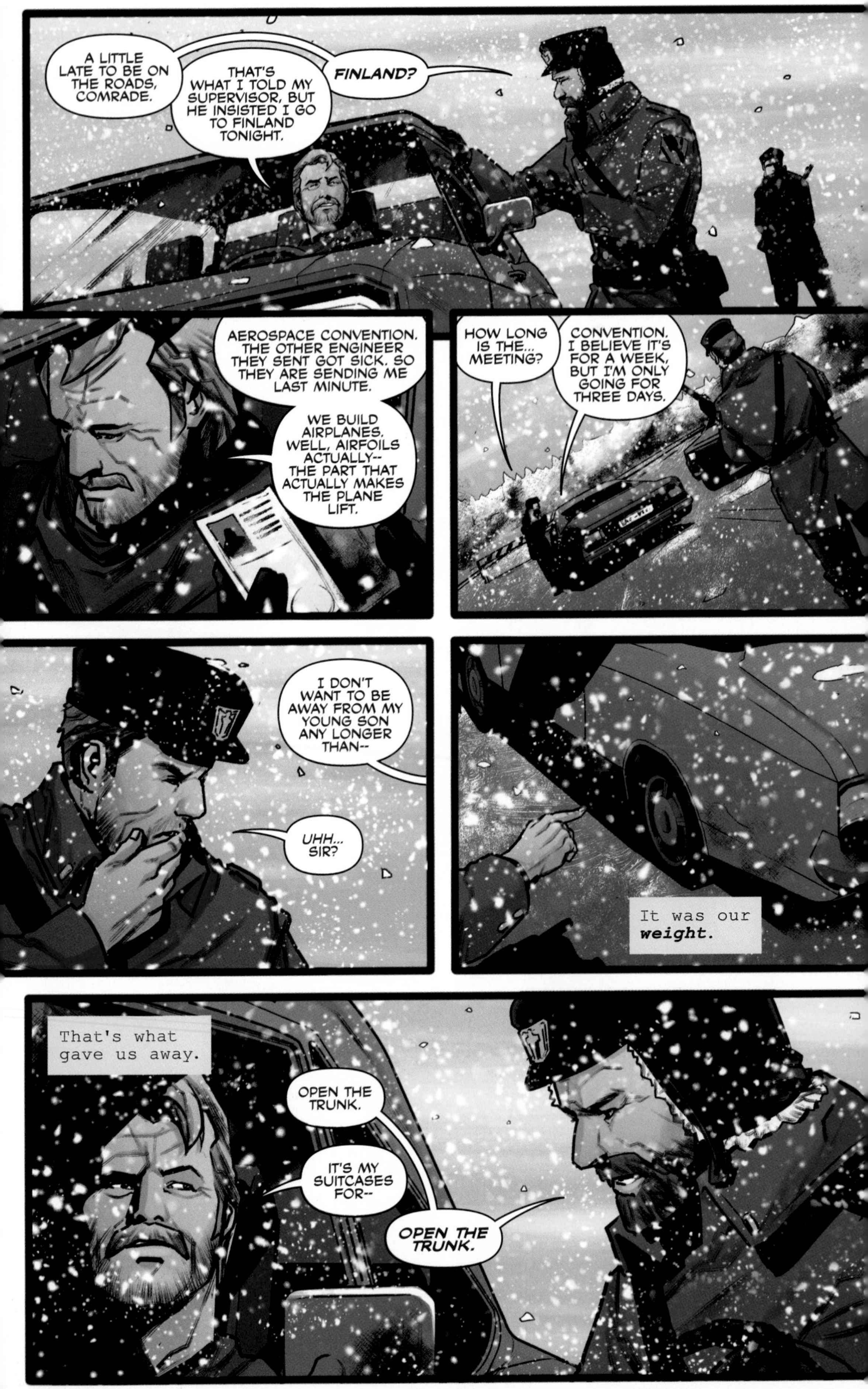
A LITTLE LATE TO BE ON THE ROADS, COMRADE.
THAT'S WHAT I TOLD MY SUPERVISOR, BUT HE INSISTED I GO TO FINLAND TONIGHT.
FINLAND?
AEROSPACE CONVENTION. THE OTHER ENGINEER THEY SENT GOT SICK. SO THEY ARE SENDING ME LAST MINUTE.
WE BUILD AIRPLANES. WELL, AIRFOILS ACTUALLY-- THE PART THAT ACTUALLY MAKES THE PLANE LIFT.
HOW LONG IS THE... MEETING?
CONVENTION. I BELIEVE IT'S FOR A WEEK, BUT I'M ONLY GOING FOR THREE DAYS.
I DON'T WANT TO BE AWAY FROM MY YOUNG SON ANY LONGER THAN--
UHH... SIR?
It was our weight.
That's what gave us away.
OPEN THE TRUNK.
IT'S MY SUITCASES FOR--
OPEN THE TRUNK.

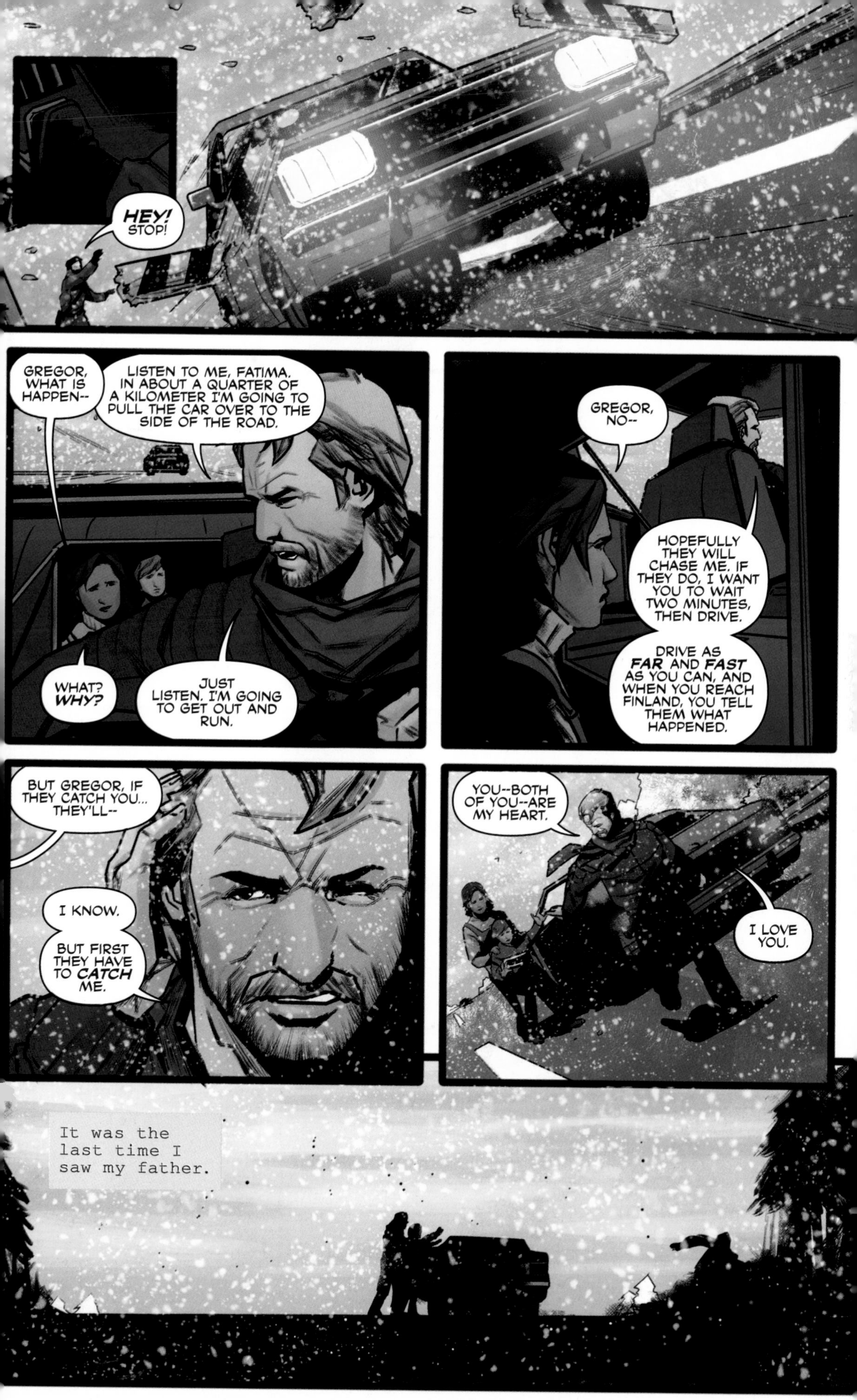

HEY! STOP!
GREGOR, WHAT IS HAPPEN--
LISTEN TO ME, FATIMA. IN ABOUT A QUARTER OF A KILOMETER I'M GOING TO PULL THE CAR OVER TO THE SIDE OF THE ROAD.
WHAT? WHY?
JUST LISTEN. I'M GOING TO GET OUT AND RUN.
GREGOR, NO--
HOPEFULLY THEY WILL CHASE ME. IF THEY DO, I WANT YOU TO WAIT TWO MINUTES, THEN DRIVE.
DRIVE AS FAR AND FAST AS YOU CAN, AND WHEN YOU REACH FINLAND, YOU TELL THEM WHAT HAPPENED.
BUT GREGOR, IF THEY CATCH YOU... THEY'LL--
I KNOW.
BUT FIRST THEY HAVE TO CATCH ME.
YOU--BOTH OF YOU--ARE MY HEART.
I LOVE YOU.
It was the last time I saw my father.

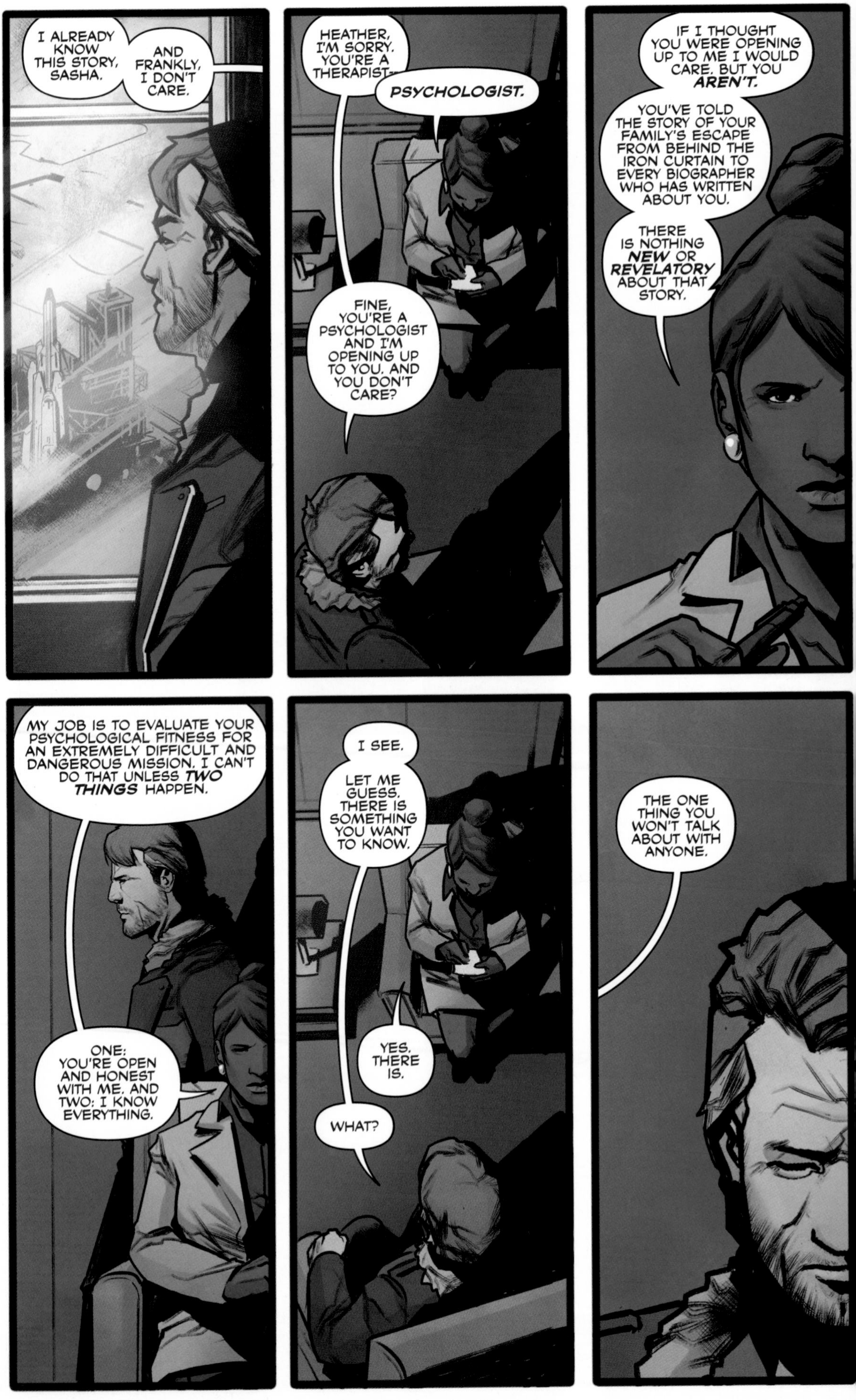
I ALREADY KNOW THIS STORY, SASHA.
AND FRANKLY, I DON'T CARE.
HEATHER, I'M SORRY. YOU'RE A THERAPIST--
PSYCHOLOGIST.
FINE, YOU'RE A PSYCHOLOGIST AND I'M OPENING UP TO YOU, AND YOU DON'T CARE?
IF I THOUGHT YOU WERE OPENING UP TO ME I WOULD CARE. BUT YOU ***AREN'T.***
YOU'VE TOLD THE STORY OF YOUR FAMILY'S ESCAPE FROM BEHIND THE IRON CURTAIN TO EVERY BIOGRAPHER WHO HAS WRITTEN ABOUT YOU.
THERE IS NOTHING ***NEW*** OR ***REVELATORY*** ABOUT THAT STORY.
MY JOB IS TO EVALUATE YOUR PSYCHOLOGICAL FITNESS FOR AN EXTREMELY DIFFICULT AND DANGEROUS MISSION. I CAN'T DO THAT UNLESS ***TWO THINGS*** HAPPEN.
ONE: YOU'RE OPEN AND HONEST WITH ME, AND TWO: I KNOW EVERYTHING.
I SEE.
LET ME GUESS. THERE IS SOMETHING YOU WANT TO KNOW.
YES, THERE IS.
WHAT?
THE ONE THING YOU WON'T TALK ABOUT WITH ANYONE.

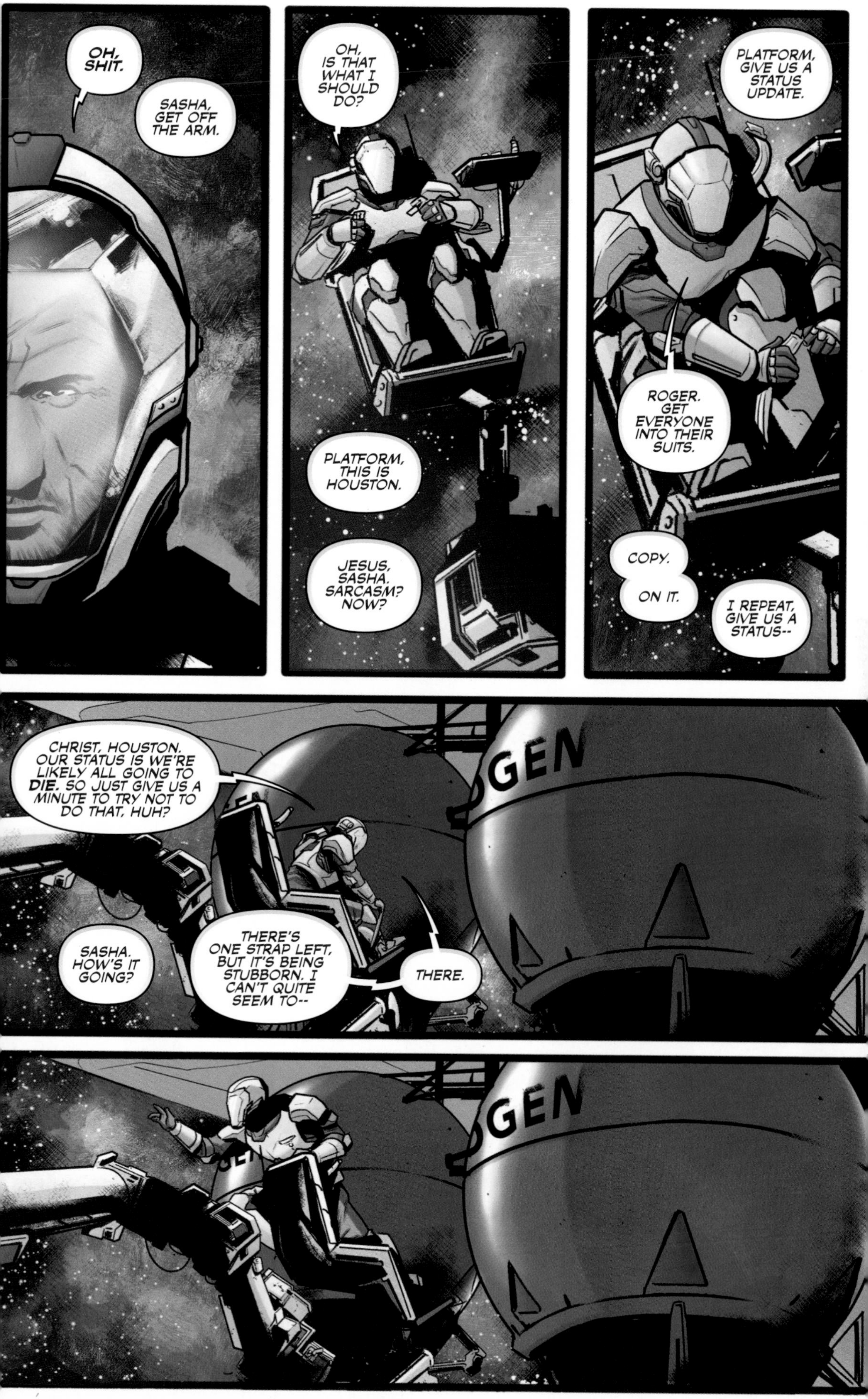

OH, SHIT.
SASHA, GET OFF THE ARM.
OH, IS THAT WHAT I SHOULD DO?
PLATFORM, THIS IS HOUSTON.
JESUS, SASHA. SARCASM? NOW?
PLATFORM, GIVE US A STATUS UPDATE.
ROGER. GET EVERYONE INTO THEIR SUITS.
COPY.
ON IT.
I REPEAT, GIVE US A STATUS--
CHRIST, HOUSTON. OUR STATUS IS WE'RE LIKELY ALL GOING TO DIE. SO JUST GIVE US A MINUTE TO TRY NOT TO DO THAT, HUH?
GEN
SASHA. HOW'S IT GOING?
THERE'S ONE STRAP LEFT, BUT IT'S BEING STUBBORN. I CAN'T QUITE SEEM TO--
THERE.
GEN

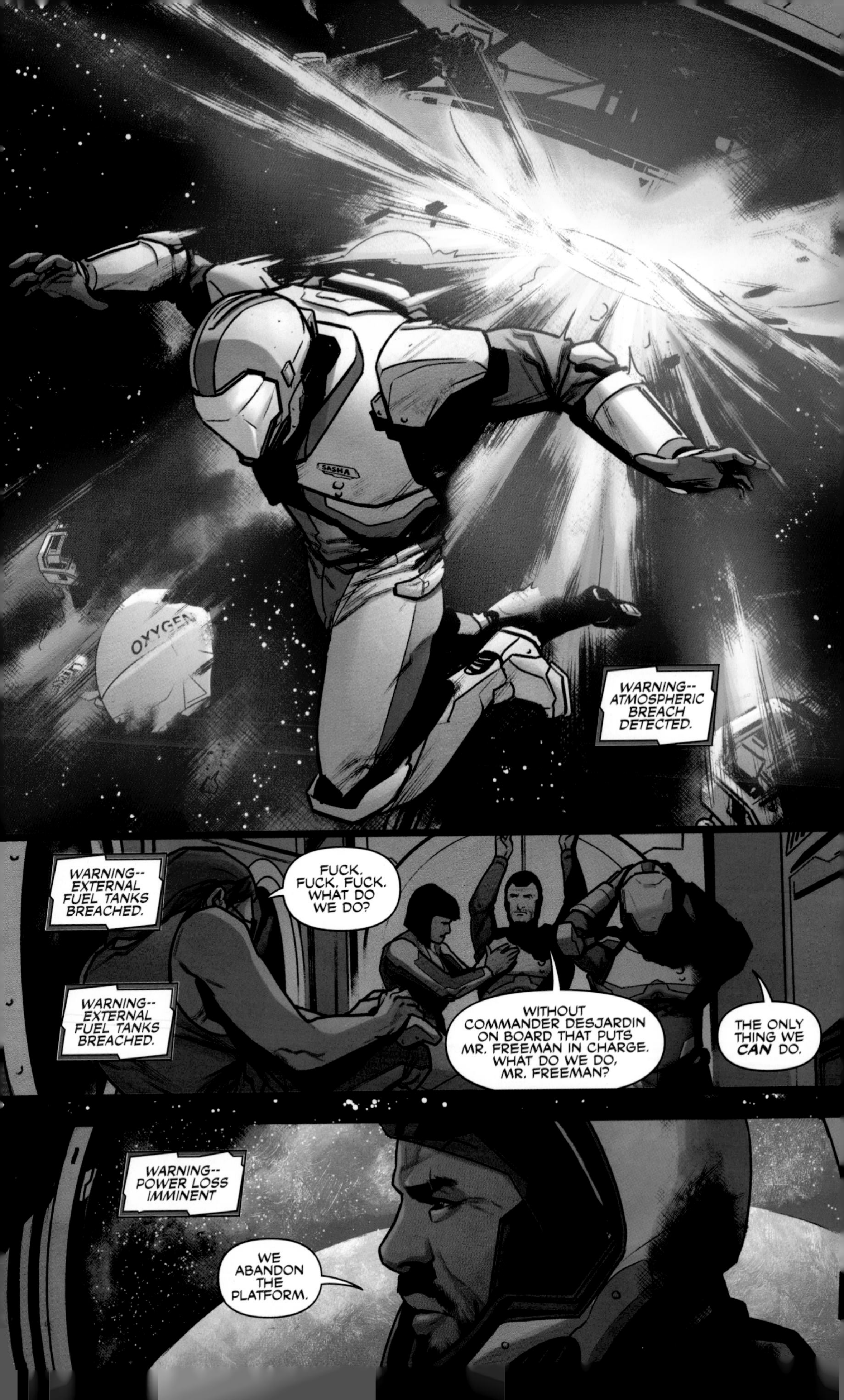
SASHA
OXYGEN
WARNING-- ATMOSPHERIC BREACH DETECTED.
WARNING-- EXTERNAL FUEL TANKS BREACHED.
FUCK. FUCK. FUCK. WHAT DO WE DO?
WARNING-- EXTERNAL FUEL TANKS BREACHED.
WITHOUT COMMANDER DESJARDIN ON BOARD THAT PUTS MR. FREEMAN IN CHARGE. WHAT DO WE DO, MR. FREEMAN?
THE ONLY THING WE *CAN* DO.
WARNING-- POWER LOSS IMMINENT
WE ABANDON THE PLATFORM.

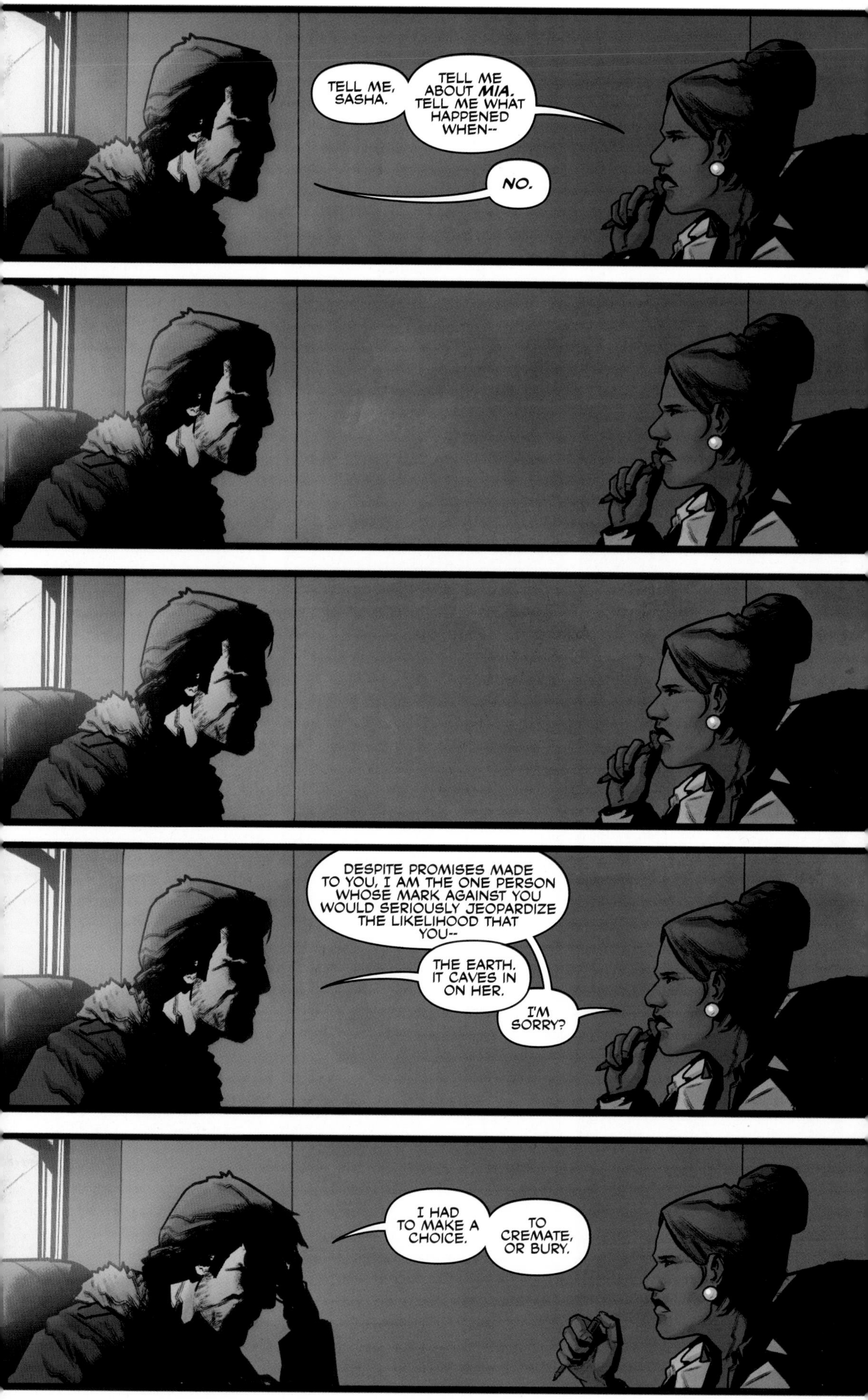
TELL ME, SASHA.
TELL ME ABOUT MIA. TELL ME WHAT HAPPENED WHEN--
NO.
DESPITE PROMISES MADE TO YOU, I AM THE ONE PERSON WHOSE MARK AGAINST YOU WOULD SERIOUSLY JEOPARDIZE THE LIKELIHOOD THAT YOU--
THE EARTH. IT CAVES IN ON HER.
I'M SORRY?
I HAD TO MAKE A CHOICE.
TO CREMATE, OR BURY.

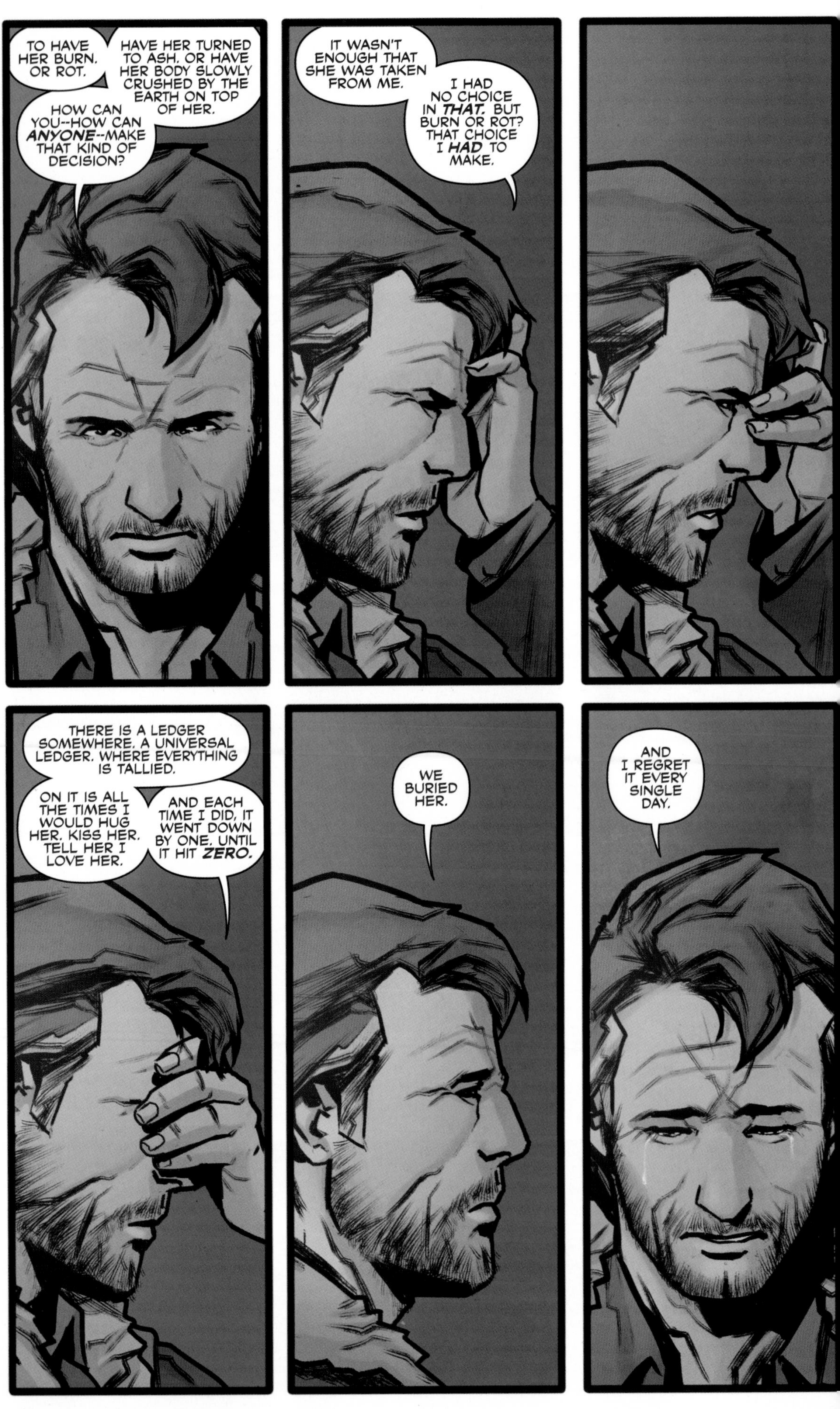
TO HAVE HER BURN. OR ROT.
HAVE HER TURNED TO ASH. OR HAVE HER BODY SLOWLY CRUSHED BY THE EARTH ON TOP OF HER.
HOW CAN YOU--HOW CAN *ANYONE*--MAKE THAT KIND OF DECISION?
IT WASN'T ENOUGH THAT SHE WAS TAKEN FROM ME.
I HAD NO CHOICE IN *THAT.* BUT BURN OR ROT? THAT CHOICE I *HAD* TO MAKE.
THERE IS A LEDGER SOMEWHERE. A UNIVERSAL LEDGER. WHERE EVERYTHING IS TALLIED.
ON IT IS ALL THE TIMES I WOULD HUG HER. KISS HER. TELL HER I LOVE HER.
AND EACH TIME I DID, IT WENT DOWN BY ONE. UNTIL IT HIT *ZERO.*
WE BURIED HER.
AND I REGRET IT EVERY SINGLE DAY.

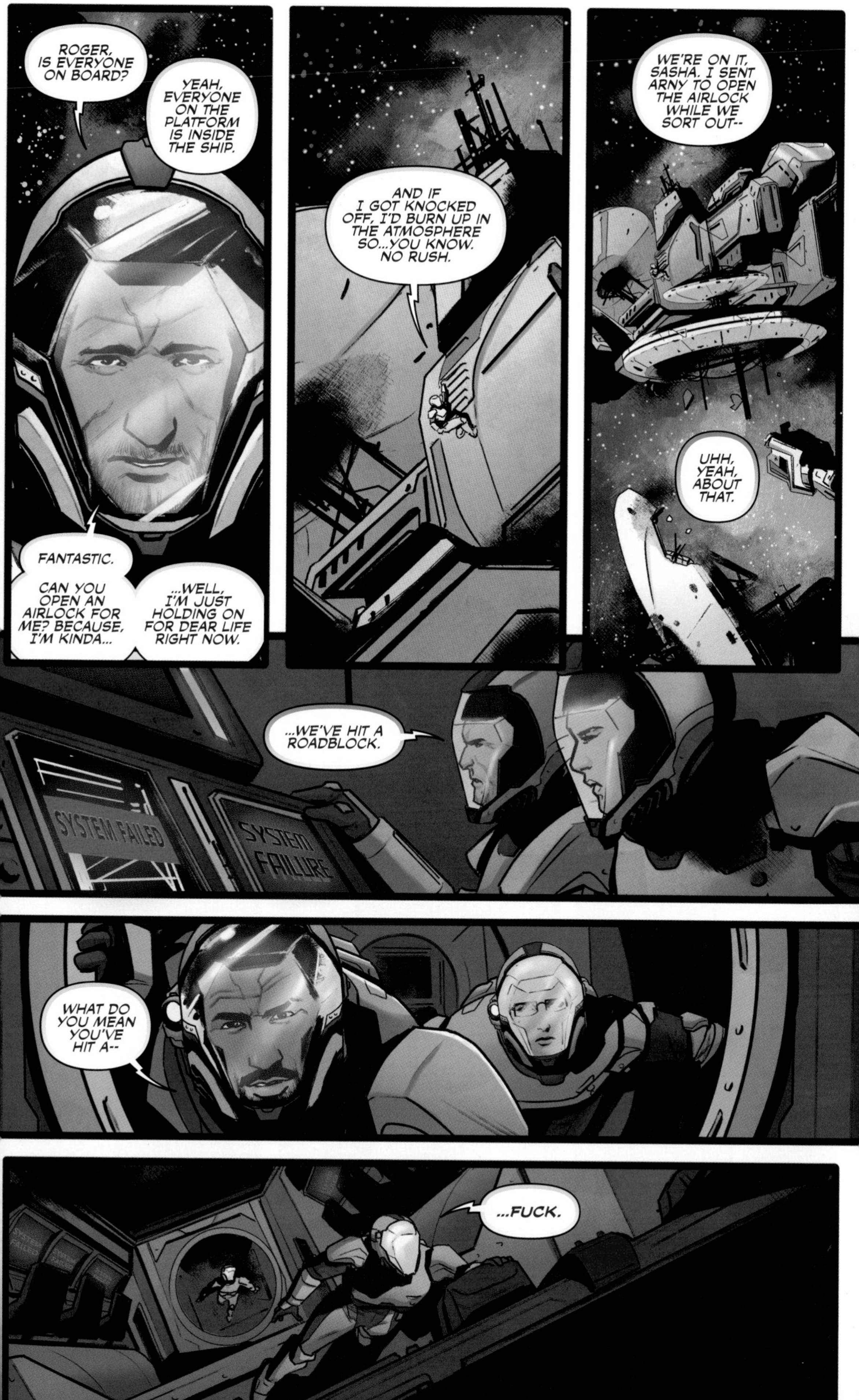
ROGER, IS EVERYONE ON BOARD?
YEAH, EVERYONE ON THE PLATFORM IS INSIDE THE SHIP.
FANTASTIC.
CAN YOU OPEN AN AIRLOCK FOR ME? BECAUSE, I'M KINDA...
...WELL, I'M JUST HOLDING ON FOR DEAR LIFE RIGHT NOW.
AND IF I GOT KNOCKED OFF, I'D BURN UP IN THE ATMOSPHERE SO...YOU KNOW. NO RUSH.
WE'RE ON IT, SASHA. I SENT ARNY TO OPEN THE AIRLOCK WHILE WE SORT OUT--
UHH, YEAH, ABOUT THAT.
...WE'VE HIT A ROADBLOCK.
SYSTEM FAILED
SYSTEM FAILURE
WHAT DO YOU MEAN YOU'VE HIT A--
...FUCK.

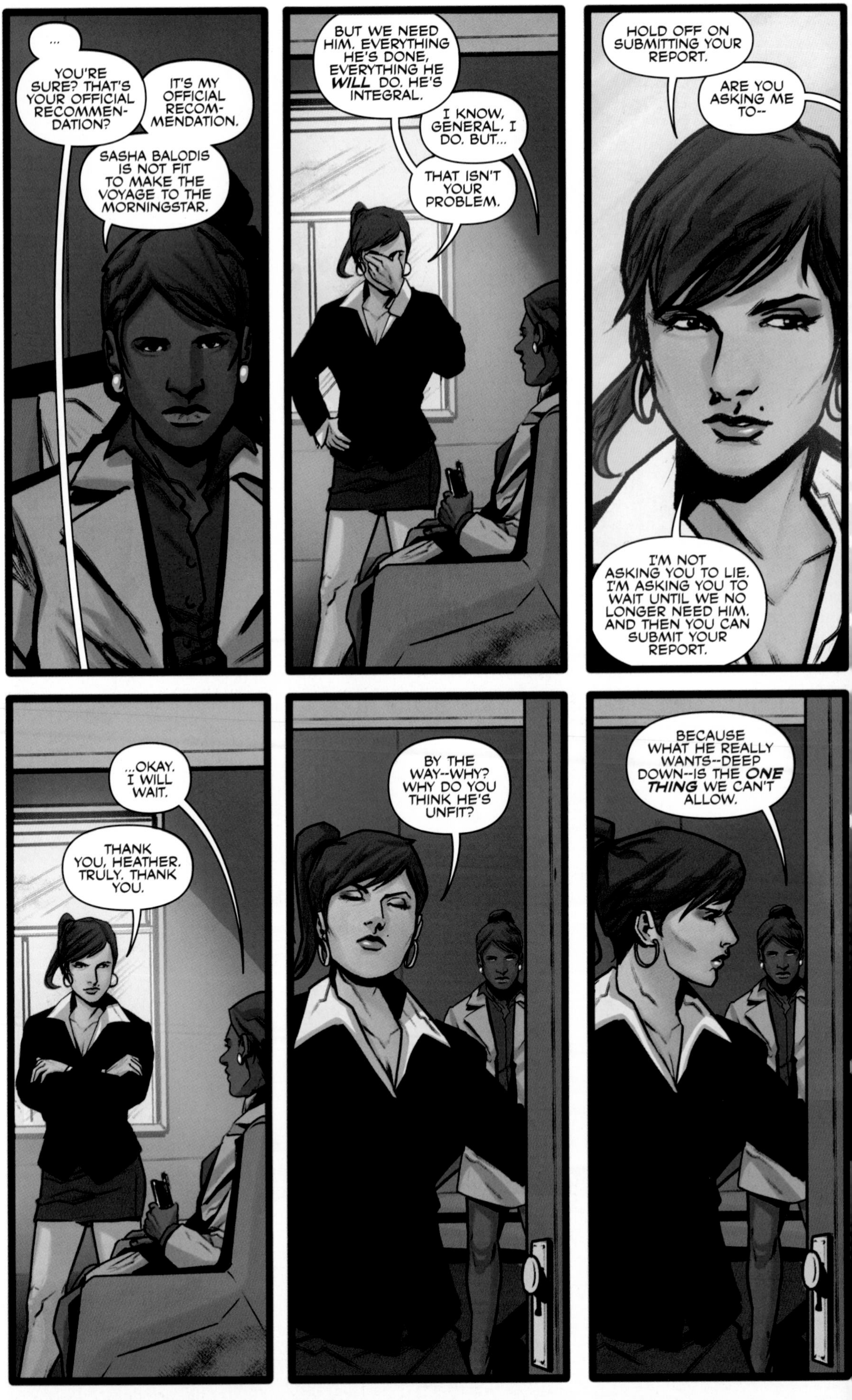
...
YOU'RE SURE? THAT'S YOUR OFFICIAL RECOMMENDATION?
IT'S MY OFFICIAL RECOMMENDATION.
SASHA BALODIS IS NOT FIT TO MAKE THE VOYAGE TO THE MORNINGSTAR.
BUT WE NEED HIM. EVERYTHING HE'S DONE, EVERYTHING HE *WILL* DO. HE'S INTEGRAL.
I KNOW, GENERAL. I DO. BUT...
THAT ISN'T YOUR PROBLEM.
HOLD OFF ON SUBMITTING YOUR REPORT.
ARE YOU ASKING ME TO--
I'M NOT ASKING YOU TO LIE. I'M ASKING YOU TO WAIT UNTIL WE NO LONGER NEED HIM. AND THEN YOU CAN SUBMIT YOUR REPORT.
...OKAY. I WILL WAIT.
THANK YOU, HEATHER. TRULY. THANK YOU.
BY THE WAY--WHY? WHY DO YOU THINK HE'S UNFIT?
BECAUSE WHAT HE REALLY WANTS--DEEP DOWN--IS THE *ONE THING* WE CAN'T ALLOW.

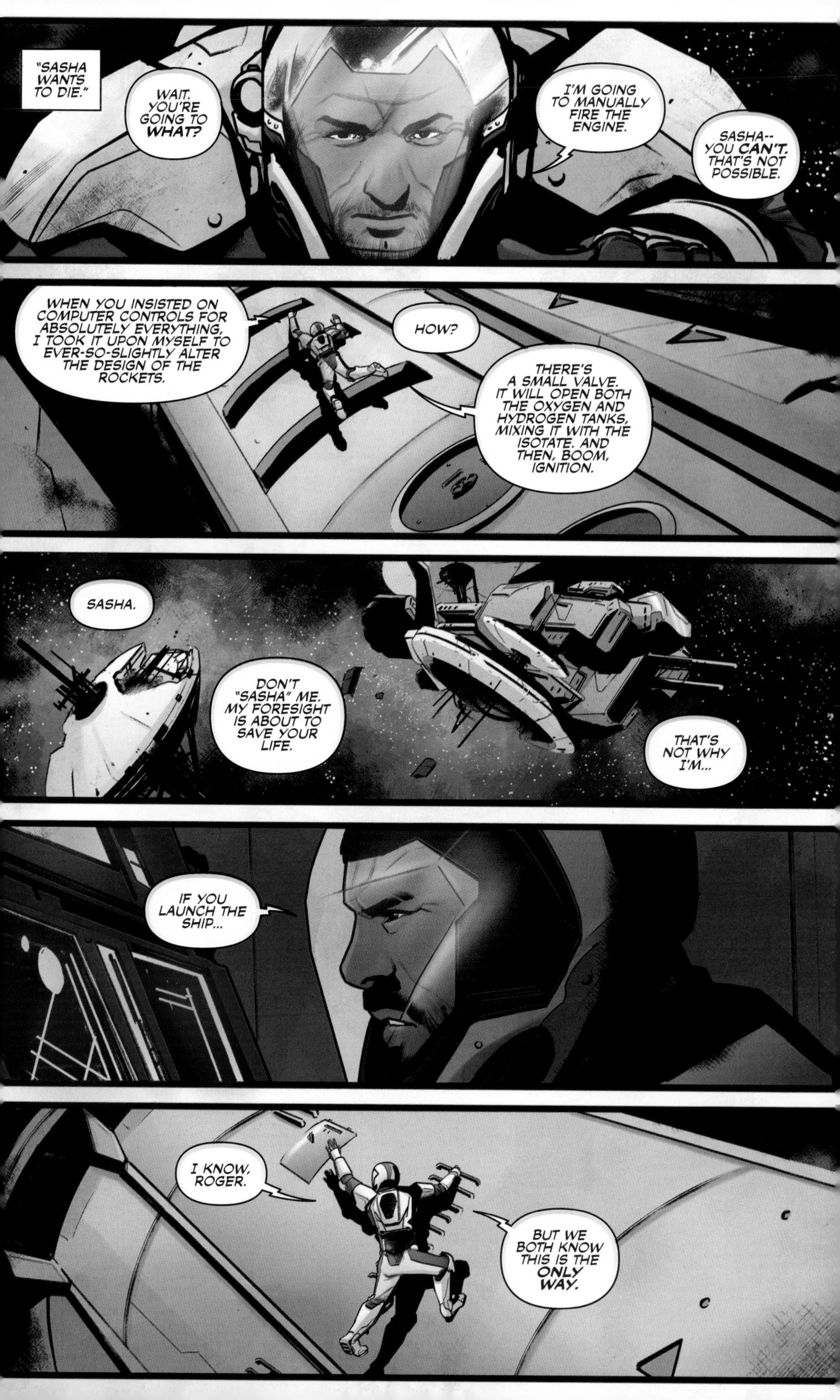
"SASHA WANTS TO DIE."
WAIT. YOU'RE GOING TO WHAT?
I'M GOING TO MANUALLY FIRE THE ENGINE.
SASHA-- YOU CAN'T. THAT'S NOT POSSIBLE.
WHEN YOU INSISTED ON COMPUTER CONTROLS FOR ABSOLUTELY EVERYTHING, I TOOK IT UPON MYSELF TO EVER-SO-SLIGHTLY ALTER THE DESIGN OF THE ROCKETS.
HOW?
THERE'S A SMALL VALVE. IT WILL OPEN BOTH THE OXYGEN AND HYDROGEN TANKS, MIXING IT WITH THE ISOTATE. AND THEN, BOOM, IGNITION.
SASHA.
DON'T "SASHA" ME. MY FORESIGHT IS ABOUT TO SAVE YOUR LIFE.
THAT'S NOT WHY I'M...
IF YOU LAUNCH THE SHIP...
I KNOW, ROGER.
BUT WE BOTH KNOW THIS IS THE ONLY WAY.

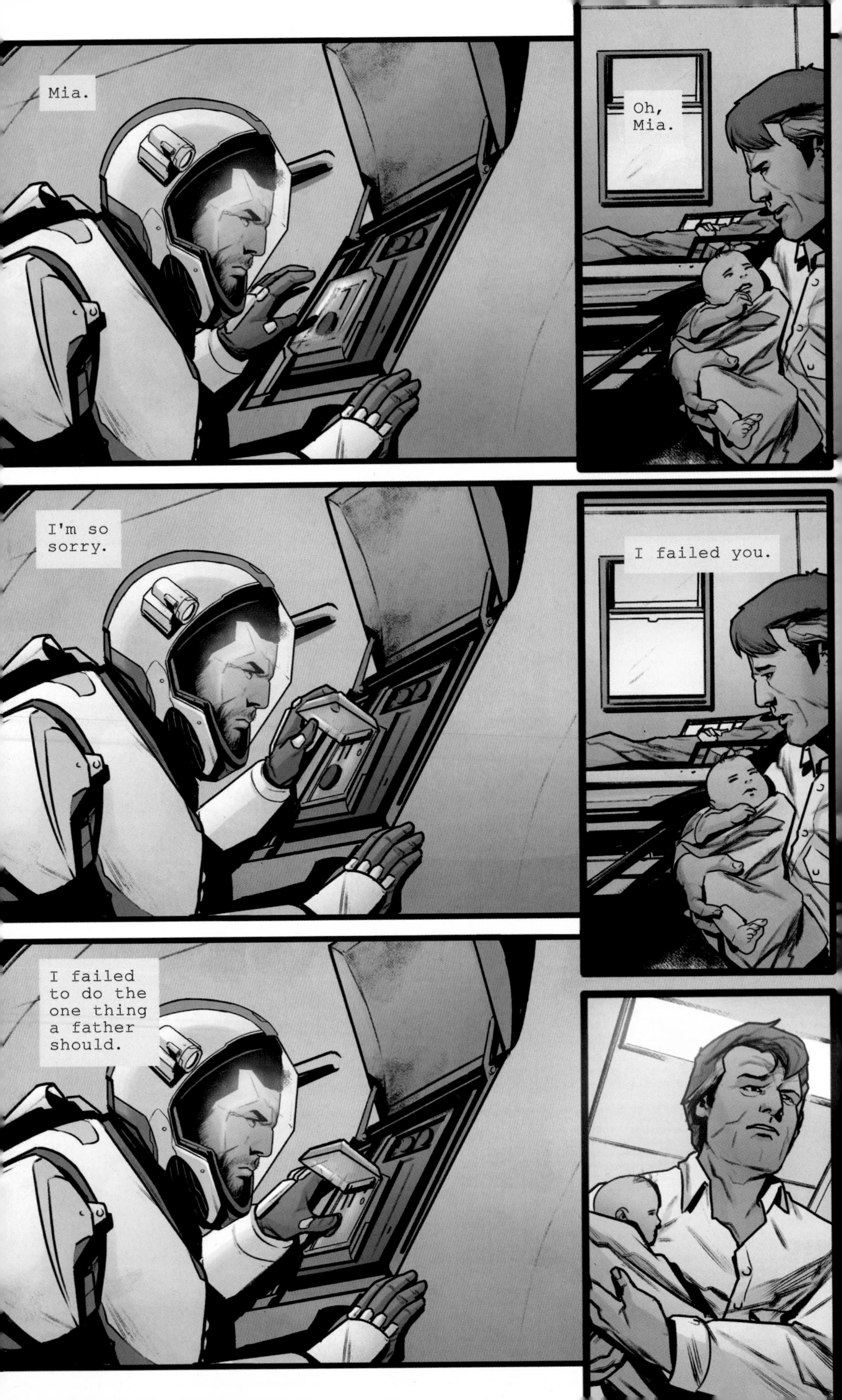

Mia.
Oh, Mia.
I'm so sorry.
I failed you.
I failed to do the one thing a father should.

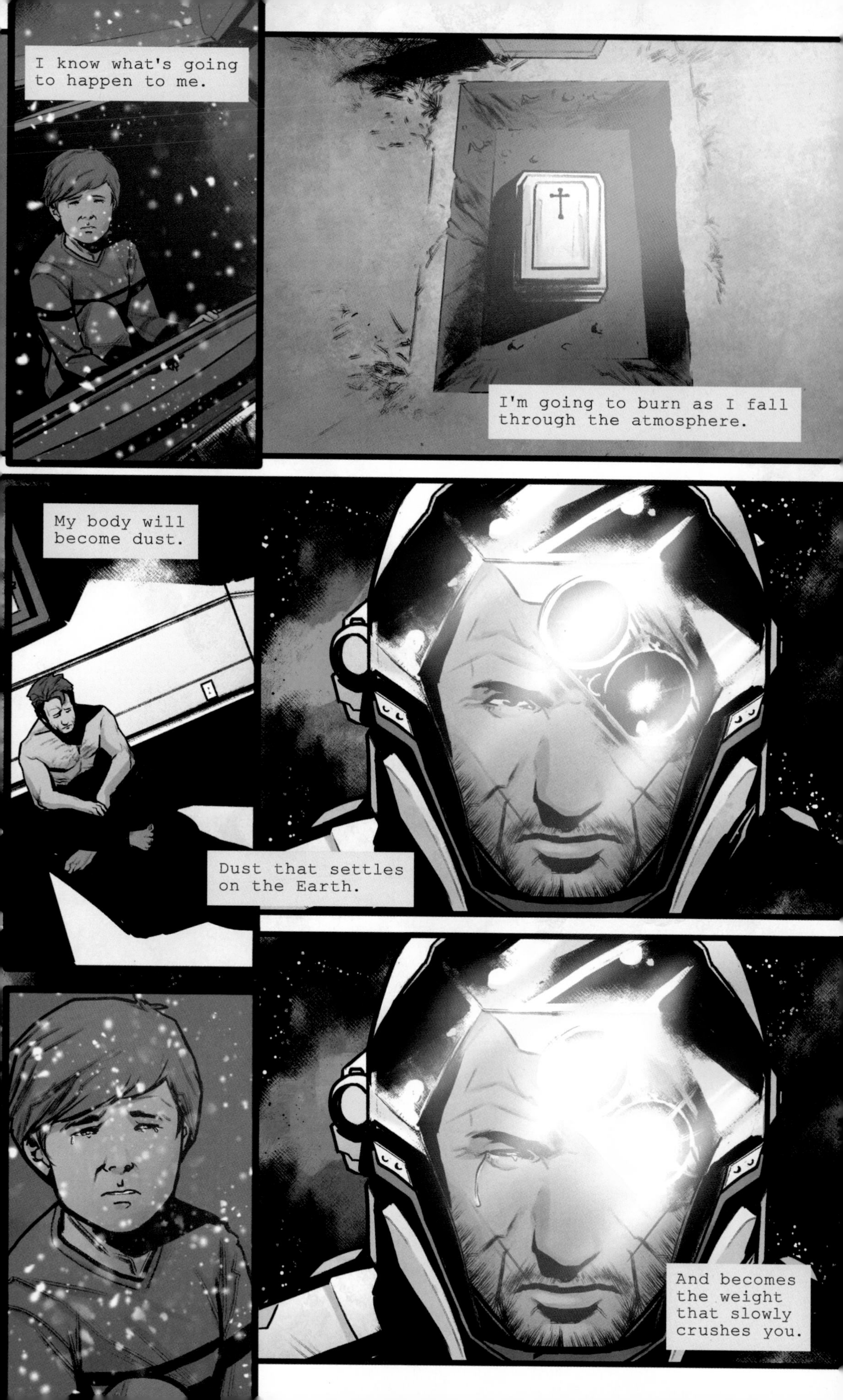
I know what's going to happen to me.
I'm going to burn as I fall through the atmosphere.
My body will become dust.
Dust that settles on the Earth.
And becomes the weight that slowly crushes you.

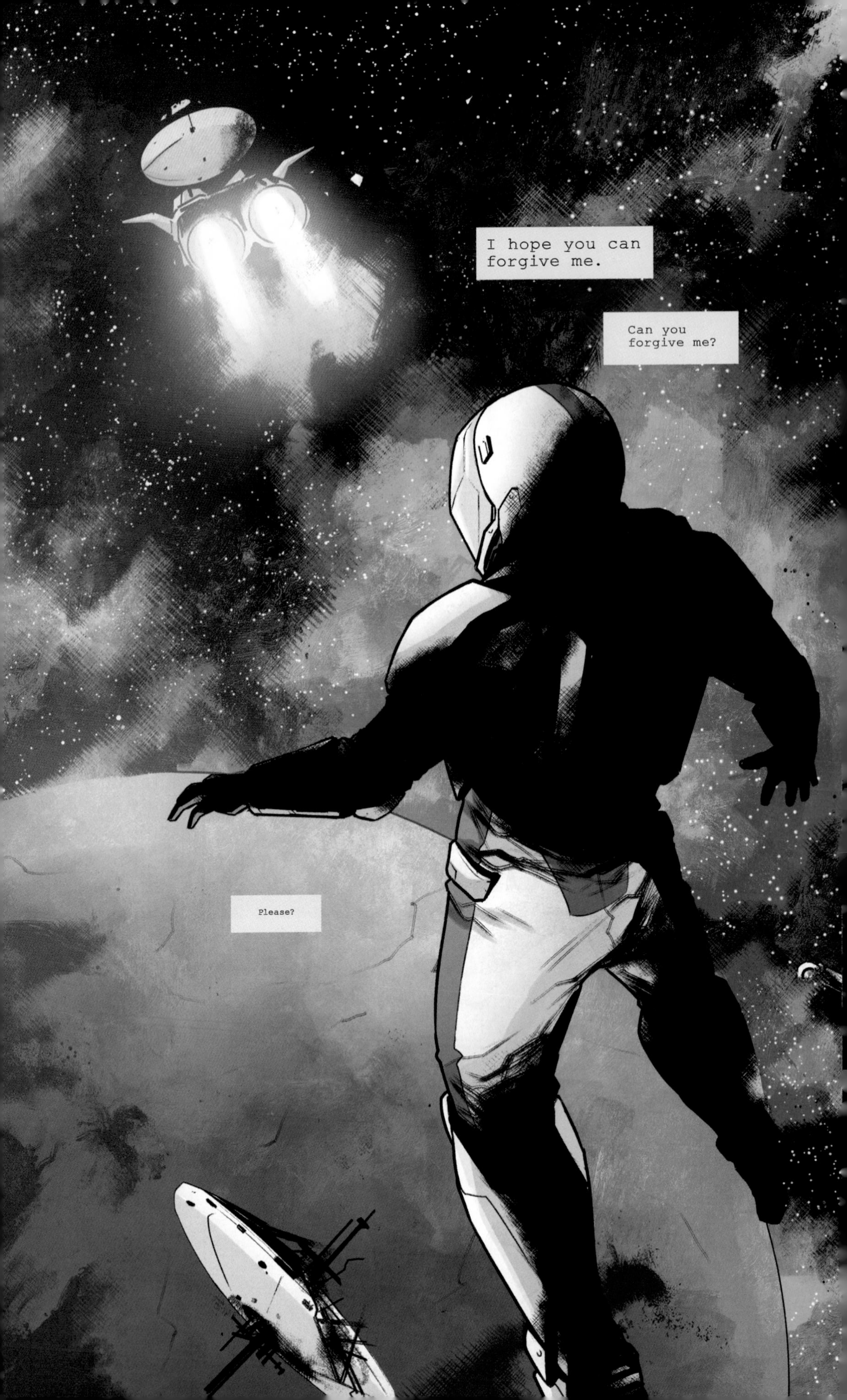
I hope you can forgive me.
Can you forgive me?
Please?

5

CATHEDRALS

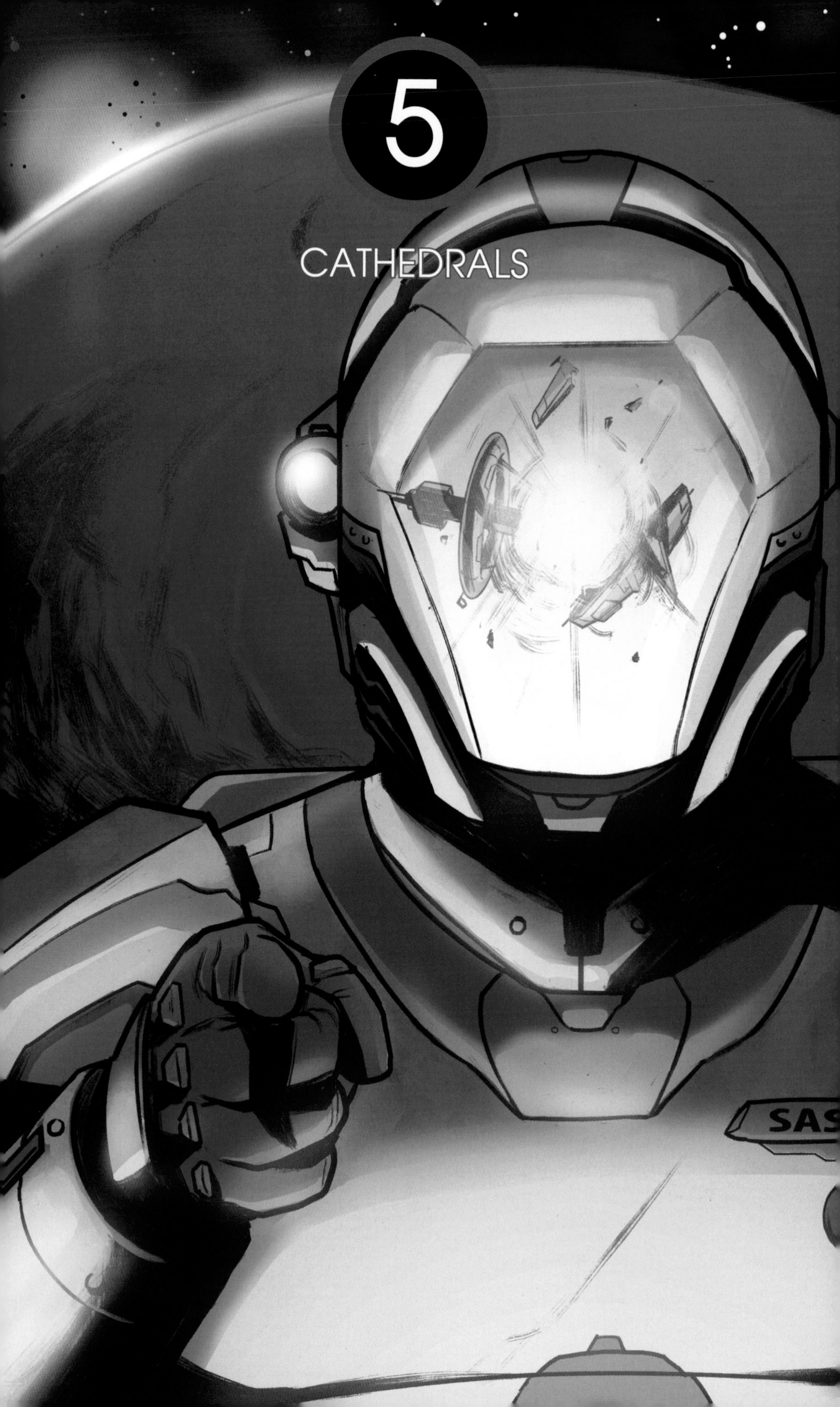
SAS

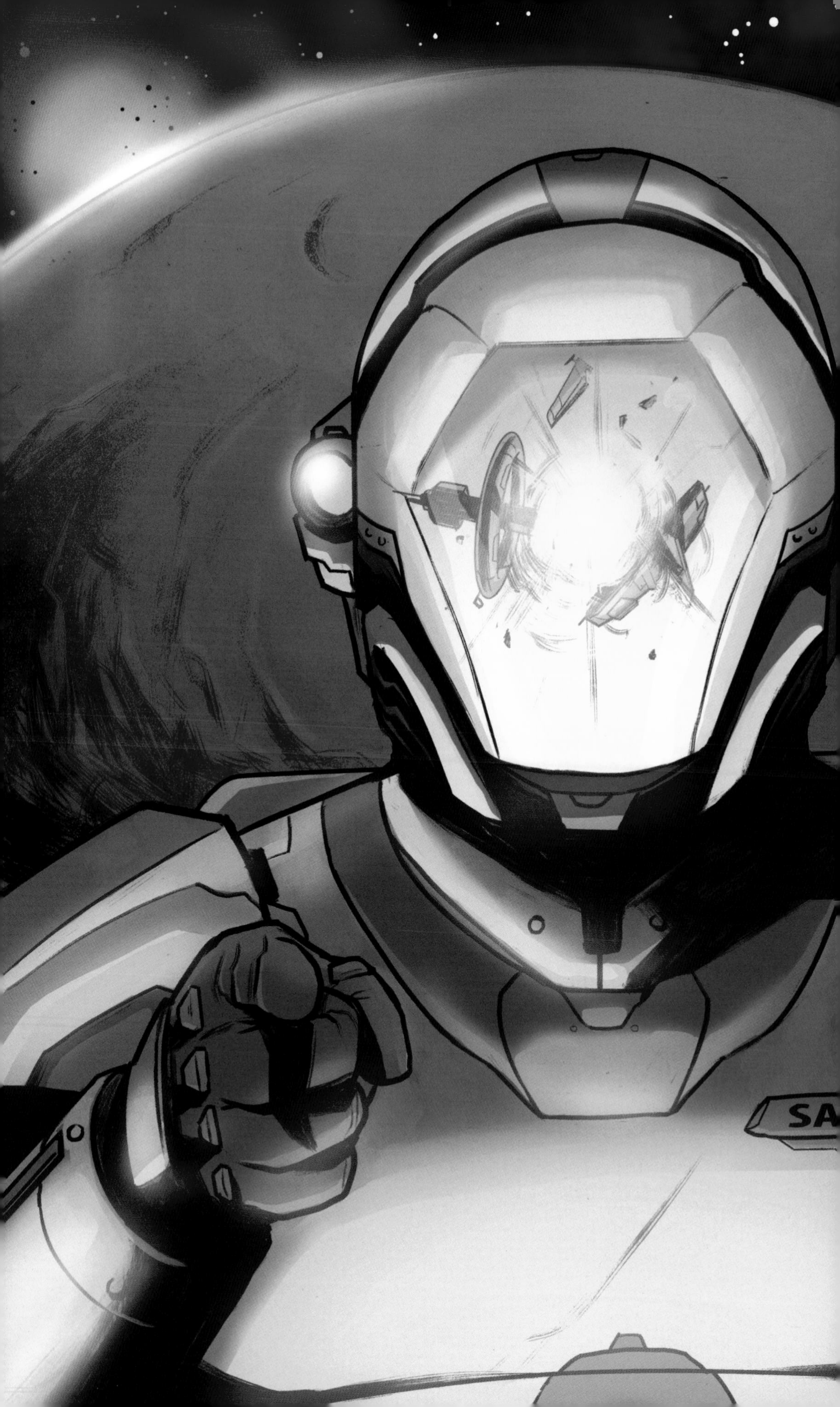

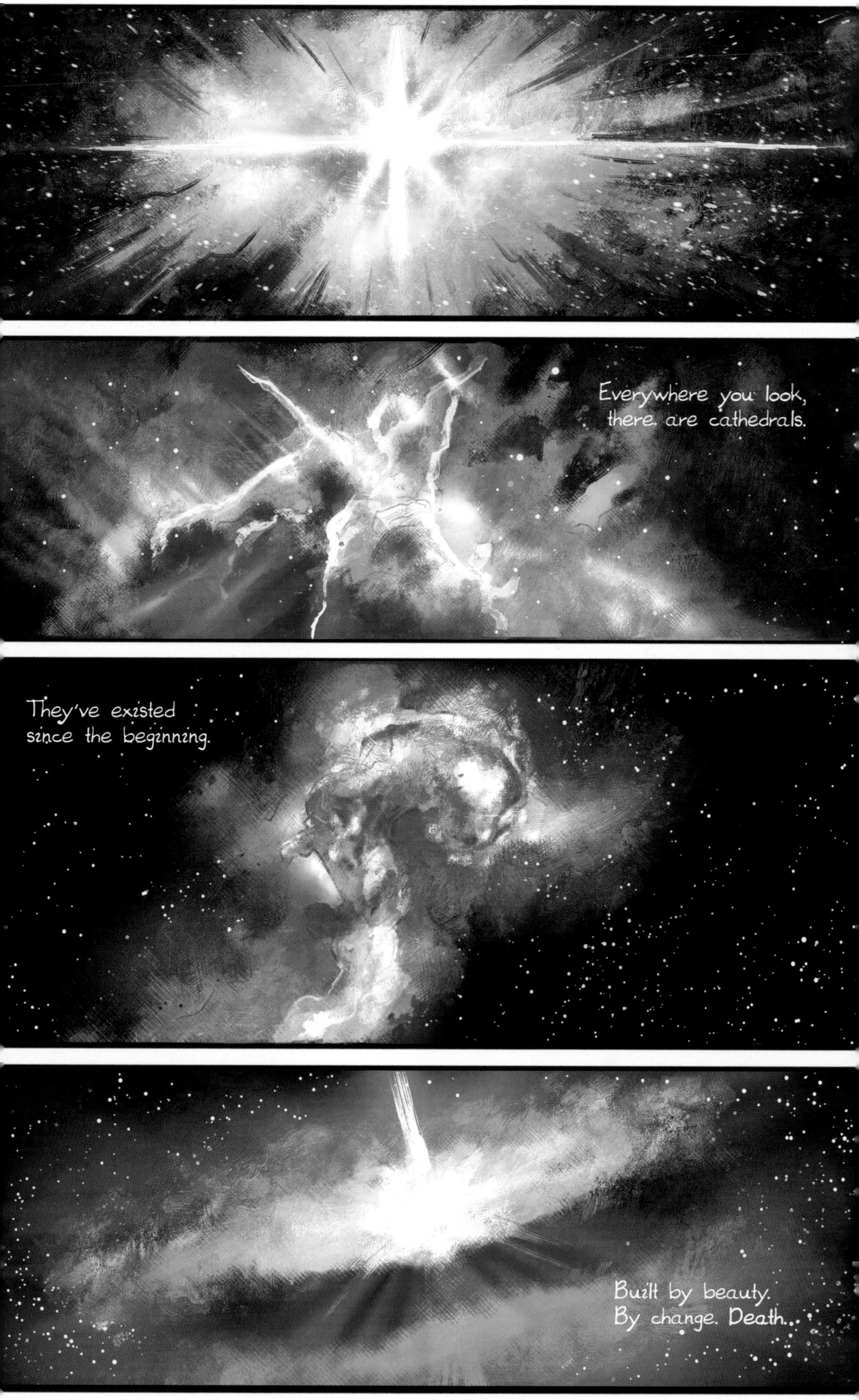
Everywhere you look, there are cathedrals.
They've existed since the beginning.
Built by beauty. By change. Death...

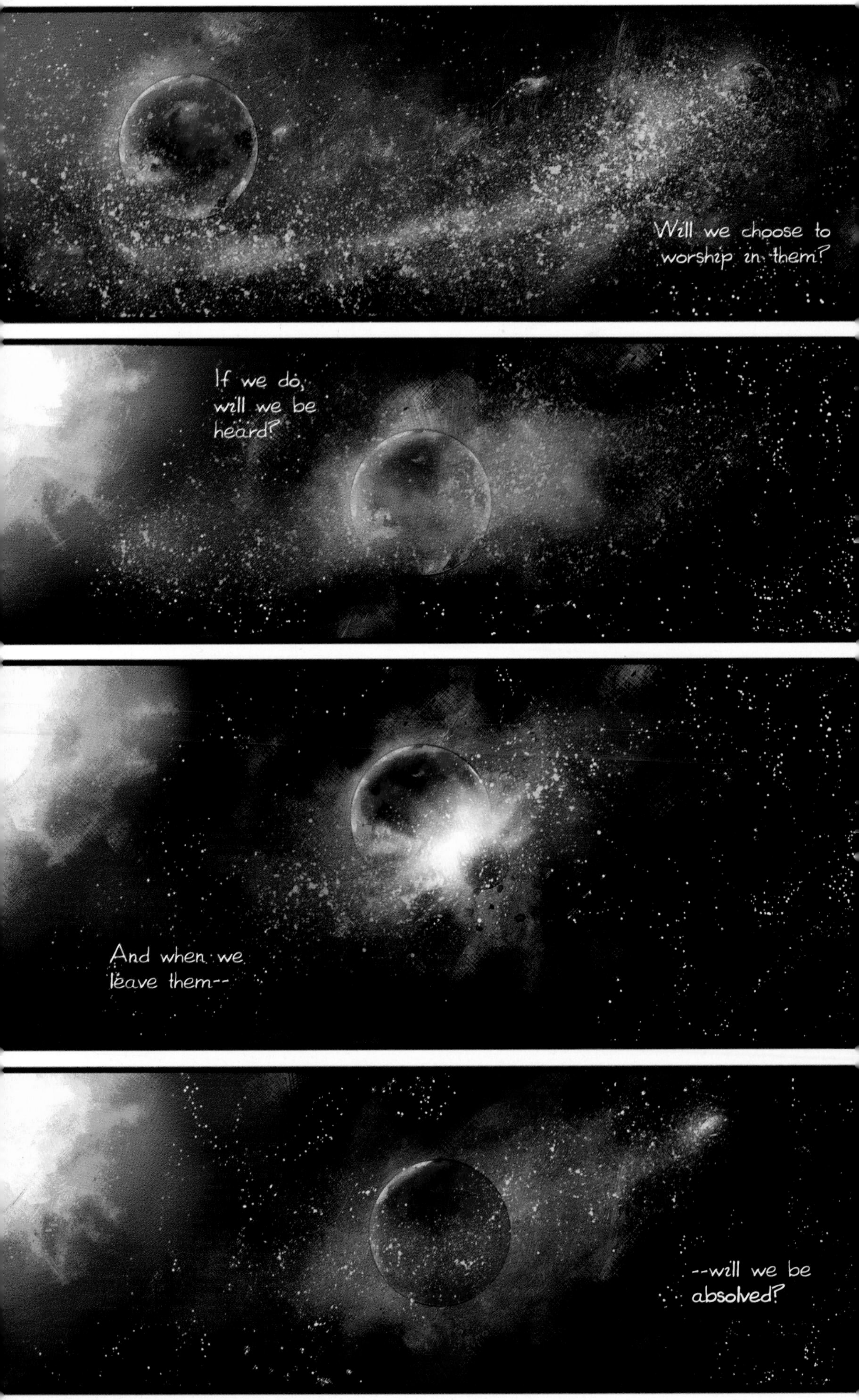
Will we choose to worship in them?
If we do, will we be heard?
And when we leave them--
--will we be absolved?

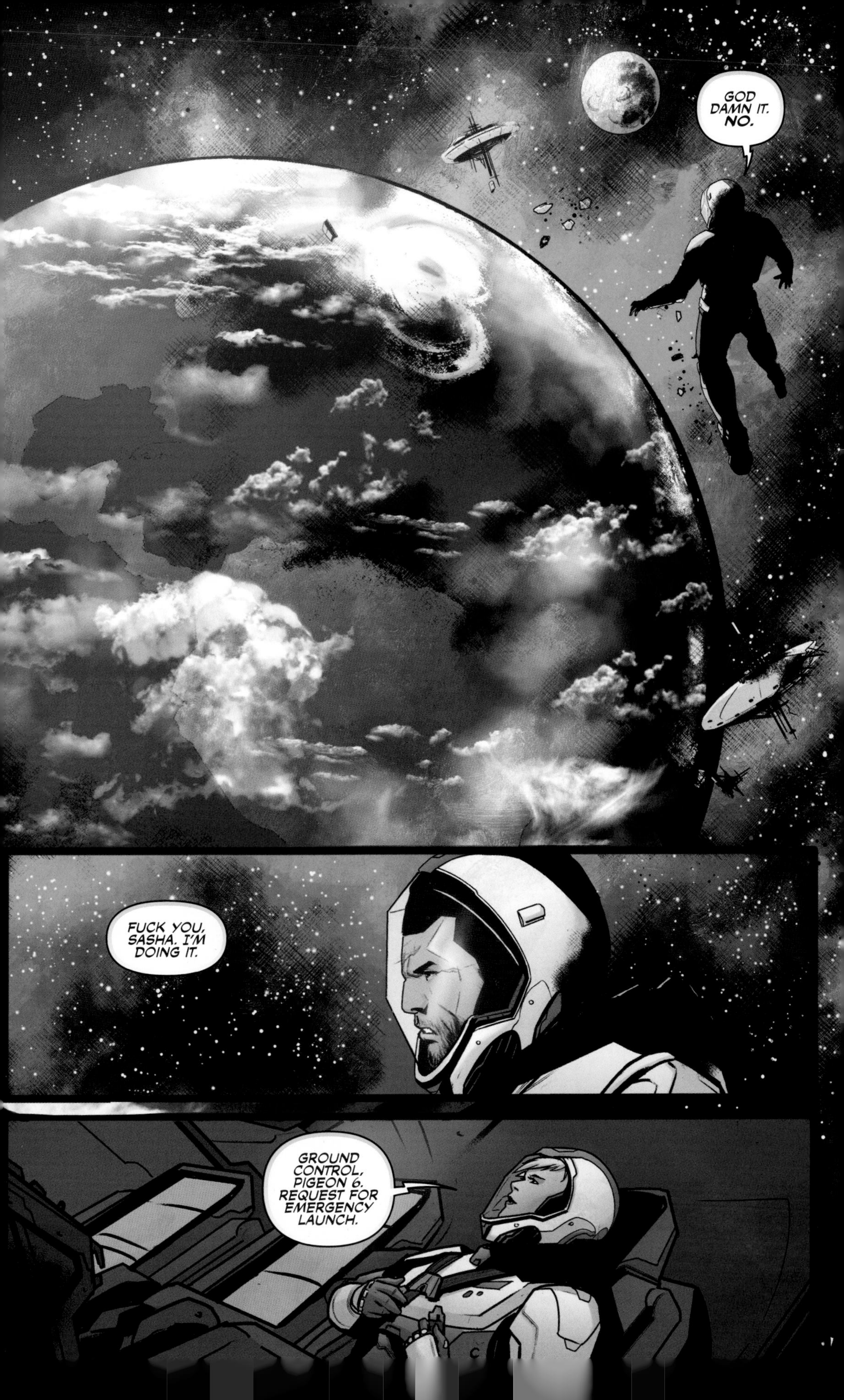
GOD DAMN IT. NO.
FUCK YOU, SASHA. I'M DOING IT.
GROUND CONTROL, PIGEON 6. REQUEST FOR EMERGENCY LAUNCH.

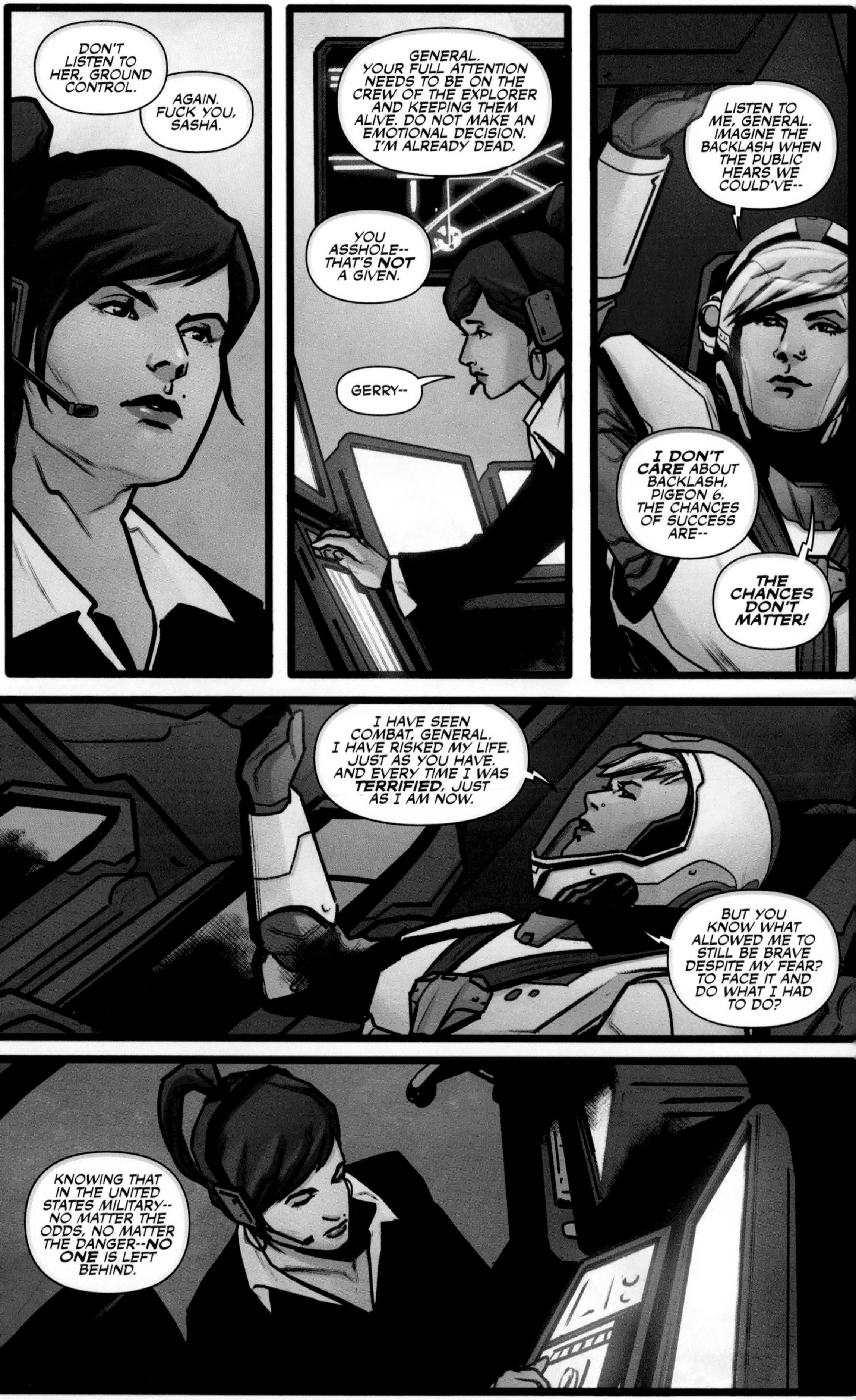
DON'T LISTEN TO HER, GROUND CONTROL.
AGAIN. FUCK YOU, SASHA.
GENERAL. YOUR FULL ATTENTION NEEDS TO BE ON THE CREW OF THE EXPLORER AND KEEPING THEM ALIVE. DO NOT MAKE AN EMOTIONAL DECISION. I'M ALREADY DEAD.
YOU ASSHOLE-- THAT'S **NOT** A GIVEN.
GERRY--
LISTEN TO ME, GENERAL. IMAGINE THE BACKLASH WHEN THE PUBLIC HEARS WE COULD'VE--
I DON'T CARE ABOUT BACKLASH, PIGEON 6. THE CHANCES OF SUCCESS ARE--
THE CHANCES DON'T MATTER!
I HAVE SEEN COMBAT, GENERAL. I HAVE RISKED MY LIFE. JUST AS YOU HAVE. AND EVERY TIME I WAS **TERRIFIED**, JUST AS I AM NOW.
BUT YOU KNOW WHAT ALLOWED ME TO STILL BE BRAVE DESPITE MY FEAR? TO FACE IT AND DO WHAT I HAD TO DO?
KNOWING THAT IN THE UNITED STATES MILITARY-- NO MATTER THE ODDS, NO MATTER THE DANGER--**NO ONE** IS LEFT BEHIND.

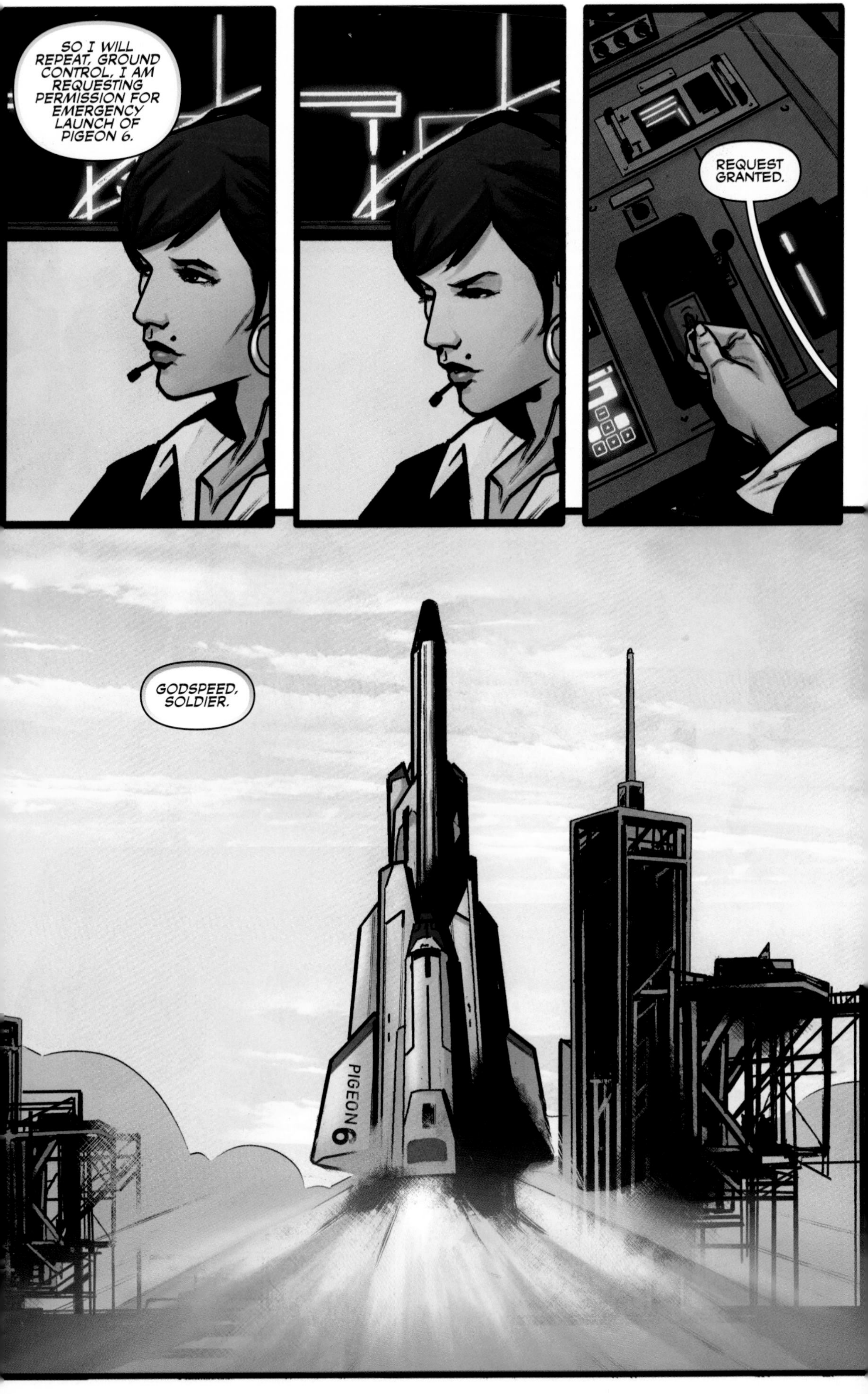
SO I WILL REPEAT, GROUND CONTROL, I AM REQUESTING PERMISSION FOR EMERGENCY LAUNCH OF PIGEON 6.
REQUEST GRANTED.
GODSPEED, SOLDIER.
PIGEON 6

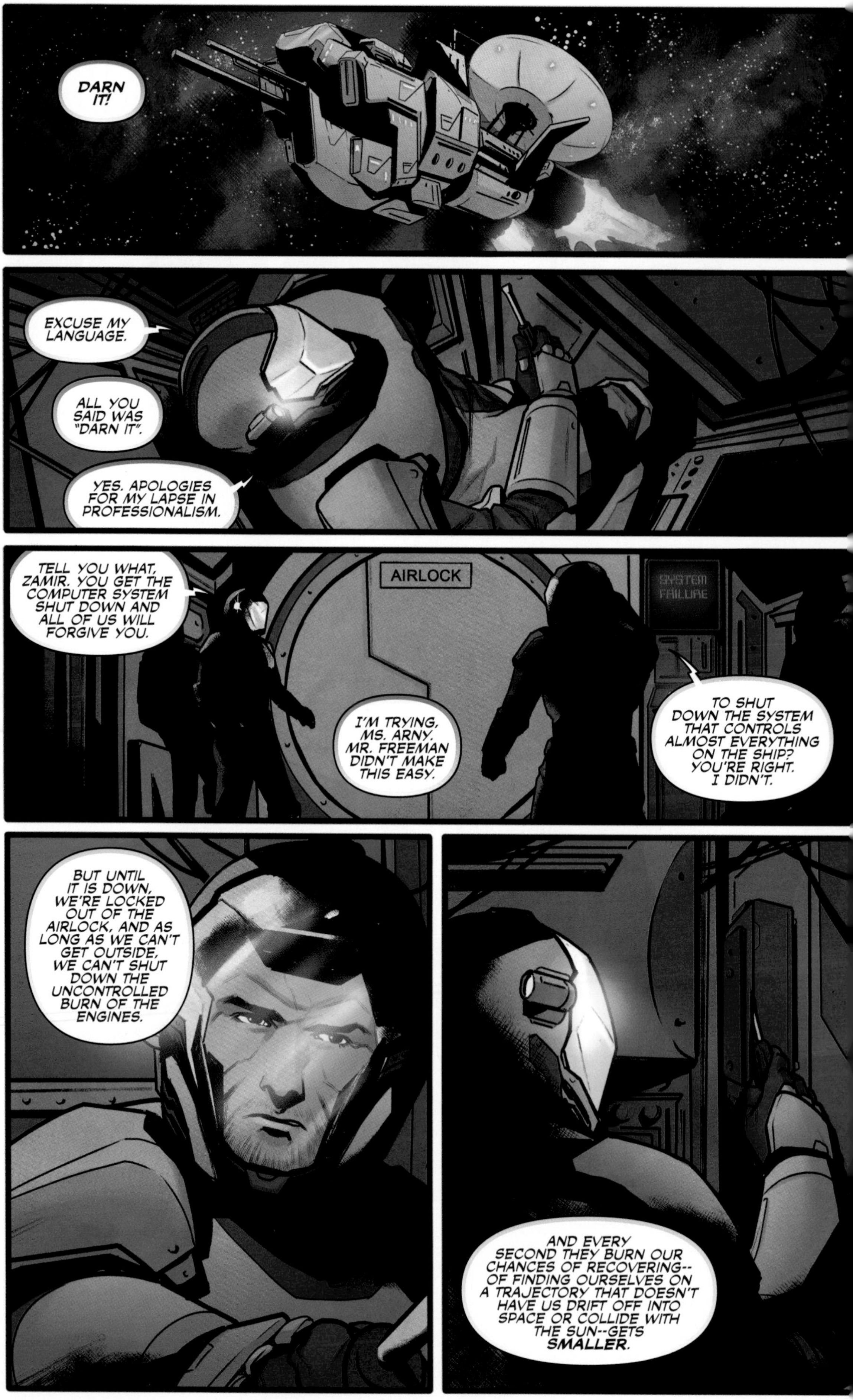
DARN IT!
EXCUSE MY LANGUAGE.
ALL YOU SAID WAS "DARN IT".
YES. APOLOGIES FOR MY LAPSE IN PROFESSIONALISM.
TELL YOU WHAT, ZAMIR. YOU GET THE COMPUTER SYSTEM SHUT DOWN AND ALL OF US WILL FORGIVE YOU.
AIRLOCK
SYSTEM FAILURE
I'M TRYING, MS. ARNY. MR. FREEMAN DIDN'T MAKE THIS EASY.
TO SHUT DOWN THE SYSTEM THAT CONTROLS ALMOST EVERYTHING ON THE SHIP? YOU'RE RIGHT. I DIDN'T.
BUT UNTIL IT IS DOWN, WE'RE LOCKED OUT OF THE AIRLOCK, AND AS LONG AS WE CAN'T GET OUTSIDE, WE CAN'T SHUT DOWN THE UNCONTROLLED BURN OF THE ENGINES.
AND EVERY SECOND THEY BURN OUR CHANCES OF RECOVERING-- OF FINDING OURSELVES ON A TRAJECTORY THAT DOESN'T HAVE US DRIFT OFF INTO SPACE OR COLLIDE WITH THE SUN--GETS SMALLER.

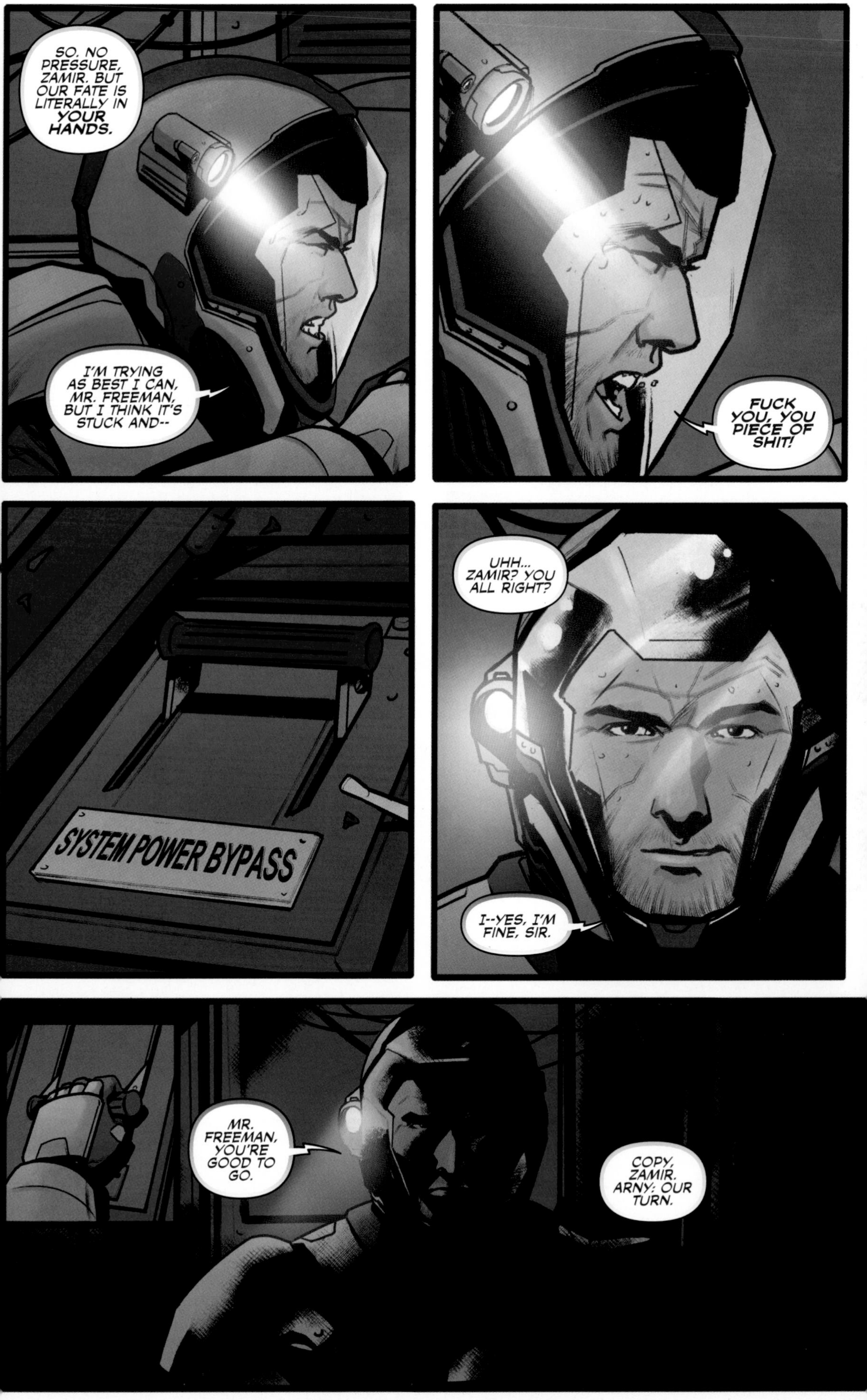
SO. NO PRESSURE, ZAMIR. BUT OUR FATE IS LITERALLY IN YOUR HANDS.
I'M TRYING AS BEST I CAN, MR. FREEMAN, BUT I THINK IT'S STUCK AND--
FUCK YOU, YOU PIECE OF SHIT!
SYSTEM POWER BYPASS
UHH... ZAMIR? YOU ALL RIGHT?
I--YES, I'M FINE, SIR.
MR. FREEMAN, YOU'RE GOOD TO GO.
COPY, ZAMIR. ARNY: OUR TURN.

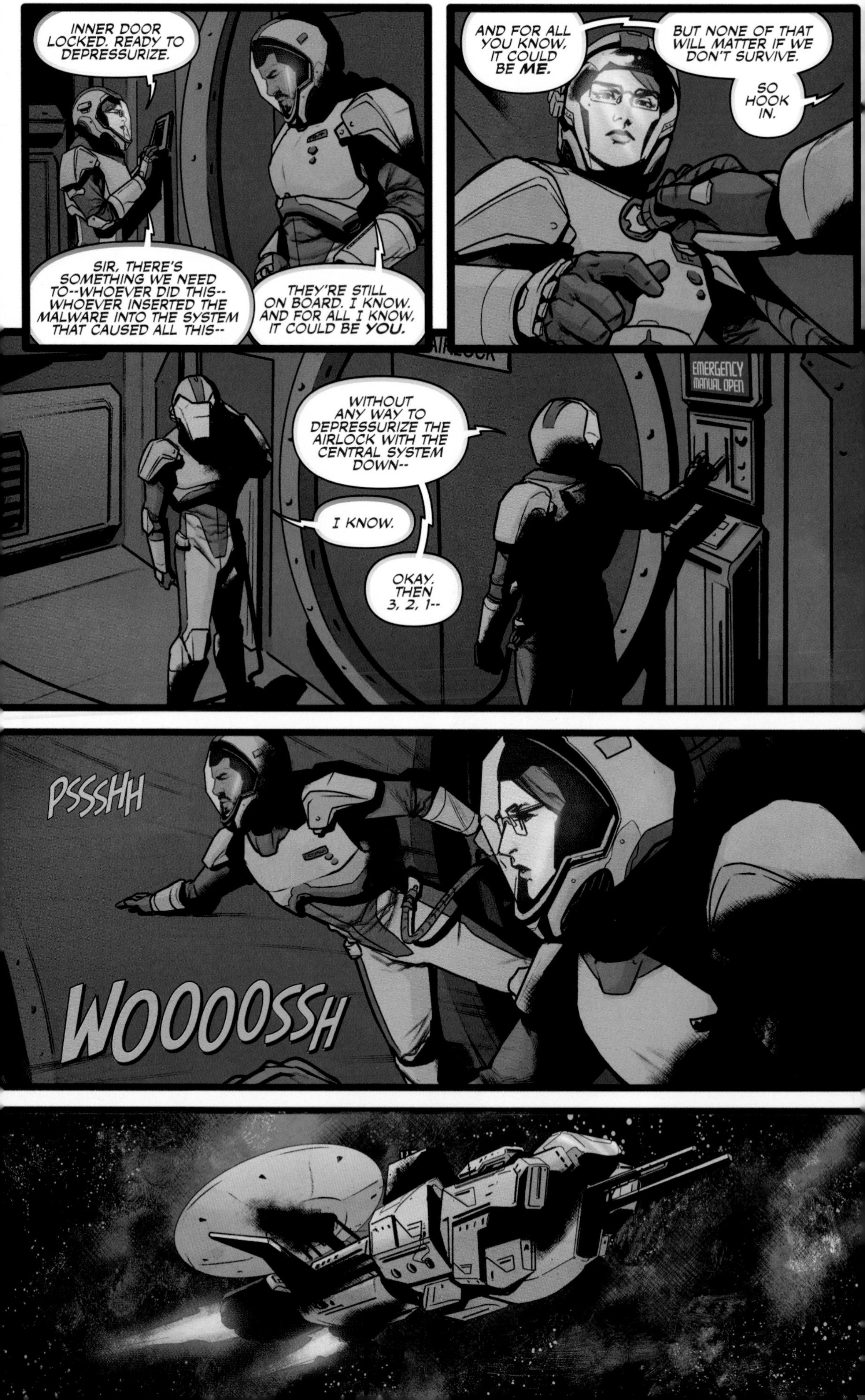
INNER DOOR LOCKED. READY TO DEPRESSURIZE.
SIR, THERE'S SOMETHING WE NEED TO--WHOEVER DID THIS--WHOEVER INSERTED THE MALWARE INTO THE SYSTEM THAT CAUSED ALL THIS--
THEY'RE STILL ON BOARD. I KNOW. AND FOR ALL I KNOW, IT COULD BE YOU.
AND FOR ALL YOU KNOW, IT COULD BE ME.
BUT NONE OF THAT WILL MATTER IF WE DON'T SURVIVE.
SO HOOK IN.
EMERGENCY MANUAL OPEN
WITHOUT ANY WAY TO DEPRESSURIZE THE AIRLOCK WITH THE CENTRAL SYSTEM DOWN--
I KNOW.
OKAY. THEN 3, 2, 1--
PSSSHH
WOOOOSSH

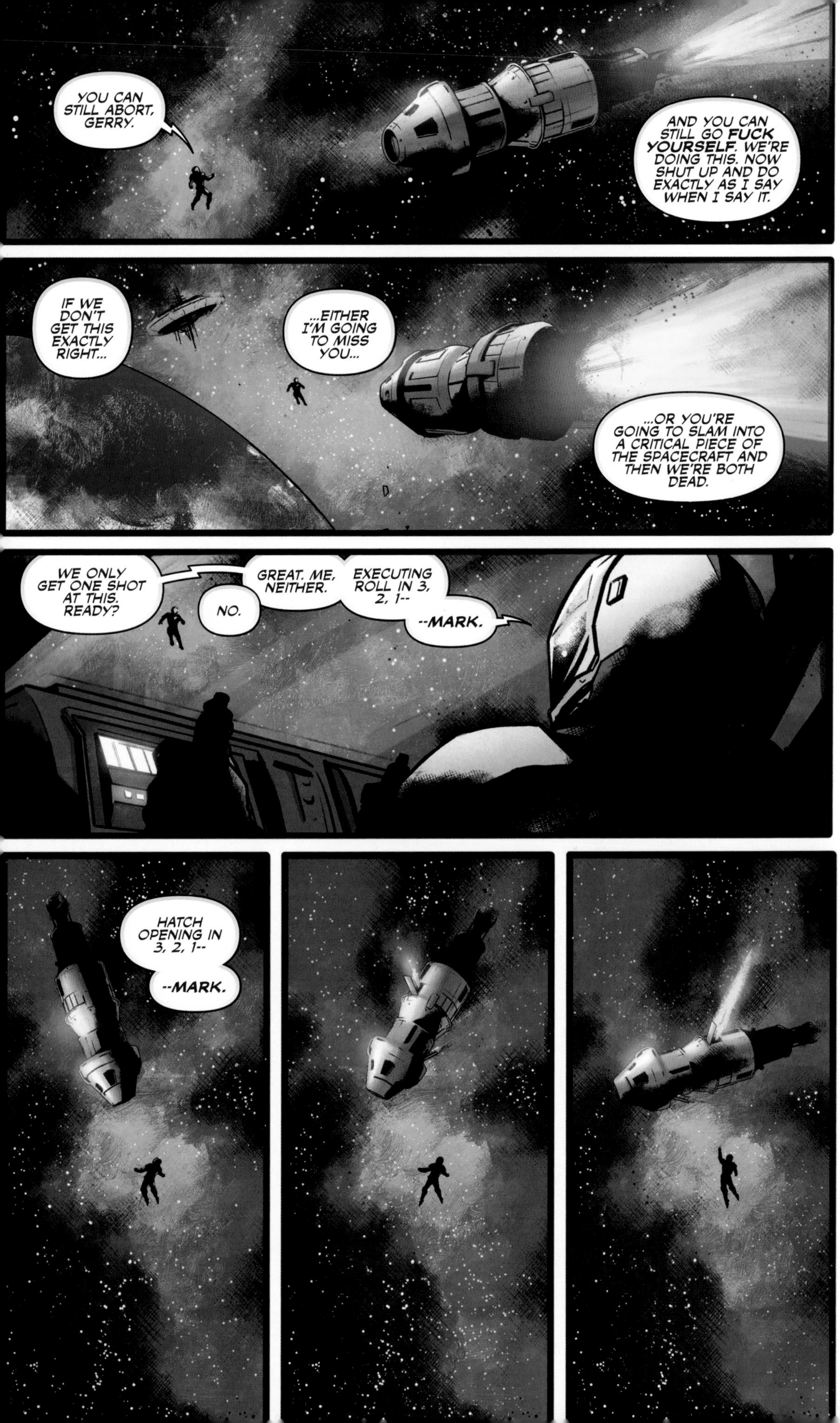
YOU CAN STILL ABORT, GERRY.
AND YOU CAN STILL GO **FUCK YOURSELF**. WE'RE DOING THIS. NOW SHUT UP AND DO EXACTLY AS I SAY WHEN I SAY IT.
IF WE DON'T GET THIS EXACTLY RIGHT...
...EITHER I'M GOING TO MISS YOU...
...OR YOU'RE GOING TO SLAM INTO A CRITICAL PIECE OF THE SPACECRAFT AND THEN WE'RE BOTH DEAD.
WE ONLY GET ONE SHOT AT THIS. READY?
NO.
GREAT. ME, NEITHER.
EXECUTING ROLL IN 3, 2, 1--
--MARK.
HATCH OPENING IN 3, 2, 1--
--MARK.

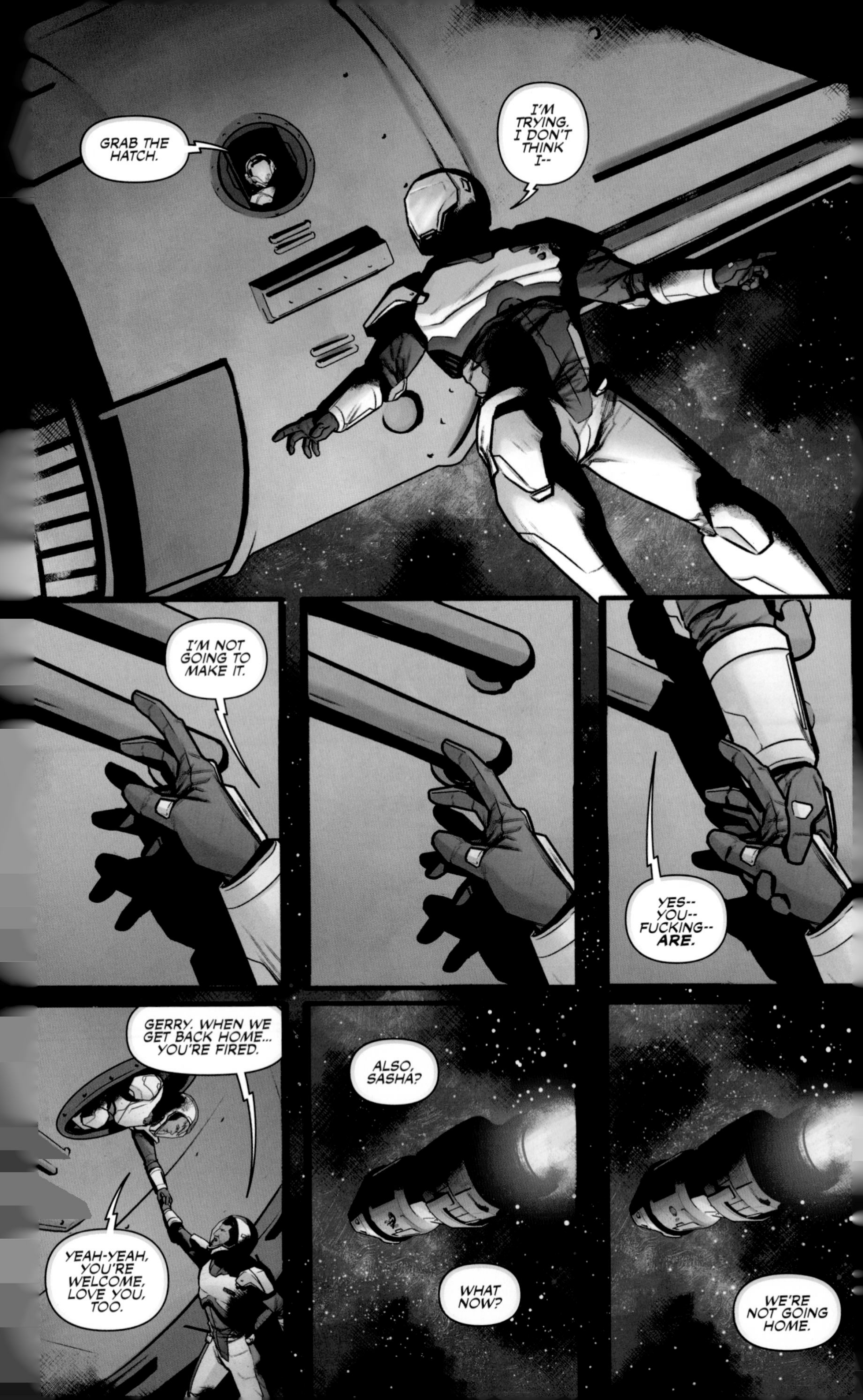
GRAB THE HATCH.
I'M TRYING. I DON'T THINK I--
I'M NOT GOING TO MAKE IT.
YES-- YOU-- FUCKING-- ARE.
GERRY. WHEN WE GET BACK HOME... YOU'RE FIRED.
YEAH-YEAH, YOU'RE WELCOME, LOVE YOU, TOO.
ALSO, SASHA?
WHAT NOW?
WE'RE NOT GOING HOME.

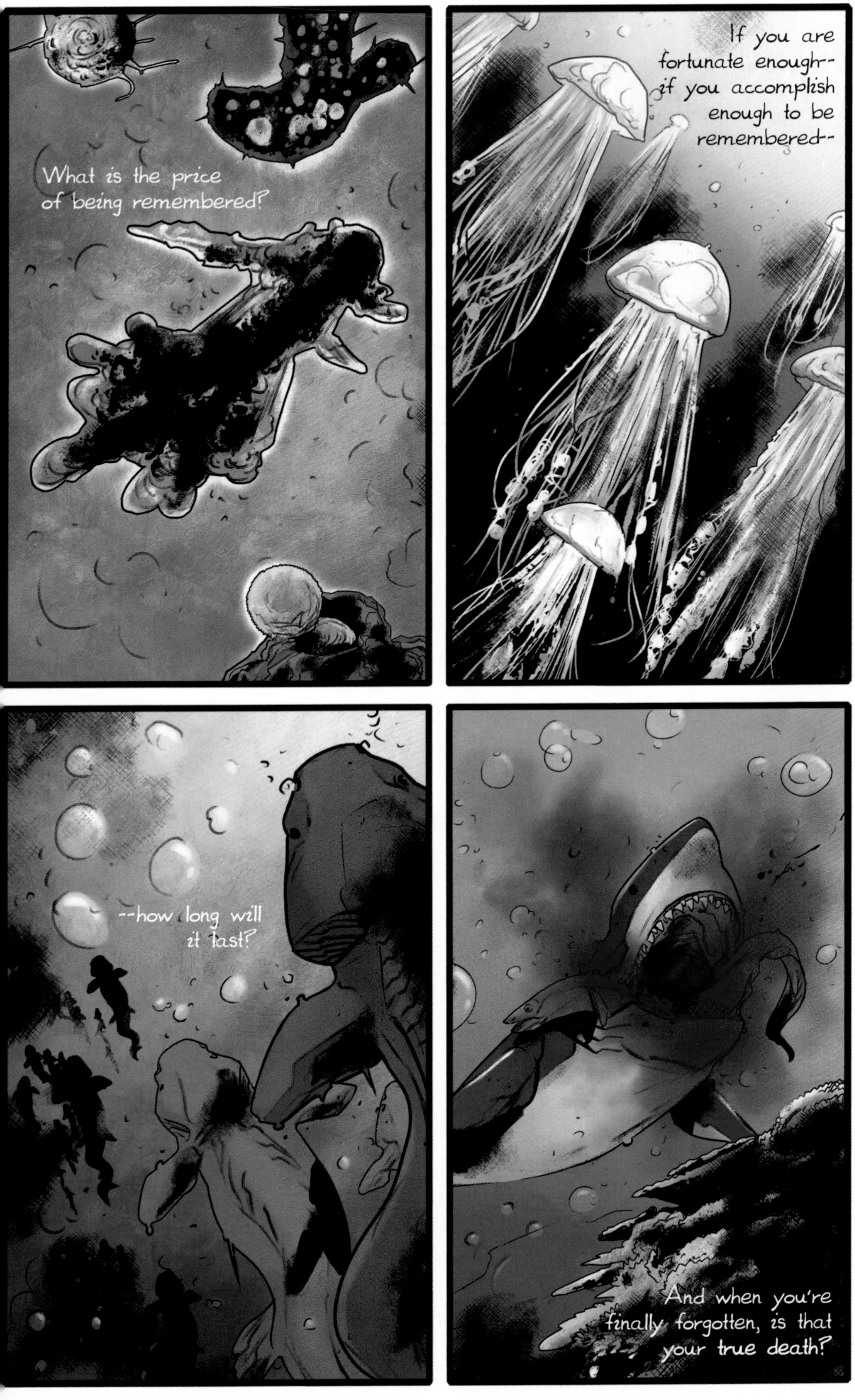
What is the price of being remembered?
If you are fortunate enough--if you accomplish enough to be remembered--
--how long will it last?
And when you're finally forgotten, is that your true death?

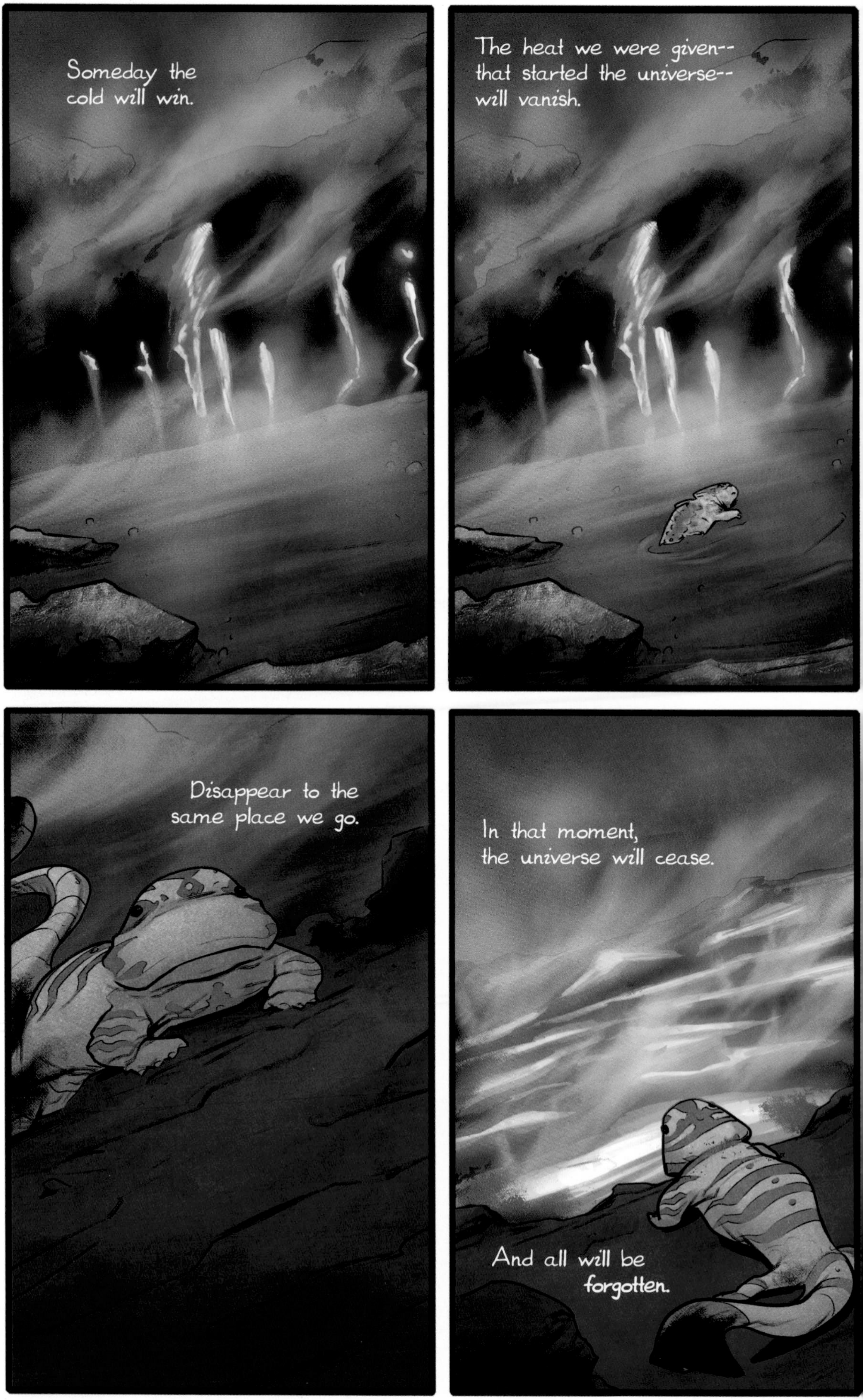
Someday the cold will win.
The heat we were given-- that started the universe-- will vanish.
Disappear to the same place we go.
In that moment, the universe will cease.
And all will be forgotten.

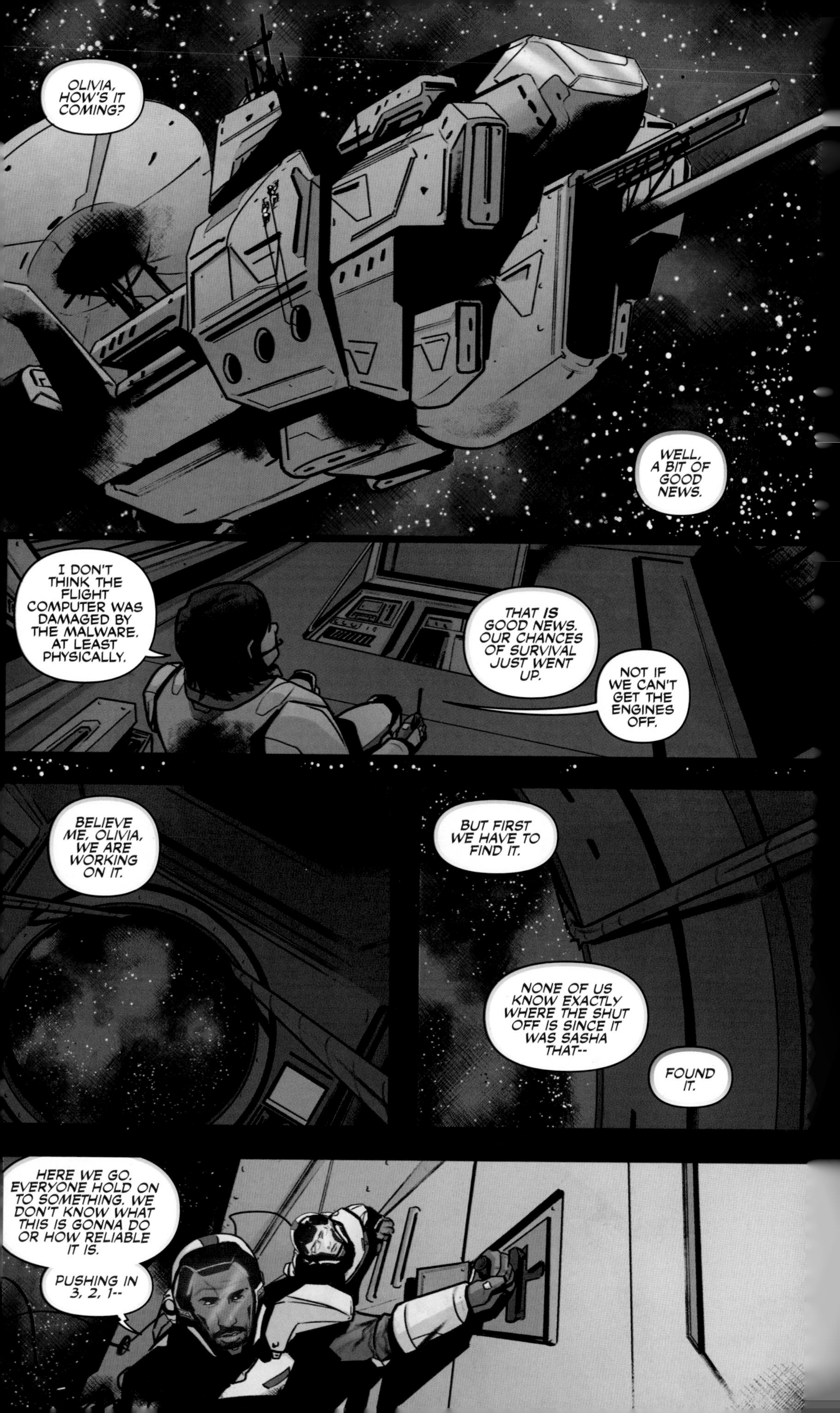
OLIVIA, HOW'S IT COMING?
WELL, A BIT OF GOOD NEWS.
I DON'T THINK THE FLIGHT COMPUTER WAS DAMAGED BY THE MALWARE. AT LEAST PHYSICALLY.
THAT IS GOOD NEWS. OUR CHANCES OF SURVIVAL JUST WENT UP.
NOT IF WE CAN'T GET THE ENGINES OFF.
BELIEVE ME, OLIVIA, WE ARE WORKING ON IT.
BUT FIRST WE HAVE TO FIND IT.
NONE OF US KNOW EXACTLY WHERE THE SHUT OFF IS SINCE IT WAS SASHA THAT--
FOUND IT.
HERE WE GO. EVERYONE HOLD ON TO SOMETHING. WE DON'T KNOW WHAT THIS IS GONNA DO OR HOW RELIABLE IT IS.
PUSHING IN 3, 2, 1--

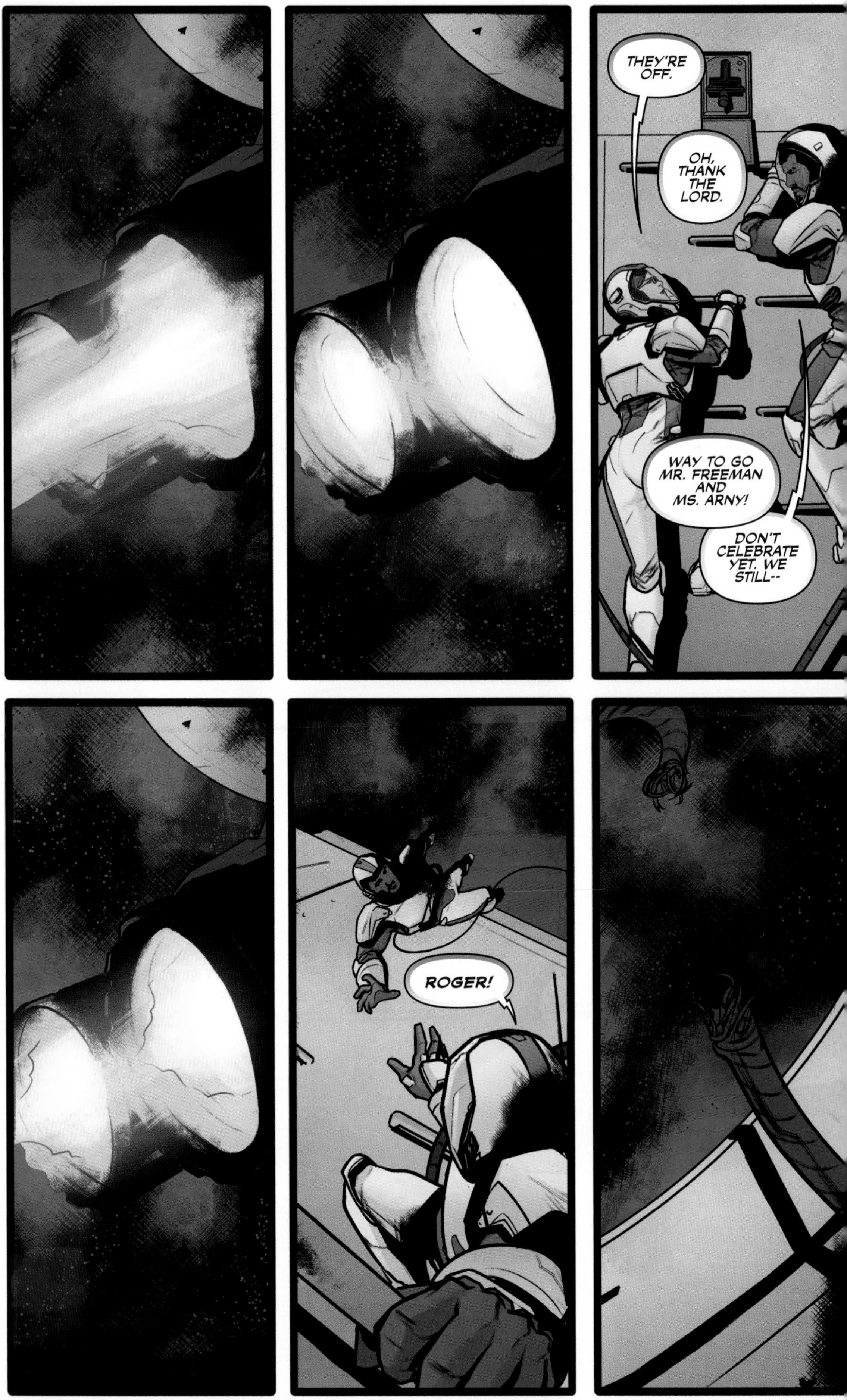
THEY'RE OFF.
OH, THANK THE LORD.
WAY TO GO MR. FREEMAN AND MS. ARNY!
DON'T CELEBRATE YET. WE STILL--
ROGER!

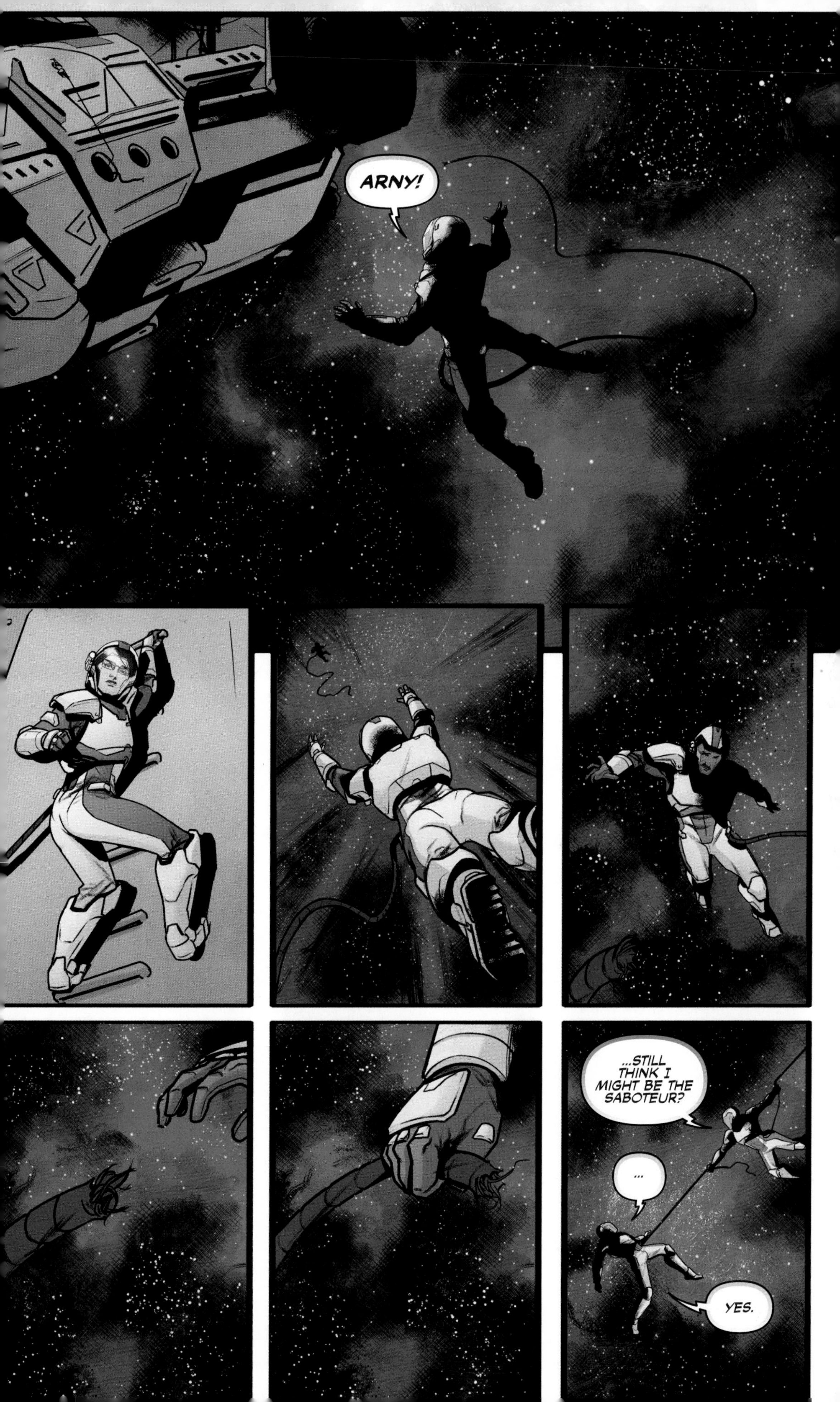
ARNY!
...STILL THINK I MIGHT BE THE SABOTEUR?
...
YES.

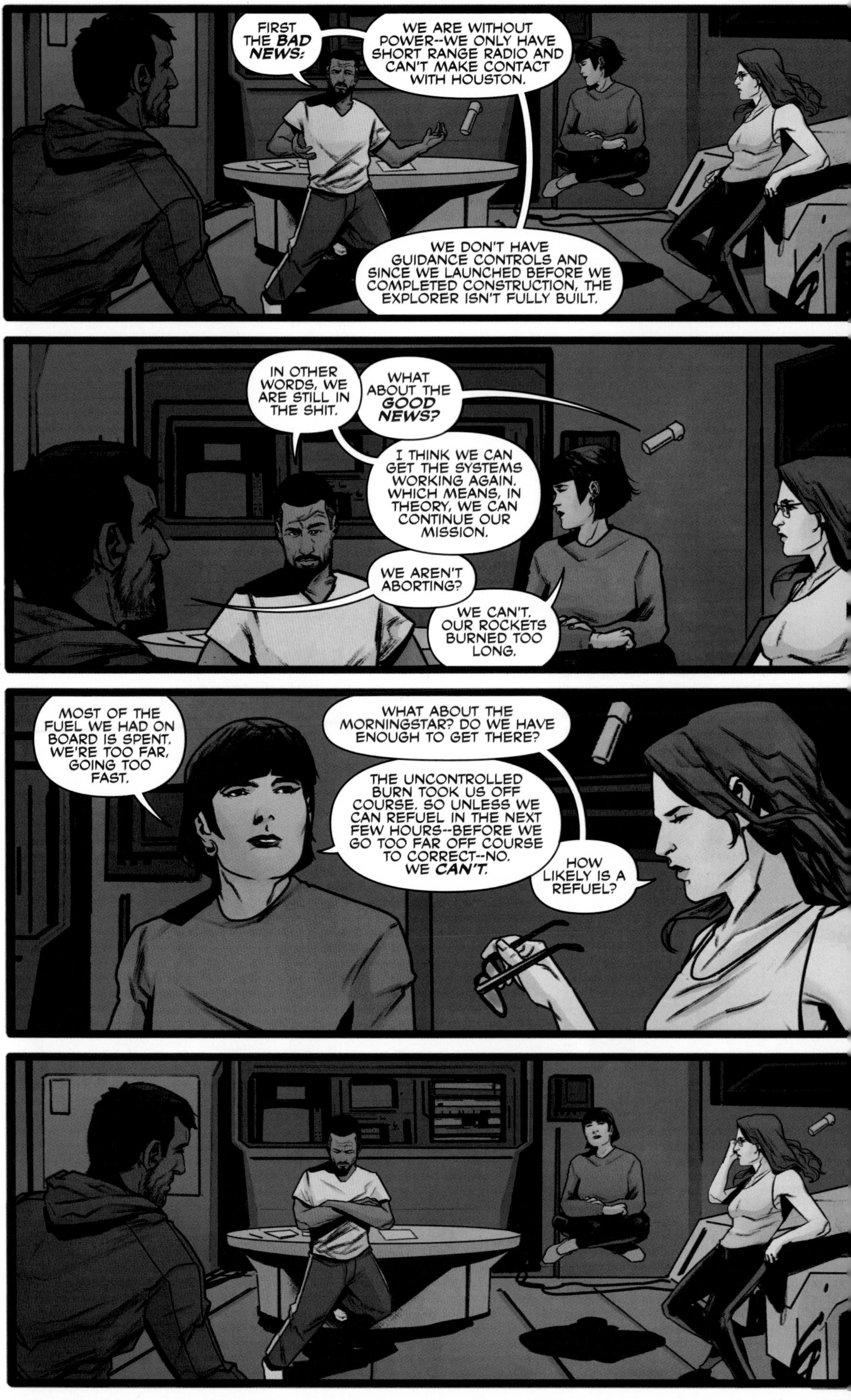

FIRST THE BAD NEWS:
WE ARE WITHOUT POWER--WE ONLY HAVE SHORT RANGE RADIO AND CAN'T MAKE CONTACT WITH HOUSTON.
WE DON'T HAVE GUIDANCE CONTROLS AND SINCE WE LAUNCHED BEFORE WE COMPLETED CONSTRUCTION, THE EXPLORER ISN'T FULLY BUILT.
IN OTHER WORDS, WE ARE STILL IN THE SHIT.
WHAT ABOUT THE GOOD NEWS?
I THINK WE CAN GET THE SYSTEMS WORKING AGAIN. WHICH MEANS, IN THEORY, WE CAN CONTINUE OUR MISSION.
WE AREN'T ABORTING?
WE CAN'T. OUR ROCKETS BURNED TOO LONG.
MOST OF THE FUEL WE HAD ON BOARD IS SPENT. WE'RE TOO FAR, GOING TOO FAST.
WHAT ABOUT THE MORNINGSTAR? DO WE HAVE ENOUGH TO GET THERE?
THE UNCONTROLLED BURN TOOK US OFF COURSE. SO UNLESS WE CAN REFUEL IN THE NEXT FEW HOURS--BEFORE WE GO TOO FAR OFF COURSE TO CORRECT--NO. WE CAN'T.
HOW LIKELY IS A REFUEL?

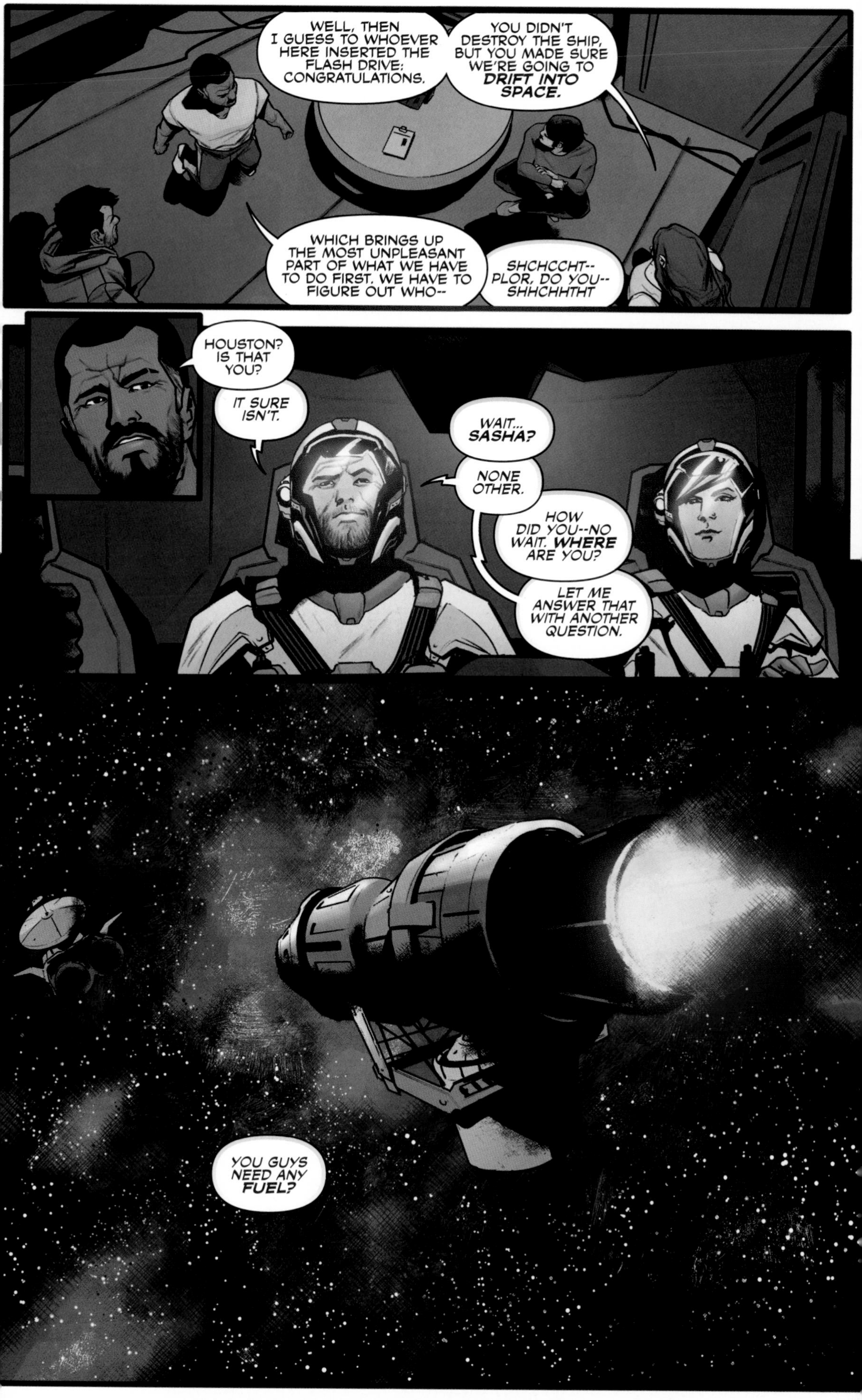
WELL, THEN I GUESS TO WHOEVER HERE INSERTED THE FLASH DRIVE: CONGRATULATIONS.
YOU DIDN'T DESTROY THE SHIP, BUT YOU MADE SURE WE'RE GOING TO **DRIFT INTO SPACE.**
WHICH BRINGS UP THE MOST UNPLEASANT PART OF WHAT WE HAVE TO DO FIRST. WE HAVE TO FIGURE OUT WHO--
SHCHCCHT--PLOR, DO YOU--SHHCHHTHT
HOUSTON? IS THAT YOU?
IT SURE ISN'T.
WAIT... **SASHA?**
NONE OTHER.
HOW DID YOU--NO WAIT. **WHERE** ARE YOU?
LET ME ANSWER THAT WITH ANOTHER QUESTION.
YOU GUYS NEED ANY **FUEL?**

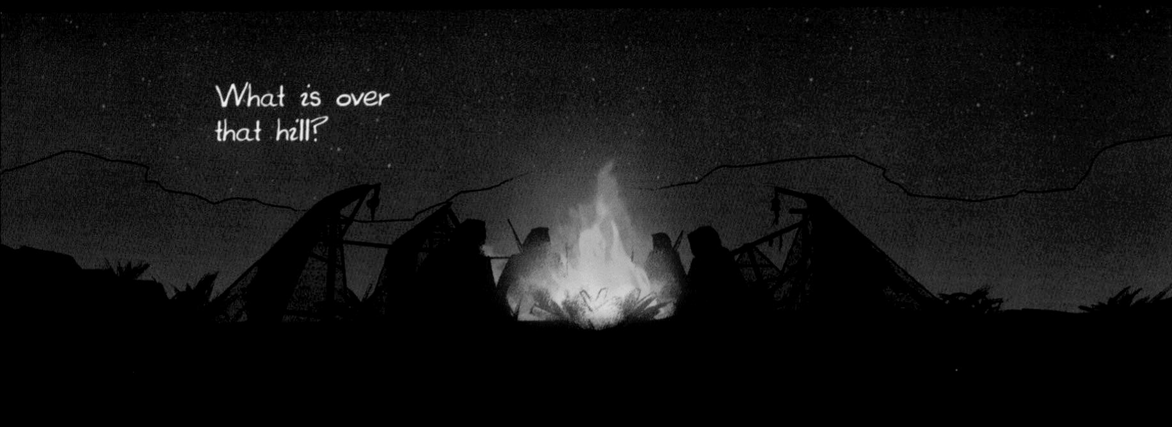
What is over that hill?

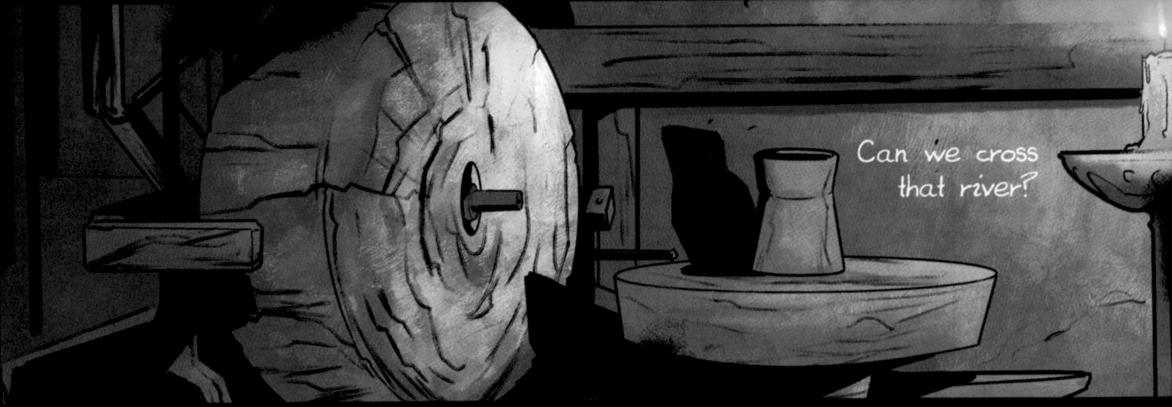
Can we cross that river?

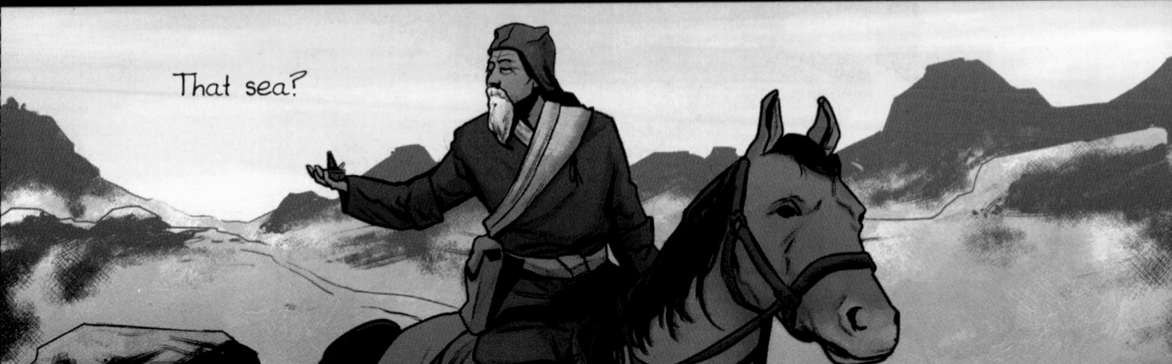
That sea?

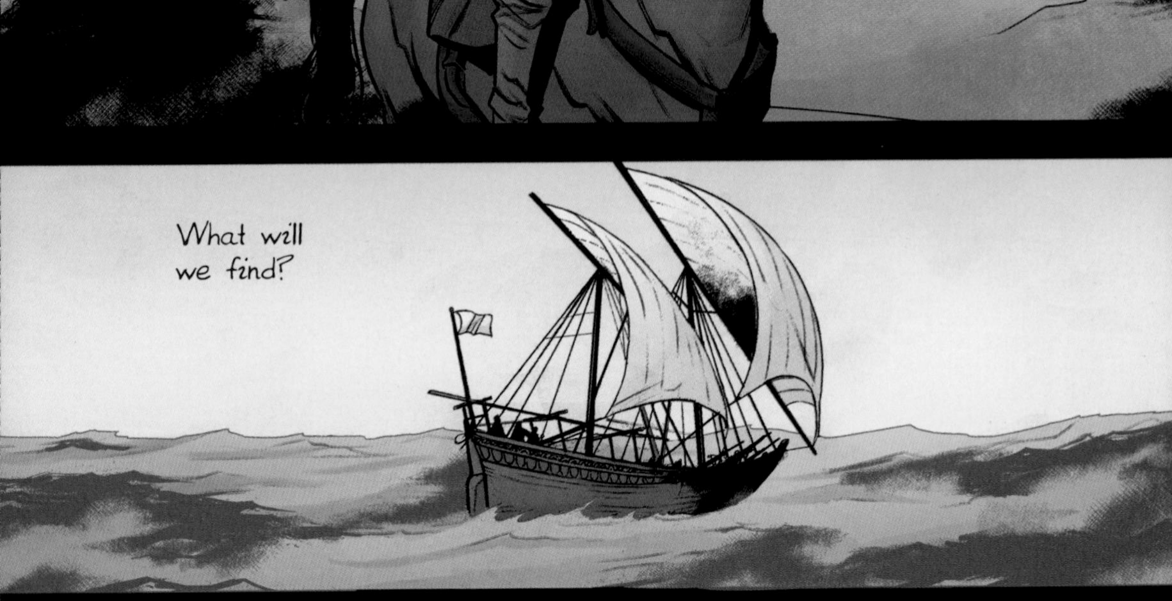
What will we find?

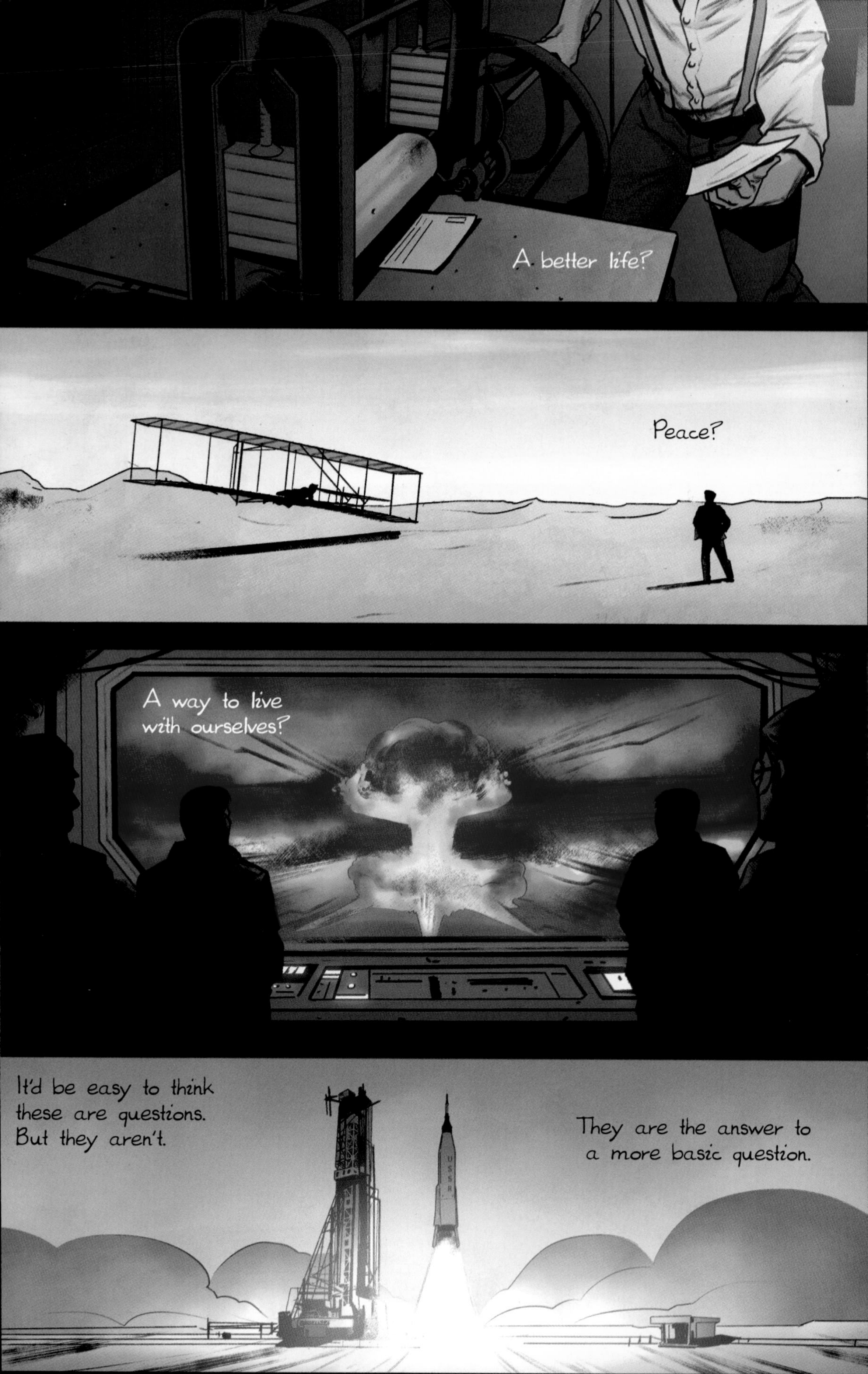
A better life?
Peace?
A way to live with ourselves?
It'd be easy to think these are questions. But they aren't.
They are the answer to a more basic question.
USSR

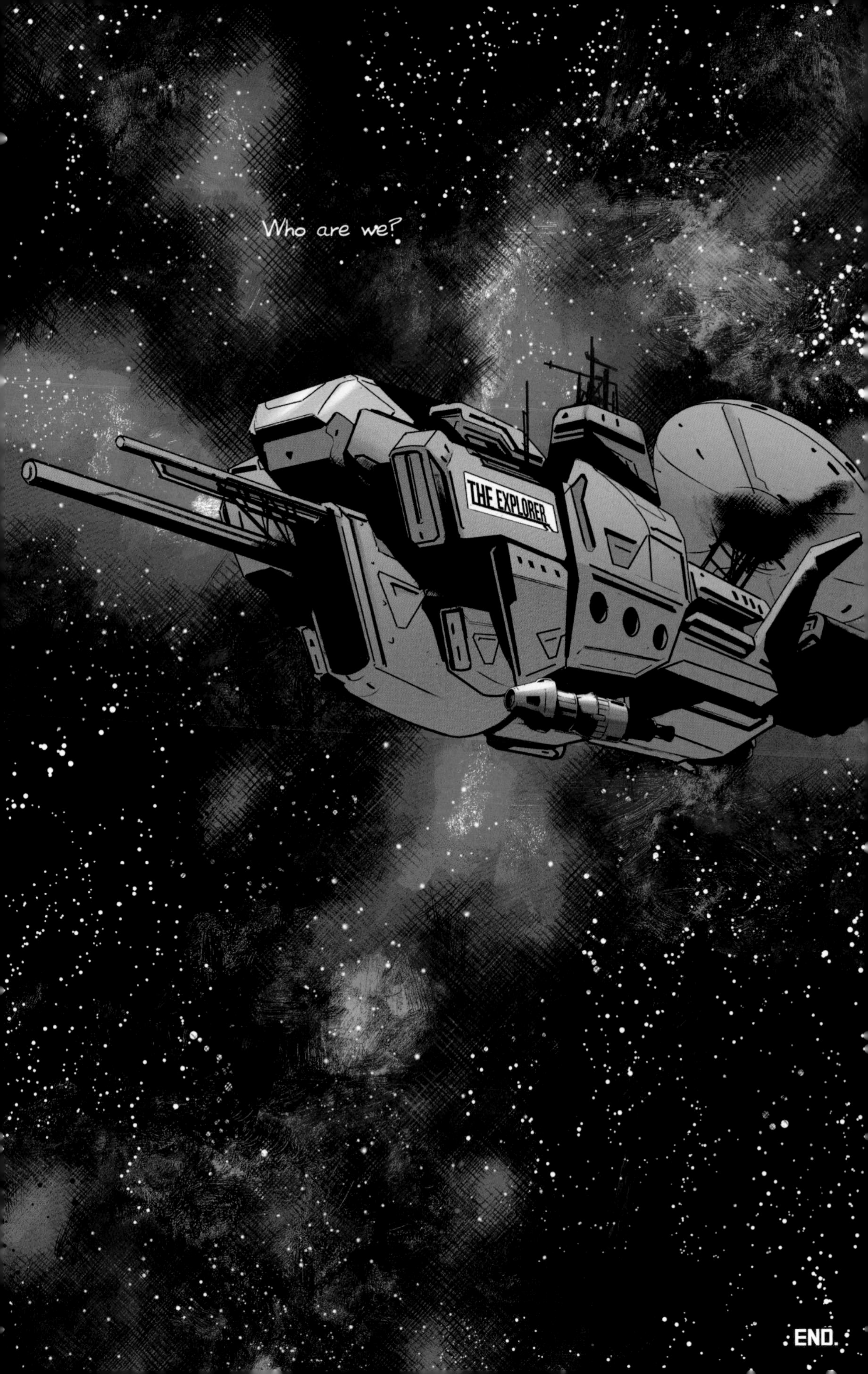
Who are we?
THE EXPLORER
END.

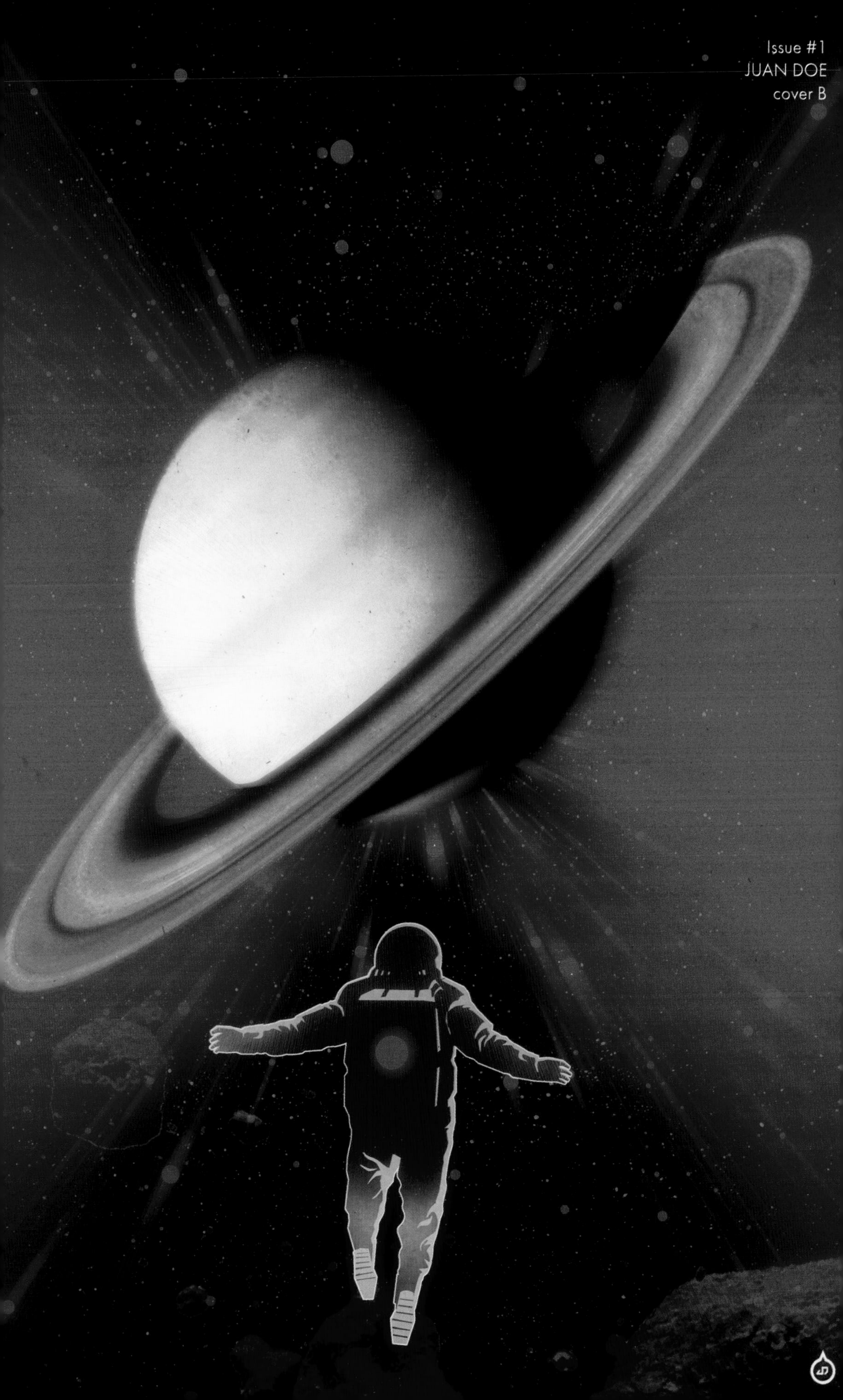
Issue #1
JUAN DOE
cover B

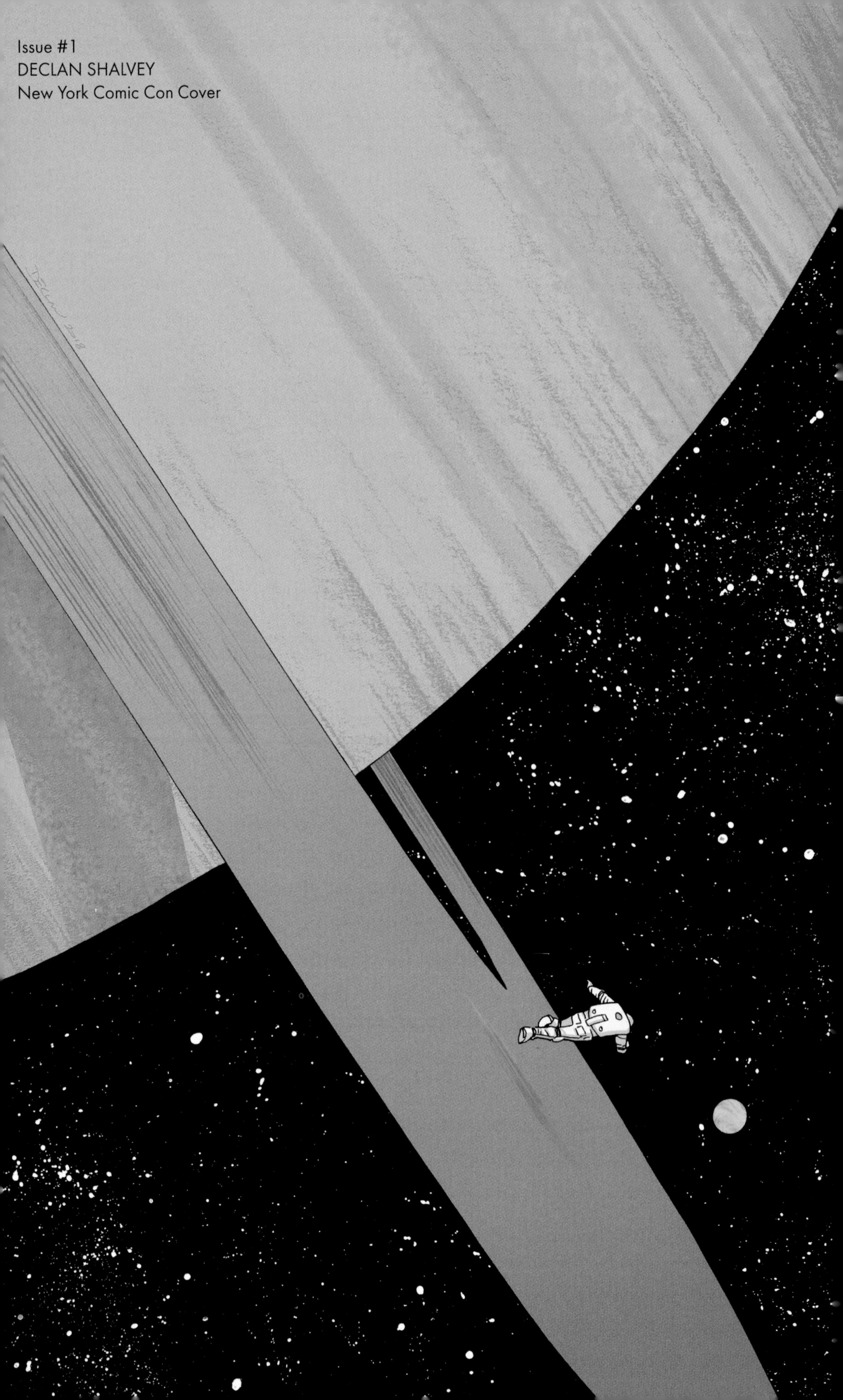

Issue #1
DECLAN SHALVEY
New York Comic Con Cover

THE LAST SPACE RACE™

sketchbook

art by ALEX SHIBAO

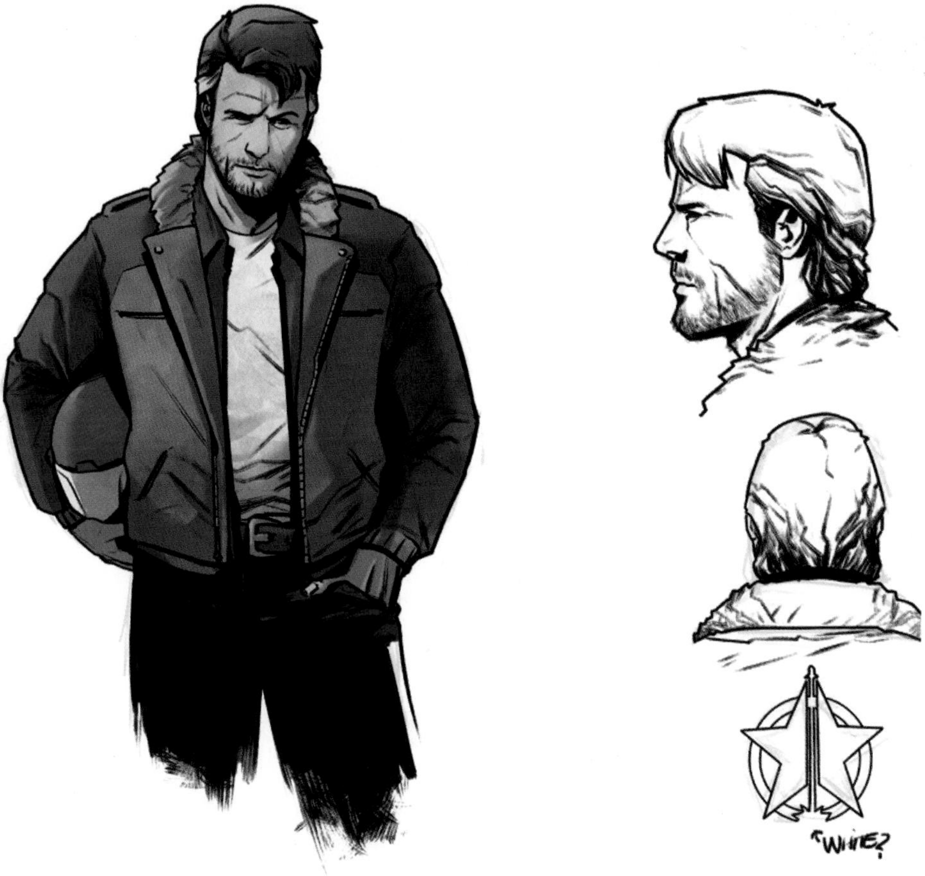
WHITE?

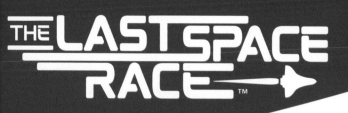

Sasha

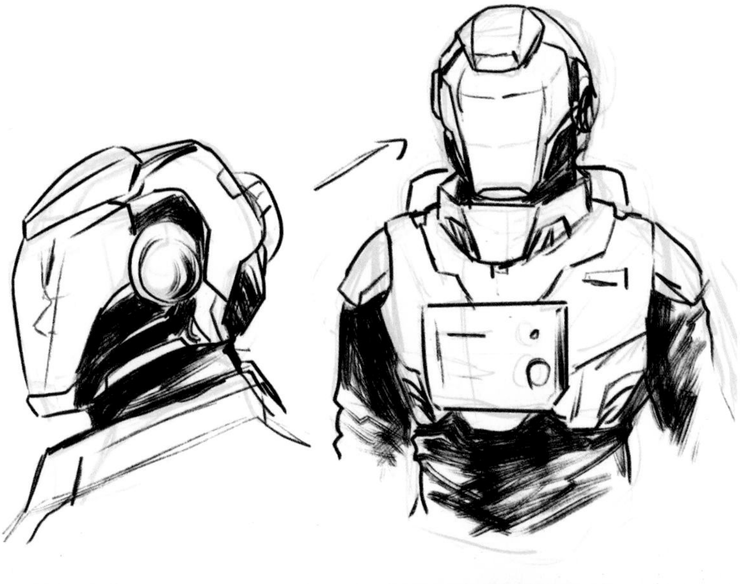

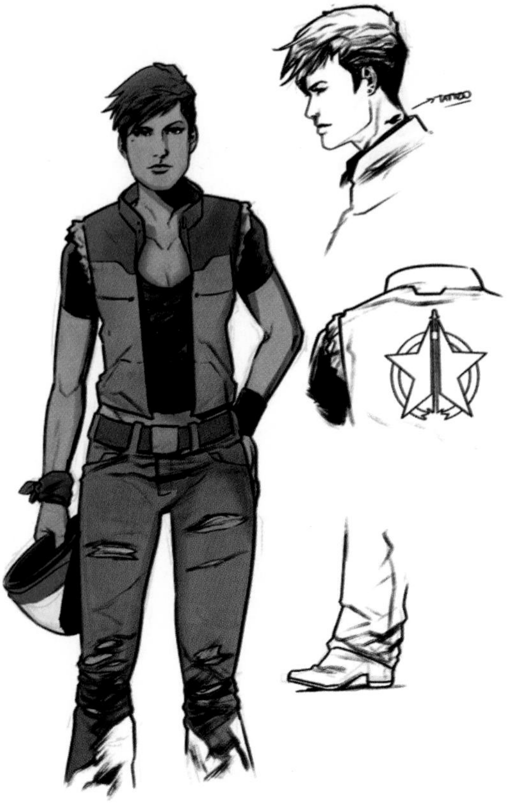
TATTOO

Gerry

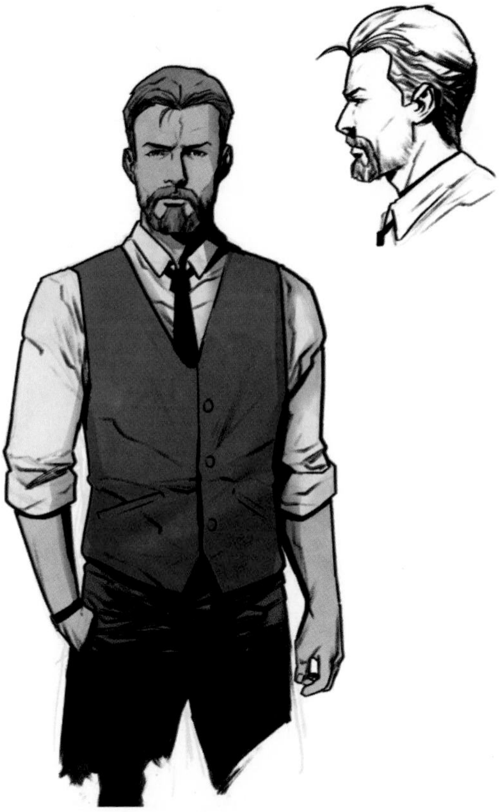

Neil

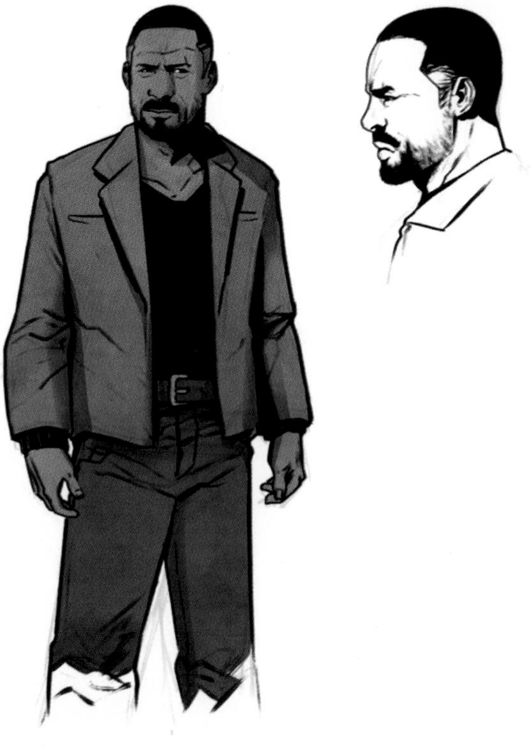

Roger

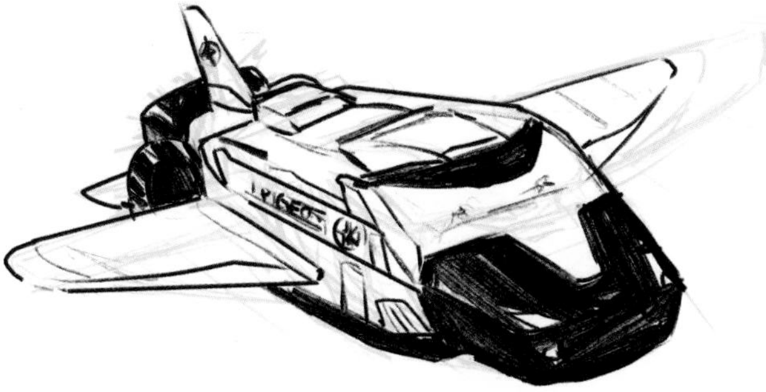

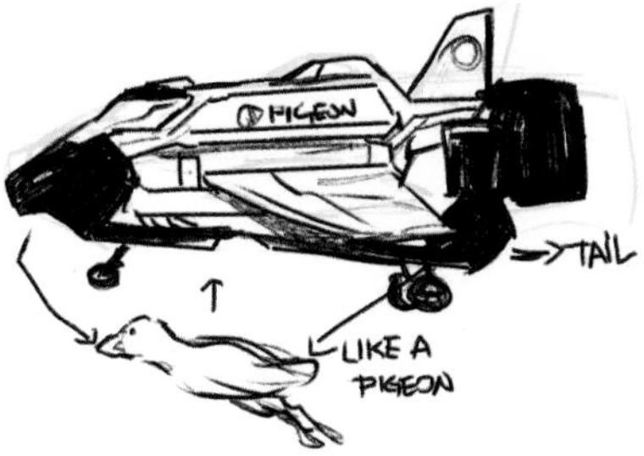
PIGEON
TAIL
LIKE A
PIGEON

Pigeon

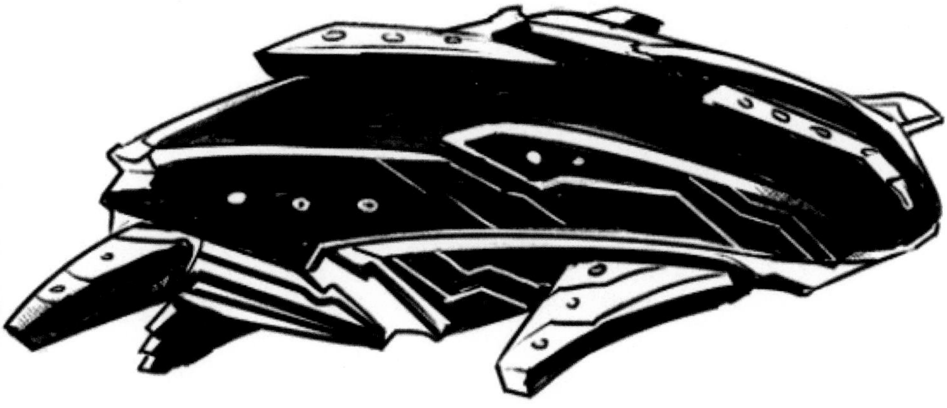

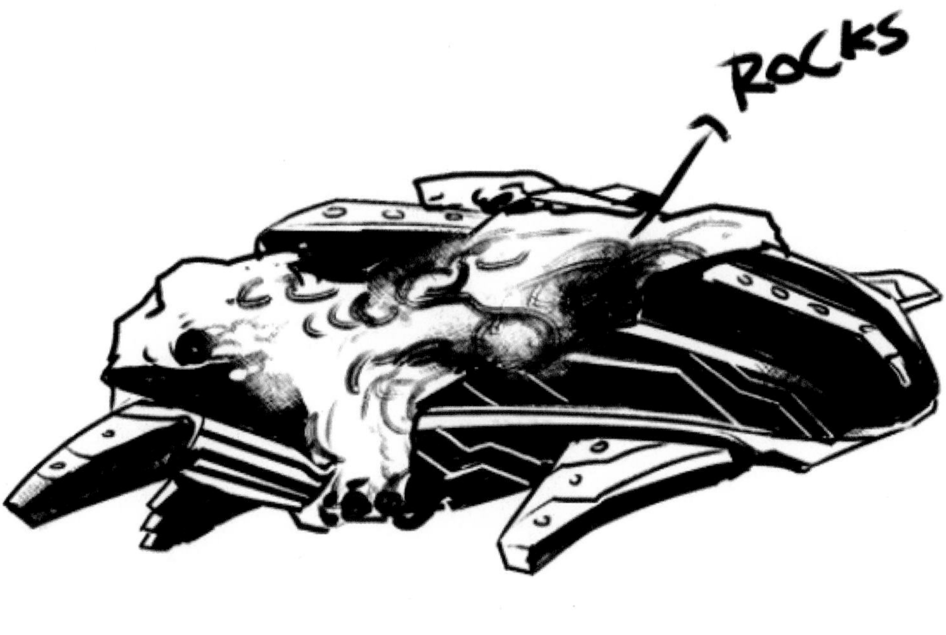
ROCKS

ABOUT THE CREATORS OF

PETER CALLOWAY
writer

@PeteCalloway

Peter Calloway is a television, movie and comic book writer. He's served as a writer and producer on hundreds of hours of television—most recently *Legion, American Gods* and Marvel's *Cloak & Dagger*. A lifelong comic book fan, he's written both his own comics on the indie side of the business, as well as titles for DC Comics, notably *Batman, Gotham City Sirens* and *Joker's Asylum*. Recently he's replaced his propane grill with a charcoal one and thinks it's superior. But a lot more work. So, is it better? This is the question he thinks about way more than he should.

ALEX SHIBAO
artist

@Alex_Shibao

Alex Shibao is a Brazilian comic book artist who has been working in the industry since 2006. Some of his works include *Silent Hill* (IDW), *Hamlet* (NEMO), *321 FAST COMIX* and *Stardust 8* by Vulgaris Magazine. Along with the studio Chiaroscuro, Alex has worked with Titan Comics as the cover artist for several titles, among them *Peepland, Normandy Gold* and *The Girl with the Dragon Tattoo*. In early 2017, Alex released his creator-owned comic, *Laser Gun*, a futuristic retro adventure. THE LAST SPACE RACE is his first AfterShock collaboration.

NATÁLIA MARQUES
colorist

Born in Brazil in the 90s, Natália Marques grew up reading comics. After many years studying various types of art, she participated in a workshop with her idol in comic book coloring, Marcelo Maiolo, and decided to become a colorist. Her first work was released in 2015, and since then she has been working in the international market, with books published in Brazil, Canada, The United States and Europe.

MARSHALL DILLON
letterer

@MarshallDillon

A comic book industry veteran, Marshall got his start in 1994, in the midst of the indie comic boom. Over the years, he's been everything from an independent self-published writer to an associate publisher working on properties like *G.I. Joe, Voltron,* and *Street Fighter*. He's done just about everything except draw a comic book, and worked for just about every publisher except the "big two." Primarily a father and letterer these days, he also dabbles in old-school paper and dice RPG game design. You can catch up with Marshall at firstdraftpress.net.